\ 원어민에게 바로 써먹는 영어표현 /

영어야 드루와

| 최창우 지음 |

- ☑ 원어민에게 바로 써먹을 수 있는 표현!
- ☑ 원어민이 농담처럼 사용하는 재밌는 표현!
- ☑ 원어민들이 자주 쓰는 상황별 표현!

KM 경문사

머리말

PREFACE

우리는 산업사회를 거쳐 이제 지식과 정보가 넘쳐나고 있는 21세기 정보화 사회를 살아가고 있으며 바야흐로 첨단기술은 나날이 눈부신 발전을 거듭하고 있다. 이와 함께 요즈음 언론이나 메스콤의 화두로 등장하고 있는 4차 산업혁명, 글로벌 혹은 국제화, 세계화와 같은 말은 이제 더 이상 우리에게 낯설지가 않다. 이러한 세계에 살고 있는 우리로서는 모름지기 외국어, 특히 세계 공용 언어인 영어는 선택이 아니라 필수가 되어버렸다.

지난날들을 돌이켜보면 기존의 기성세대들은 학창시절을 보내면서 그렇게 많은 영어수업을 받았음에도 정작 외국인을 만났을 때 말 한마디 하지 못했던 것이 우리의 현실이었다. 여러 가지 이유에 기인하겠지만 주된 이유 중의 하나는 아마도 입시위주의 우리나라 교육제도 때문이라 해도 과언이 아닐 것이다.

그러나 이제는 시대의 흐름에 발맞추어 어려서부터 조기에 영어에 많은 시간을 할애하는 우리 교육의 현실을 모두는 직시하고 있다.

이러한 이유로 대학에서 영문학을 부전공한 저자는 평소 영어에 남다른 관심을 가지고 있었고 해외에서 연구년을 보내며 현지인들이 사용하는 표현, 심지어 도로나 공원 등 길을 걷다가도 간판이나 표지판에 표기된 영어, 신문이나 잡지, 인터넷, 방송 등 여러 곳에서 게재되거나 방송되고 있는 문장이나 자료들을 틈틈이 기록 또는 수집하여 21세기를 살아가는 독자 여러분들에게 조금이라도 도움을 주고자 이 책을 집필하게 되었다.

이 교재에서 사용된 표현들은 독자들의 편의를 위하여 생활에서 유용하게 활용할 수 있는 단어와 숙어 및 관련 표현들을 유형별로 분류하여 제시하였다.

모름지기 영어를 우리말처럼 잘 하기 위해서는 독자 여러분들은 아래의 말을 꼭 명심하기 바란다.

If you wish to improve your knowledge of english conversation, please keep the followings in mind.

Don't be bashful of speaking.
Don't be afraid of making mistakes.
Practice your english at all times.

끝으로 저자로서는 최선을 다하여 조금이라도 독자의 입장에서 많은 부분을 배려하고자 하였으나 여러 가지 미비한 점은 독자 여러분들의 조언에 따라 꾸준히 수정·보완해 나갈 것임을 약속하는 바이다.

2020년을 보내며
상록동산에서 저자 씀

차례
CONTENTS

PART 1

우리의 삶과 함께하는 생활영어

CHAPTER 01

일상생활

일상생활

01 You're making me blush.

얼굴이 다 화끈거리네요.

A And then when I saw you score the winning goal... I was really impressed.

B Stop it. **You're making me blush.** It was nothing, really.

A Nothing? If it weren't for you, your team wouldn't be in the finals!

A 그러다가 네가 결승골을 넣는 걸 봤을 때… 굉장히 인상적이었어.

B 그만해. 네가 그러니까 얼굴이 다 화끈거리잖아. 별 거 아니었어, 정말.

A 아니라고? 너 아니었다면 너희 팀은 결승전에 나가지도 못했을 거라고!

일상생활

02 I get that a lot.

그런 말 자주 들어요.

A Hi, I'm Aaron Young. It's nice to meet you.

B Hi. I'm sorry, but has anyone ever told you that you look exactly like a young Tom Hanks?

A Yeah, **I get that a lot.** People say it's something about my eyes. It's just a coincidence, though. I'm not related to him.

A 안녕하세요. 저는 애런 영입니다. 만나서 반가워요.

B 안녕하세요. 죄송하지만 누군가 당신에게 젊었을 때의 톰 행크스와 꼭 닮았다고 한 적 없나요?

A 네, 그런 말 자주 들어요. 사람들이 제 눈 때문에 닮은 것 같다고 하더라고요. 단지 우연의 일치일 뿐이지만요. 저는 그 사람과 관계가 없어요.

일상생활

03 Do I know you?

저를 아세요?

A Jenny! It's been a while. I never would've expected to see you here.

B Excuse me, but **do I know you?**

A C'mon! It's me, Mike! We graduated from the same high school. Don't you remember?

A 제니! 오랜만이야. 여기서 너를 보게 될 줄 전혀 예상 못 했어.

B 실례하지만 저를 아세요?

A 왜 그래! 나야 마이크! 우리 같은 고등학교를 나왔잖아. 기억 안나?

일상생활

04 That's a steal.

횡재했네요.

A Congratulations. You finally bought your own house downtown. It looks great.

B Thanks. I found it on the first day I started seriously looking. And I was able to buy it at half price because the owner needed some quick cash.

A Oh my goodness! **That's a steal.** You're so lucky.

A 축하해요. 드디어 시내에 당신 집을 장만했네요. 좋아 보여요.

B 고마워요. 본격적으로 보기 시작한 첫날에 이 집을 찾았어요. 그리고 집 주인이 급하게 현금이 필요해서 반값에 살 수 있었죠.

A 오, 세상에나! 횡재했네요. 정말 운이 좋군요.

일상생활

05 My ears are plugged.

귀가 막혔어요.

A Why do you keep using Q-tips again and again?

B **My ears are plugged.** I think some water got into them while I was taking a shower this morning.

A I see. But don't poke around in there too much. It could cause problems.

A 왜 면봉을 계속 쓰는 거야?

B 귀가 막혔어. 오늘 아침에 샤워할 때 물이 귀에 좀 들어간 것 같아.

A 그렇구나. 하지만 너무 많이 귀를 찌르지 마. 문제가 생길 수 있어.

일상생활

06 I wasn't born yesterday.

저도 알 건 다 압니다.

A Here, Mary. You just dropped a coin.... Oh! Are you all right?

B What do you mean? Oh, because my eyes are red? That's just because of my allergies.

A Look, **I wasn't born yesterday.** I can see you've been crying. What's going on?

A 이봐요, 메리. 지금 막 동전을 떨어뜨렸어요…. 아! 괜찮은 거예요?

B 무슨 뜻이에요? 아, 제 눈이 빨개져서 그런 거예요? 이건 그냥 알러지 때문이에요.

A 이봐요, 저도 알 건 다 압니다. 당신이 계속 운 것을 알겠어요. 무슨 일이에요?

일상생활

07 I didn't lift a finger.

손가락 하나 까딱 안 했어요.

A Ow, my back hurts. I don't know how I'm going to move everything to my new place next week.

B You should call a moving company. It costs more than moving by yourself, but they do everything from A to Z. When I moved last year, **I didn't lift a finger.**

A That sounds really convenient. I've got to give them a call.

A 악, 허리 아파. 다음 주에 어떻게 새 집으로 모든 물건들을 옮겨야 할지 모르겠어.

B 이삿짐 회사에 전화해야 해. 혼자서 옮기는 것보다 비용이 더 들지만 하나부터 열까지 다 해 주잖아. 내가 작년에 이사했을 때 손가락 하나 까딱 안했어.

A 정말 편리한 것 같네. 나도 연락해야겠어.

일상생활

08 Catch you later.

나중에 봐요.

A What a great concert that was! Look at me! I'm all soaked with sweat.

B Me too! Plus, I think I have a sore throat from singing along so loudly.

A I bet we'll be tired tomorrow. Oh – this is my stop! **Catch you later!**

A 정말 멋진 콘서트였어! 나 좀 봐! 땀으로 흠뻑 젖었어.

B 나도야! 게다가 나는 노래도 엄청 크게 따라 불러서 목도 아픈 것 같아.

A 우리 내일 엄청 피곤하겠다. 아, 나 여기서 내려! 또 만나!

일상생활

09 That was a close call.

큰일 날 뻔했어요.

A Okay, come over here next to me and we'll take a picture of ourselves in front of the ocean. Hmm, I can't get the angle right.... Oh, My phone!

B Yikes, it hit the ground hard. Did the screen break?

A No, but you saw how it almost bounced through the railing, right? It could've fallen straight into the water! **That was a close call.**

A 그래, 여기 내 옆으로 와. 그리고 우리는 바다 앞에서 사진을 찍을 거야. 음, 각도가 잘 안 나오네…. 아, 내 휴대폰!

B 이키, 땅에 세게 떨어졌네. 액정이 깨졌어?

A 아니, 근데 하마터면 난간 사이로 어떻게 튕겨 나갈 뻔했는지 봤지? 물속으로 바로 떨어질 수도 있었어! 큰일날 뻔했어.

일상생활

10 You're a real buzz kill.

당신 때문에 분위기 망했어요.

A Wanna hear a funny joke? A horse walks into a bar and the bartender says….

B Why the long face? I get it."Long face"means sad, and a horse has a long face.

A You ruined my joke. You know, **you're a real buzz kill.** What a downer!

A 웃긴 얘기 하나 해 줄까요? 말 한 마리가 술집 안으로 걸어 들어왔대요. 바텐더가 하는 말이….

B "왜 그렇게 시무룩한 얼굴을 하고 있어?"라고 한 거? 알고 있어요. "long face"는 우울하다는 뜻인데 말이 얼굴이 기니까.

A 망했어요. 분위기 망치는 데 뭐 있군요. 완전히 김샜어요!

일상생활

11 That's that.

이거로 이야기는 끝이다.

A Honey, are you ready to go to church?

B Mom, can I just stay home today? I feel a little tired. You know I started to work part-time recently.

A Listen, you're going to church today and **that's that**. Now, get dressed.

A 얘야, 교회 갈 준비 됐니?

B 엄마, 오늘은 그냥 집에서 쉬면 안 돼요? 좀 피곤해서요. 최근에 아르바이트 시작한 거 아시잖아요.

A 잘 들어라, 오늘 교회 가는 거야. 이걸로 이야기 끝! 자, 옷 입어.

일상생활

12 Nature's calling.

화장실에 가야 해요.

A So, I think the most efficient way to promote our clothing would be by using social media. What do you think? Oof!

B Are you OK? What's going on?

A Uh, **nature's calling**. Could you excuse me for a second?

A 그래서 소셜 미디어를 활용하는 것이 우리의 의류를 홍보하는 가장 효율적인 방법이라고 생각하는데, 어떻게 생각해요? 아이구!

B 괜찮아요? 왜 그래요?

A 어, 화장실에 가야 해서요. 잠시만 실례해도 될까요?

일상생활

13 Give it a rest.

그쯤 해 둬요.

A Everything in China is much cheaper. You can drink as much beer as you want for 10 dollars. And th food is....

B **Give it a rest** about China already! You've been talking about it nonstop for an hour!

A Oh, have I? I'm sorry. But you know what? There really is a lot to like about it.

A 중국은 모든 게 훨씬 싸요. 10달러면 맥주도 맘껏 마실 수 있어요. 그리고 음식도….

B 이제 중국 이야기 좀 그만해요! 한 시간 내내 쉬지 않고 계속 그 이야기만 하고 있잖아요!

A 아, 그랬나요? 미안해요. 그런데 말이죠, 중국은 맘에 드는 것이 너무 많아요.

일상생활

14 You get what you pay for.

싼 게 비지떡

A That's the used computer you bought online, right? What's wrong with it?

B Well, it was okay for the first few days, but it's totally dead now.

A See? I told you to get a new one. **You get what you pay for.**

A 그게 온라인으로 산 중고 컴퓨터 맞죠? 뭐가 문제예요?

B 음, 처음 며칠은 괜찮았는데 지금은 전혀 작동을 하지 않네요.

A 거 봐요. 내가 새것 사라고 했죠? 싼 게 비지떡이라고요.

일상생활

15 It went viral.

인터넷에 쫙 퍼졌어.

A Did you see the music video for that K-pop boy band's latest song?

B No, I didn't. I'm not a big fan of the group. But I am curious about the video. Where can I watch it?

A **It went viral**, so I'm sure you can find it on any major video site.

A 너 그 K팝 보이 밴드의 최신곡 뮤직비디오 봤어?

B 아니. 난 그 그룹의 열성 팬이 아니야. 그런데 그 비디오는 좀 궁금하네. 어디서 볼 수 있어?

A 인터넷에 쫙 퍼졌기 때문에 분명 주요 비디오 사이트에서는 어디서나 찾을 수 있을거야.

일상생활

16 Times have changed.

세상이 많이 변했습니다.

A According to recent statistics, every fourth newly wed couple in Korea will eventually divorce.

B Well, **times have changed.**
When I was young, divorces were very rare.

A So, Kenny, please don't push your son-in-law.

B How dare! None of your business.

A Calm down. I am saying as a friend.
Don't get me wrong.

A 최근 통계에 따르면 한국은 신혼부부 네 쌍 중 한 쌍은 결국 이혼한다는군.

B 그래, 세상 많이 변했군.
내가 젊었을 때는 참 드문 일이었는데.

A 그러니, 케니, 자네 사위를 몰아세우지 말게.

B 감히 어디다. 자네 상관할 바 아니야.

A 진정하게. 친구로서 하는 말일세.
곡해하지 말게.

일상생활

17 My condolences!

삼가 조의를 표합니다.

A **My condolences!**

B Please accept my condolences.

C Please accept my deepest sympathy.

D I am so sorry to hear that your grandmother had passed away.

E I am so saddened to hear of your beloved grandmother passing away.

A 삼가 조의를 표합니다.

B 조의를 받아주세요.

C 슬픔을 같이 나누고 싶습니다.(애도합니다.)

D 할머니께서 돌아가셨다니 유감입니다.

E 사랑하는 할머니께서 별세하셨다는 소식을 들으니 매우 애통하군요.

※ C에서 sympathy는 동정이 아니라 '슬픔을 같이 나눔'을 뜻한다.

일상생활

18 I'm afraid I have a cramp in my foot.

발에 쥐가 난 것 같아.

A **I'm afraid I have a cramp in my foot.**

B It feels like I'm walking on pins and needles.

A My leg is asleep, too.

B I'm not surprised. You have sat cross-legged over five hours playing cards.

A 발에 쥐가 난 것 같아요.

B 나는 다리가 저려요.

A 내 다리도 저려요.

B 그럴 수밖에 없지요. 다섯 시간 이상 다리를 꼬고 앉아 포커를 치니 그럴지요.

일상생활

19 A penny for your thoughts.

네 생각을 말해 봐.

A Hey. You look so serious. What are you thinking?

B Nothing.

A It can't be nothing.
You didn't say a word for half an hour. What is it?

B Well.... Just a couple of things about you and me.
Nothing big.

A About us? Now, I've gotta know. What's brewing in your mind? **A penny for your thoughts.**

B If you insist. Do you really think we can work out well?

A 되게 심각하네. 무슨 생각해?

B 아무 생각 안 해.

A 그럴 리가.
30분 동안 한마디도 안 했잖아. 뭔데?

B 그냥…. 너랑 나에 대해서 좀.
별거 아니야.

A 우리에 대해서? 이제, 진짜 알아야겠어. 무슨 생각인데? 말 좀 해봐.

B 네가 정 알고 싶다면. 우리가 정말 잘 어울린다고 생각해?

일상생활

20 No dice!

절대로 안 돼!

A What's going on with you and your father?

B What? Something weird?

A Yeah. You guys didn't say anything to each other at dinner.

B Actually, I asked him for a raise in my allowance.
And you know what he said? **"No dice!"**

A Is that why? How old are you?
Don't be such a baby!

B Come on! Do you have any idea how hard it is to live it up with 20 bucks a week?

A 너 아버지랑 무슨 일 있어?

B 왜? 이상해 보여?

A 당연하지. 저녁 식사 동안 서로 한마디도 안했잖아.

B 사실은 아빠한테 용돈을 좀 올려달라고 말씀드렸는데 뭐라 그러신 줄 알아? "절대로 안 돼!"

A 그게 이유야? 너 몇 살이야?
철 좀 들지!

B 뭐야? 일주일에 20달러로 사는 게 얼마나 힘든지 너 알아?

일상생활

21 It's a bed of roses.

이건 천국이지.

A Hello, Justin. Long time no see.

B Hi, Neo. What's up? I've lost track of you.

A Oh, I got a new job on Madison Avenue.

B You did? Wow.... So, how's your new job?

A Pretty good. Compared to my old one, **it's a bed of roses.**

B That's awesome!

A 안녕, 저스틴. 정말 오랜만이다.

B 그래, 네오. 잘 있었어? 어떻게 지내나 궁금했는데.

A 아, 나 광고 쪽에 새로 취직했어.

B 그래? 와…. 새 일은 어때?

A 꽤 좋아. 예전 직업에 비하면 이건 천국이야.

B 정말 잘됐다!

일상생활

22 The fruit will get crushed at the bottom of the cart.

과일을 카트 바닥에 놓으면 뭉개질 거야.

A I guess we should start over on the other side of the supermarket.

B Why walk all the way there and then back again? We can start here, in the fruit section.

A But then **the fruit will get crushed at the bottom of the cart.**

B I see. Let's go to the canned goods first, then.

A 슈퍼마켓 저쪽 끝에서부터 쇼핑을 시작하는 게 어때.

B 왜 저기까지 걸어갔다가 다시 돌아와야 하는데? 여기 과일 코너부터 보자.

A 하지만 과일을 먼저 사서 카트 바닥에 놓으면 뭉개질거야.

B 그렇구나. 그럼 통조림류 코너부터 가자.

일상생활

23 It's a once-in-a-lifetime chance!

평생에 한 번 올까 말까 한 기회야.

A You should invest heavily in Acme Company.
I've heard some hot tips about it!

B I don't know.
It seems like a risky company to invest in.

A But you could make millions.
It's a once-in-a-lifetime chance!

A Acme 회사에 집중 투자해.
좋은 정보를 들었거든.

B 글쎄.
투자하기엔 좀 불안한 회사 같은데.

A 하지만 떼돈을 벌 수 있을걸.
평생에 한 번 올까 말까한 기회야!

일상생활
24 Can I ring of these up for you?
이것으로 계산해 드릴까요?

A Can I ring of these up for you?
B I still haven't made up my mind, thanks.

A 이것으로 하나 계산해 드릴까요?
B 아직 결정을 못 내렸어요. 감사합니다.

일상생활
25 Can I see something a little more compact?
좀 소형으로 볼 수 있나요?

A Can I see something a little more compact?
B Sure. our ultra-compact video cameras are here.

A 좀 소형으로 볼 수 있나요?
B 물론이죠. 초소형 비디오카메라가 이쪽에 있습니다.

일상생활
26 Paper or plastic?
종이 백 드릴까요, 비닐 백 드릴까요?

A Paper or plastic?
B Are those my only choices? I'm worried the paper bags might rip, but I hate to use too much plastic.
A We also sell re-usable cotton bags.
B Perfect. I'll take two, please.

A 종이 백 드릴까요, 비닐 백 드릴까요?
B 그 두 가지 뿐인가요? 종이 백은 찢어질까봐 걱정되고, 비닐 백을 너무 많이 쓰는 건 싫은데
A 재사용할 수 있는 면 가방도 팔고 있습니다.
B 좋군요. 두 개 주세요.

일상생활
27 You can count on me.
제게 맡기세요.

A My wife says, "No boys allowed."
B Don't worry.
I have a bunch of homework to do anyway.
A Then, if the phone rings, just let the machine get it.
And don't answer the door.
B You can count on me. if there are any problems, your number is on the fridge, right?

A 아내가 남자는 절대로 데려오지 말라고 하네요.
B 걱정 마세요.
해야 할 숙제도 많아요.
A 그리고 전화가 오면 자동응답기가 받도록 두세요.
누가 와도 문을 열어 주지 말고요.
B 제게 맡기세요. 문제가 생기면
냉장고에 써 있는 번호로 연락드리면 되죠?

일상생활

28 I'm green with envy.

매우 부러워하는

A You'll never guess what happened to me last Saturday.

B You found tha man of your dreams?

A Oh, very funny, but you're not so far off. I got Stephen Laure's autograph.

B You mean that really gorgeous looking actor in the detective series on TV?

A Well they were filming some scenes on location just round the corner from my apartment and I managed to catch him during a break.

B Oh, **I'm green with envy.** What did he say to you.

A 너는 지난 토요일에 내게 무슨 일이 일어났는지 짐작도 못할거야.

B 너 이상형이라도 만났니?

A 오 아주 웃겨. 하지만 아예 틀리진 않아. 내가 스태픈로리의 사인을 받았어.

B TV탐정 시리즈에 나오는 외모가 멋진배우 말이지?

A 우리 아파트 근처에서 몇 장면을 찍고 있어서 휴식시간에 가까스로 그를 만날 수 있었어.

B 오, 정말 부럽군. 그가 너에게 무슨 말이라도 했니?

일상생활

29 Bob's your uncle!

걱정할 필요 없어. 그렇게 하면 되는 거야.

A What are you wailing about?
Has your computer crashed?

B No, I am trying to make this photo bigger on the screen.

A Oh, it's not difficult.

B I've been trying to do it for half an hour without success.

A I'll show you. Look, you open this menu. click here, click on the percentage you want, say 200% and **Bob's your uncle.** There it is, twice as large.

B It's easy when you know how. Thanks a lot.

A 너 왜 울부짖고 있니?
너의 컴퓨터가 부서졌니?

B 아니, 이 사진을 화면에 확대하려고 하고 있어.

A 오, 그건 어렵지 않지.

B 30분 동안 해매고 있었어.

A 내가 보여주지. 봐. 이 메뉴를 연 후, 여기를 클릭한 후에 네가 원하는 퍼센트로 클릭해봐 200%로,
그렇게 하면 되는 거야. 2배로 말이야.

B 방법을 알고 나니 쉽군, 고마워.

일상생활

30 He's a handful.

귀찮은 것

A Good afternoon. Jessica. How's the baby?

B **He's a handful.** but very healthy.

A You know, you're looking great. I'm amazed you were able to get back into such good shape so soon after having a baby.

B Oh, thanks, Sue.

A What's your secret?

B I don't know.
I have been trying to exercise a lot, I guess.

A Well, whatever you're doing. it's working.

B If you keep this up, I'm going to start blushing.

A 안녕, 제시카 애기는 좀 어때?

B 애보기가 너무 귀찮지만 애기는 건강해.

A 너 정말 멋져 보여. 애기를 낳은 후로 그렇게 빨리 몸매가 돌아올수 있다니 놀라워.

B 고마워, 슈.

A 비법이 뭐야?

B 모르겠어.
꾸준히 운동한 덕분이 아닐까?

A 넌 무엇을 하든 효과가 있구나.

B 네가 계속 칭찬하면 내 얼굴이 붉어진다니까!

일상생활

31 Every cloud has a silver lining.

고생 끝에 낙이 온다.

A I heard you went to Jan's wedding. It must be strange seeing your high school sweetheart marry another guy.

B I was not looking forward to going, but it worked out fine. I met a nice girl at the reception, and now we're dating.

A Well, I guess it's true what people say.
Every cloud has a silver lining.

A 조앤 결혼식에 갔다고 들었어요. 고등학교 때 애인이 다른 남자랑 결혼하는 걸 보는 기분이 좀 묘했을 거예요.

B 가고 싶지 않았는데 가길 잘했어요.
피로연에서 괜찮은 여자를 만나서 지금 사귀고 있어요.

A 흠, 옛말이 맞는 것 같아요.
고생 끝에 낙이 온다잖아요.

일상생활

32 The thorn just poked me.

가시에 찔렸어.

A Well, Betty, what do you think?
Are you having a good time so far?

B What a perfect day! I loved the chocolates.
They're sweet, just like you are.

A And what about the card and the poem?

B Right. And the flowers are so....
Ouch! **The thorn just poked me!**

A 베티, 어때? 오늘 즐거웠어?
B 정말 멋진 하루였어! 초콜릿도 마음에 들어.
당신처럼 달콤한 것 같아.
A 그럼 카드와 시는 어때? 그것도 나처럼 로맨틱하지?
B 맞아. 그리고 꽃은 아주….
아야! 가시에 찔렸어!

일상생활

33 Their work ethic might rub off on you.

그 아이들 학습태도를 네가 배울 수 있어.

A I found the perfect way to stick to my resolution to improve my grades.

B Good for you.

A I'm going to get together with all the other students who are having problems.

B Why not hang out with successful students instead?
Their work ethic might rub off on you.

A 성적 향상 결심을 지키기 위한 좋은 방법을 알았어.
B 잘됐구나.
A 성적 때문에 골치 썩이는 다른 애들과 어울릴 생각이야.
B 그러지 말고 공부 잘하는 애들과 어울리지 그러니?
걔네 학습태도를 네가 배울 수 있어.

일상생활

34 New cameras are idiot-proof.

새로 나온 카메라는 전자동이야.

A My father has an old film camera he still uses.

B A lot of people are like that. They're called purists.
They think using a digital camera is cheating.

A Because the camera does everything for you?

B Right. **New cameras are idiot-proof**, and purists think that's no fun at all.

A 우리 아버지는 필름 카메라를 갖고 계신데 아직도 사용하셔.
B 많이들 그래. 그런 사람들은 '순수주의자'라고 하지. 그들은 디지털 카메라로 사진을 찍는 건 진짜 사진이 아니라고 생각해.
A 카메라가 다 알아서 해주니까 그런 거야?
B 맞아. 새로 나오는 카메라는 전자동이라서 그들한테는 전혀 흥미롭지 않지.

일상생활
35 The years have sure been unkind to her.
그녀는 힘든 세월을 보낸 거 같아.

A Look over there, It's Jill Henson.
Boy, **the years have sure been unkind to her.**
B You can say that again. Although, to be fair, I heard she's had two kids.
A Wow. I never expected her to settle down and start a family.
B Oh, she never settled down.
She has two kids by two different men.

A 저기 좀 봐. 질 헨더슨이야.
저런, 힘든 세월을 보낸 거 같네.
B 정말 그렇네. 거짓말 안 보내고, 쟤한테 아이가 두 명 있대.
A 와. 쟤가 결혼해서 가정을 꾸릴 거라곤 상상도 못했는데.
B 아, 결혼은 한 번도 안했어.
아빠가 다른 아이가 둘이래.

일상생활
36 It's sort of cliche, isn't it?
그건 좀 뻔하지 않니?

A What do you think about giving my girlfriend a box of chocolates for Valentine's Day?
B That's it? **It's sort of cliche, isn't it?**
A I guess you're right. I don't want to get her the same thing everyone else is.
B But at the same time, it is aort of a tradition.

A 밸런타인데이에 여자 친구에게 초콜릿 한 상자를 주는 건 어떨까?
B 그게 다야? 초콜릿을 주는 건 좀 뻔하지 않니?
A 네 말이 맞는 것 같아. 다른 사람들이랑 똑같은 걸 주고 싶지는 않은데.
B 그런데 또 그게 관례이긴 해.

일상생활
37 He struck it rich in computers soon after graduation.
그는 졸업하고 얼마 후 컴퓨터로 벼락부자가 됐어.

A Is that Ted Johnson over there? That suit looks like it's worth more than my house.
B I bet it is.
He struck it rich in computers soon after graduation.
A That figures. He was a huge math nerd in school.
B Look at him now. All the single women here are fawning over him.

A 저기 저 사람 테드 존슨이니? 쟤가 입은 정장이 우리 집값보다 더 비싸 보여.
B 틀림없이 그럴 거야. 졸업하고 얼마 후에 컴퓨터로 벼락부자가 됐대.
A 생각한 대로네.
학교 다닐 때도 수학밖에 모르는 따분한 애였잖아.
B 쟤 좀 봐. 결혼 안 한 여자애들이 다 쟤한테 비위를 맞추고 있어.

일상생활
38 Did you turn him down?
너 그 사람 말 거절했어?

A Tom invited us out for drinks this evening.

B What did you tell him? **Did you turn him down?**

A Of course. My resolution was not to drink during the week.

B Good for you. Now, I think I'll call Tom and accept his invitation. My resolution was to get out of the house more often.

A 톰이 오늘 저녁에 술 한잔 하자고 우리를 초대했어.

B 그래서 톰에게 뭐라고 했어? 거절했어?

A 물론이지. 내 새해 결심은 평일에 술을 마시지 말자는 거였잖아.

B 잘했네. 난 톰한테 전화해서 간다고 해야지. 내 결심은 외출을 더 자주 하자는 거였어.

일상생활
39 I have terrible handwriting.
내 글씨는 엉망이야.

A Look at this job application!
It's going to take forever to fill out.

B The company really wants to know a lot about the applicants.

A Well, I guess that's to be expected.
It's not just some fast food, part-time job.

B Let me get a pen. Actually, can you write in the answers? **I have terrible handwriting.**

A 이 입사지원서 좀 봐!
다 쓰려면 끝도 없겠네.

B 회사에서 지원자에 대해 속속들이 알고 싶은 거야.

A 예상했던 일이긴 해. 패스트푸드점 아르바이트를 뽑는 것도 아니니까.

B 내가 펜을 가지고 올 테니 지원서 좀 써줄 수 있어? 난 글씨가 엉망이라서.

일상생활
40 Proper posture is essential.
올바른 자세가 가장 중요해요.

A Now that I can read music a little bit, I'm all ready to learn to play.

B The first thing you have to do is sit up straight.
Don't bend your back at all.

A Like this? It feels a bit awkward.

B **Proper posture is essential.**
Otherwise, you'll hurt your back.

A 악보를 조금 읽을 수 있으니까
연주할 준비가 된 거네요.

B 가장 먼저 해야 될 일은 똑바로 앉는 거예요.
허리를 구부리지 마시고요.

A 이렇게요? 어색한데요.

B 올바른 자세가 가장 중요해요.
그렇지 않으면 허리가 아플 거예요.

일상생활
41 Looks don't matter.
겉모양은 중요하지 않아.

A What do you think of these hiking shoes? They look great, don't they?

B **Looks don't matter.** How do they fit? Are they tight anywhere?

A A little bit around the toes, but I still think they look good. They match my pants.

B They'll give you blisters if they're not the right size. Try on another pair.

A 이 하이킹 신발 어때? 괜찮아 보이는데, 안 그래?

B 겉모양은 중요하지 않아. 잘 맞아? 꽉 끼는 데 있니?

A 발가락 주위가 좀 끼는데 그래도 모양이 괜찮잖아. 바지와 잘 어울리고.

B 사이즈가 안 맞으면 물집이 생길 거야. 다른 걸로 신어봐.

일상생활
42 What else will I need besides the monitor?
모니터 말고 뭐가 더 필요할까요?

A **What else will I need besides the tower and the monitor?**

B Will you just install the OS from your old computer onto the new one?

A Can't I buy something that already has an OS?

B Sure. We'll put everything together and load the OS right here in the store.

A 탑이랑 모니터 말고 뭐가 더 필요할까요?

B 예전 컴퓨터의 OS를 새 컴퓨터에 설치하시겠어요?

A OS가 이미 깔려 있는 것을 살 수는 없나요?

B 사실 수 있죠. 여기 가게에서 저희가 다 편집하고 OS를 깔아 드립니다.

일상생활
43 It says an honorarium is available.
사례금이 있다고 나와 있구나.

A The center for the blind actually pays money!

B Well, **It says an honorarium is available.**

A But they give you money, right?

B The center is far away, so the money is to help volunteers pay for the subway rides there and back.

A 시각장애인 센터에서는 보수를 지급한대요!

B 사례금이 있다고 나와 있구나.

A 그럼 거기서 돈을 준다는 거 맞죠?

B 센터가 멀어서 왕복 지하철 요금을 보태주는 거란다.

일상생활

44 I'm not a picky eater.

나는 아무거나 잘 먹어.

A Do you like Italian cuisine?
I find a website full of recipes.

B I love pizza. Can you make us one for dinner?

A Actually, these are authentic Italian dishes.
Real Italian pizza is different from what you'd expect.

B Well, I'll give it a try anyway. **I'm not a picky eater.**

A 이탈리아 요리 좋아하니? 요리법으로 가득한 웹사이트를 찾았어.

B 피자 정말 좋아해. 저녁에 피자 만들어 주는 게 어때?

A 그런데 이건 정통 이탈리아 요리야. 네가 생각하는 것과 다른 진짜 이탈리아 피자지.

B 그럼 일단 먹어보지 뭐. 나는 아무거나 잘 먹어.

일상생활

45 It's a point-and-shoot camera.

이건 보고 누르기만 하면 되는 전자동 카메라야.

A I don't know what half of these buttons do.

B Set the camera to full auto.
Then, **it's like a point-and-shoot camera.**

A But I spent all this money to get one with all the bells and whistles.

B You can learn how to use it one feature at a time.
Eventually, you'll be shooting in full manual.

A 이 버튼들 중에서 절반은 뭔지 모르겠어.

B 카메라를 전부 자동으로 설정해봐. 그럼 완전 자동카메라 같이 돼.

A 그렇지만 카메라 부속품 사는데 들인 돈이 얼마인데.

B 한 번에 기능 하나씩 배우면, 나중엔 전부 수동 기능으로 사진을 찍을 수 있을 거야.

일상생활

46 We just try to get the most out of each volunteer.

자원봉사자들을 최대한 활용하려는 거예요.

A Excuse me.
I'm here to sign up for the volunteer project.

B Great. Fill in this form and I'll get you a T-shirt.

A Hey, way are there questions about my work experience on this form?

B Don't worry, it's not an interview. **We just try to get the most out of each volunteer.**

A 실례합니다만 자원봉사 프로젝트에 등록하러 왔어요.

B 좋아요. 서류를 작성해주시면 티셔츠를 갖다 드릴게요.

A 저기요, 이 서식에 왜 경력을 묻는 질문이 들어있죠?

B 인터뷰가 아니니 걱정 마세요. 자원봉사자들을 최대한 활용하려는 거예요.

일상생활

47 He's half the size he used to be.

그는 몸이 반쪽이 됐어.

A Did you see Mark Hill?
He's half the size he used to be.

B A few years back he dropped all the weight and opened a chain of gyms.

A I heard he married Jane Henderson. She was the most popular girl at school.

B Good for him. In the end, he got the girl.

A 너 마크 힐 봤어?
몸이 반쪽이 됐어.

B 걔 몇 년 전에 살을 전부 빼고 체육관 체인점을 열었어.

A 제인 헨더슨과 결혼했다고 하던데, 그 애가 학교에서 제일 예뻤잖아.

B 잘됐네. 결국 헨더슨과 결혼했구나.

일상생활

48 It's not easy to find someone on such short notice.

급하게 부탁할 수 있는 사람을 찾기가 쉽지 않네요.

A **It's not easy to find someone on such short notice.**

B Let me call my sister.

A You mean, she'll come over and look after the kids for a few hours?

B No, but she should be able to recommend someone.
I know she has a few babysitters she usually uses.

A 급하게 부탁할 수 있는 사람을 찾기가 쉽지 않네요.

B 여동생한테 전화해볼게요.

A 처제가 와서 몇 시간 동안 아이를 본다는 말이에요?

B 아니요, 그 애가 아이 봐줄 사람을 추천해줄 거예요.
자주 부르는 사람이 몇 명 있거든요.

일상생활

49 You can leave any valuables at the front desk

귀중품은 카운터에 맡길 수 있습니다.

A Do I have to bring my own lock for the lockers?

B No. All the lockers have built-in locks and we'll give you a key every time you come.

A Are the locks any good?
I don't want my stuff to get stolen.

B **You can leave any valuables at the front desk** if you're worried.

A 사물함을 잠글 자물쇠를 제가 갖고 와야 하나요?

B 아니요, 모든 사물함에 자물쇠가 붙어 있어서 오실 때 마다 열쇠를 드려요.

A 자물쇠는 잘 잠기나요?
소지품을 도난당하면 안 되잖아요.

B 걱정되시면 귀중품은 카운터에 맡길 수 있습니다.

일상생활

50 That depends on how old she is

그녀의 나이에 따라 달라요.

A What's a good CD for my daughter?

B **That depends on how old she is** and what sort of music she likes.

A She's twelve and to be honest I have no idea what kind of music she listens to.

B The new Cindy is a safe bet.
She is really popular with young girls.

A 딸에게 줄 CD로 뭐가 좋을까요?

B 몇 살인지, 또 어떤 음악을 좋아하는지에 따라 달라요.

A 12살인데, 솔직히 어떤 음악을 듣는지 잘 모르겠어요.

B 새로 나온 신디음악이라면 틀림없이 좋아할 거예요.
여자아이들에게 인기가 아주 많아요.

일상생활

51 What would you describe as your worst quality?

본인의 단점을 말해 볼래요?

A **What would you describe as your worst quality?**

B In the past, I used to work too hard.
What I mean is, I would push myself too much.

A And is this something you still do?

B A little bit, but I also try not to be so hard on myself.

A 본인의 단점을 말해 볼래요?

B 예전에는 일을 너무 열심히 했습니다. 제 스스로를 지나치게 다그쳤다는 뜻이죠.

A 그럼 지금도 그런 가요?

B 조금 그렇긴 하지만, 제 자신에게 너무 심하게 하지는 않으려고 노력합니다.

일상생활

52 The machine is beeping

기계에서 삑 소리가 나요.

A I'd like to pay for everything with my credit card.
Here it is.

B Thank you. I'll just swipe the card and then ask you to sign the receipt.

A **The machine is beeping.**
It looks like there's something wrong with the card.

B Actually, it says your card has been declined.
You might have to try another one.

A 신용카드로 다 계산할게요.
여기 있습니다.

B 감사합니다. 제가 카드를 긁고 나면 영수증에 서명을 부탁드릴게요.

A 기계에서 삑 소리가 나는데요.
카드에 무슨 문제가 있는 거 같아요.

B 손님, 카드가 승인되지 않았다고 나오네요.
다른 카드로 해봐야겠네요.

일상생활 53 It's a great chance to see a living legend.

유명인을 볼 수 있는 굉장한 기회야.

A How much longer are we going to have to stand in line?

B Be patient. This is a once in a lifetime chance to meet the author.

A I know. **It's a great chance to see a living legend.**

B Well, I just want him to sign this book.
Then I can double my money selling it on e-bay.

A 줄을 얼마나 더 서야 할까?

B 조금만 참아. 작가를 만날 기회는 평생 한 번 뿐이야.

A 알아. 유명인을 볼 수 있는 굉장한 기회라는 거.

B 난 이 책에 사인을 받을 거야.
그러면 이-베이에서 이걸 두 배 가격으로 팔 수 있어.

일상생활 54 You don't need a lot of detergent.

세제는 많이 필요 없어요.

A **You don't need a lot of detergent.**

B Right. Look at this shirt. Everything looks OK, but the collar is really dirty.

A "Ring around the collar." You'll need to add some stain remover directly to the fabric.

B OK. Let me take care of that for you.

A 세제는 많이 필요 없어요.

B 맞아요. 이 셔츠 좀 봐요. 깃의 때만 아니면 다 멀쩡해 보여요.

A "깃 주위에 때 탄 거네요." 옷깃에 직접 얼룩 제거제를 뿌려요.

B 알겠어요. 당신 거니까 신경 쓸게요.

일상생활 55 Did you make your payment last month?

지난달 카드 대금 냈어?

A It says my card was declined. What should I do?

B **Did you make your payment last month?**
The bank might have cancelled your card.

A That can't be it. Could it be something else?

B Well, if the purchase is really large, it might exceed your daily limit.

A 카드 사용이 정지됐다고 나오네. 어떻게 해야 하니?

B 지난달 카드 대금 냈어?
은행에서 네 카드를 취소했을지도 몰라.

A 그건 아닐 거야. 다른 이유 때문 아닐까?

B 음, 구매 금액이 아주 클 경우 하루 사용 한도액을 초과할 수도 있어.

일상생활

56 I guess they're afraid of credit card fraud.

신용카드 사기를 염려하는 거 같아.

A The guy in the store spent a long time looking at my card.

B He was just making sure your signature matched the one on the card.

A **I guess they're afraid of credit card fraud.**

B Sure. If you lose your card, you should call and cancel is as soon as possible.

A 가게 점원이 내 카드를 오랫동안 살펴보고 있었어.

B 저 사람은 네 서명이 카드에 있는 것과 같은지 확인하고 있던 거야.

A 신용카드 사기를 염려하는 거구나.

B 그럼, 만일 카드를 잃어버리면 최대한 빨리 전화해서 카드사용을 금지시켜야 해.

일상생활

57 I guess a fixer-upper is out of the question.

리모델링용 주택은 안 되겠군요.

A Tell me about your husband. Is he handy with tools?

B My husband has to hire someone to change light bulbs.

A **I guess a fixer-upper is out of the question**, then.

A 남편에 대해 얘기를 좀 해주세요. 연장을 잘 다루시나요?

B 제 남편은 전구 바꿀 때도 사람을 불러야 해요.

A 그럼 리모델링용 주택은 어렵겠군요.

일상생활

58 The lyrics are all about violence.

가사가 전부 폭력에 관한 거예요.

A What does this label on the front of the CD mean?

B That's the parental advisory sticker.

A I guess **the lyrics are all about violence.**

B Right. It's store policy to not sell any CD with that sticker on it to kids under the age of fifteen.

A CD 앞에 붙은 이 라벨은 뭔가요?

B 부모의 동의가 있어야 판다는 스티커입니다.

A 가사들이 전부 폭력에 관한 거군요.

B 네. 이런 스티커가 붙은 CD는 15세 이하의 아이들에게 팔지 않는 게 가게 방침입니다.

일상생활
59 What if the market crashes?
집값이 떨어지면 어떡해요?

A This house has a lot of potential.
You're looking at a really nice ROI.

B ROI? What's that?

A It's "return on investment" You buy the house, do some quick cosmetic improvements and then sell it at a profit.

B But **what if the market crashes?**

A 이 집은 개발 가능성이 많아요.
로이가 정말 괜찮네요.

B 로이? 그게 뭐예요?

A '투자 수익률'요. 집을 사서 빨리 외관을 바꾸어 팔면 이익이 남죠.

B 그런데 집값이 떨어지면 어떡해요?

일상생활
60 That's the last straw.
더 이상 못 참아!

A **That's the last straw** Sam.
You don't respect me at all.

B I do. You have done great work as the vice-president of this company.

A Then why do you constantly refer to me as "honey"?

B I just thought that you looked sexy in that red dress.

A That's borderline sexual harassment.
Do you want me to sue you?

B You know that's the last thing I want, honey.

A That's it. I'm finished here. I quit.
I'm cleaning out my office this afternoon.

A 더 이상 못 참겠어요.
당신은 나를 전혀 생각하지 않는군요.

B 그래요. 당신은 이 회사의 부회장으로 많은 일을 했어요.

A 근데 당신은 왜 나를 계속해서 애인으로 취급하나요?

B 당신이 빨간 드레스를 입으면 섹시해 보일거라 생각했지요.

A 그건 성희롱에 가까운데요.
내가 고소하길 바라세요?

B 아니 그러고 싶지 않아요.

A 그럼 여기까지 하죠. 오늘 오후에 회사를 정리하겠어요.

일상생활
61 You are a sight for sore eyes.
만나서 정말 반갑다.

A Brian! How are you? **You are a sight for sore eyes!**

B It has been a while hasn't it? How have you been?

A I've been okay, but it's great to see a friendly face.

A 브라이언! 잘 지냈어? 만나서 정말 반갑다!

B 정말 오랜만이네. 그동안 어떻게 지냈어?

A 난 잘 지냈지. 오랜만에 반가운 얼굴을 보니 정말 좋다.

일상생활

62 Don't get me started.

말도 꺼내지 마세요.

A Have you seen Tom's latest numbers? It looks like the department is having some real problems.

B **Don't get me started.** The whole department needs to be fired. they're driving me nuts.

A Well, it's something that needs to be deal with. let's schedule a meeting for this afternoon, at the latest.

A 톰의 최근 실적 봤어요? 그 부서는 심각한 문제가 있는 것 같아요.

B 말도 꺼내지 마요. 부서 직원을 전부 다 해고시켜야 해요. 그 부서 때문에 정말 미치겠어요.

A 음, 이건 꼭 짚고 넘어가야 할 문제예요. 늦어도 오늘 오후에는 회의 일정을 잡으세요.

일상생활

63 That's a wrap.

끝났어요.

A And **that's a wrap!** Thanks everyone for all your hard work. I really appreciate it.

B That's it? But I thought we would spend more time hammering out the details.

A Nope. I just needed your help with the general ideas. I can take it from here and finish it on my own.

A 오늘은 여기까지요! 모두들 정말 수고 많았어요. 정말 고마워요.

B 끝이라고요? 세부적인 내용들을 좀 더 논의할 줄 알았는데요.

A 아니요. 전반적인 계획에 대해서만 여러분들의 도움이 필요했어요. 오늘 의견을 바탕으로 제가 혼자서 끝내도록 할게요.

일상생활

64 I'd rather not ask someone in the family.

가족에게 부탁하고 싶진 않아요.

A We're running out of options.
Thereis only a few more names on our list.

B If worse comes to worst, we can call your nephew and ask him.

A **I'd rather not ask someone in the family.**
It's better to hire a stranger.

B I agree. It feels strange to pay someone in your own family.

A 선택할 수 있는 사람이 얼마 없어요.
생각나는 사람이 거의 없거든요.

B 정 안되면 당신 조카한테 전화해서 물어봐요.

A 가족에게 부탁하고 싶진 않아요.
아예 모르는 사람이 낫죠.

B 그러게요. 가족에게 돈을 주기가 좀 껄끄럽긴 해요.

일상생활

65 What a trip down memory lane!

그리운 추억이여!

A **What a trip down memory lane!**

B I agree.

It was interesting to see how everyone turned out.

A For some people, high school was the only happy part of their lives.

B And it's been all down hill for them. But for a lot of people, they moved on to bigger and better things.

A 그리운 추억이여!

B 맞아.

다들 어떻게 변했는지 보니까 정말 즐겁다.

A 몇몇 친구들에겐 고등학교 때가 인생에서 유일하게 행복한 시절이었어.

B 그들에게는 그 후로 쭉 내리막길이었나 봐. 하지만 많은 사람들이 더 성공하고 발전했어.

일상생활

66 It's my treat.

내가 한턱 낼께.

A Put your wallet away. These coffees are on me.

It's my treat.

B But I thought you didn't have any cash on you.

How are you going to pay?

A I'll charge it. I've got my credit card with me.

B In that case, thanks.

A 지갑은 넣어둬. 이 커피는 내가 살게.

내가 한턱 낼 거야.

B 그런데 너 돈 없는 거 같던데 어떻게 계산하려고?

A 카드로 계산할 거야. 신용카드를 가져왔거든.

B 그렇다면 고마워.

일상생활

67 He's had his eye on you.

그가 너를 눈여겨 봐왔어.

A Do you remember George from my office?

He's had his eye on you since last Christmas.

B Really? He is kind of cute. Can you set us up?

A No sweat. I'll invite the two of you over for dinner on the same night.

B Good, That way it won's feel like a blind date at all.

A 우리 회사 다니는 조지 기억나?

그가 지난 크리스마스부터 너를 눈여겨봐왔어.

B 정말? 그 사람 멋있잖아. 우리 주선 좀 해줄래?

A 물론이지. 너희 둘을 같은 날 밤 저녁 식사에 초대할게.

B 좋아 그런 경우 소개팅 같은 분위기도 없을 거야.

일상생활

68 Time is really dragging on for me today.

오늘은 시간이 지독히도 안 가는군.

A May I spreak to Il-Hyung Kim?

B Speaking.

A Hi, Il-Hyung. This is Kenny. How is it going today?

B **Time is really dragging on for me today.**

A You must be tired or something.

B No. This job I'm doing is really boring.

A 김일형씨 부탁합니다.

B 접니다.

A 일형아, 나 케니인데, 오늘 어떻게 지내고 있냐?

B 오늘 진짜 시간 안 가네.

A 피곤한 모양이구나.

B 아니. 내가 하고 있는 일이 지겨워서 그래.

일상생활

69 I was just in the neighborhood.

잠깐 근처에 들렀어요.

A What's new with you?

B **I was just in the neighborhood.**

I couldn't resist sneaking a preview of the opening.

A Did Nancy come along with you?

B No, she couldn't make it,

because she is swamped with work.

A What a pity!

By the way, what time does the opening start?

B 1 p.m. on the dot.

A 어쩐 일이야?

B 잠깐 근처에 들렀어.

개업식을 미리 보고 싶어서 참을 수가 없었거든.

A 낸시도 같이 왔니?

B 아니, 그녀는 오지 못했어.

그녀는 너무 일이 많거든.

A 유감이군!

그런데 개업식은 몇 시에 시작이야?

B 오후 1시 정각이야.

일상생활

70 Not your usual slapdash work.

늘 하듯 대충하지 마세요.

A Kenny, could you mow the lawn today?

B Don't worry, Dad.

A And **not your usual slapdash work.** Lately you've been getting sloppy in a lot of things.

B I've got a lot of things to do. I don't have enough time for all your work.

A 케니야, 오늘 잔디 좀 깎아줄래?

B 걱정 마세요, 아빠.

A 네가 늘 하듯 대충하지 말거라. 요즘 들어 많은 일을 대강 아무렇게나 해왔잖니.

B 저도 할 일이 많이 있어요. 아빠가 시키시는 일을 다 할 시간이 충분치 못해요.

일상생활

71 Let's face it.

현실을 직시하세요.

A I want my daughter to go to Princeton no matter what.

B **Let's face it.** Mr. Huh.

Your daughter's high school GPA and SAT score are not good enough for her to be admitted to Princeton.

A My daughter's extra curricular activities and writing skills are perfect.

B Whatever you say,

the most important thing is school GPA.

A 내 딸을 무슨 일이 있어도 프린스턴 대학에 보내고 싶어요.

B 허 선생님. 현실을 직시하시죠.

따님의 학교성적과 수능성적은 프린스턴대학에 입학하기에 충분치 못해요.

A 내 딸의 과외 활동과 글 솜씨가 완벽하잖아요.

B 뭐라 하시건,

가장 중요한 것은 내신성적입니다.

일상생활

72 I'm about ready to wrap it up.

거의 끝나가요.

A Kenny, please finish building the dog house.

B Morn! Don't worry. **I'm about ready to wrap it up.**

A Your nephew, Sebastian, wants you to go to a movie with him.

B Really? I scolded him just before.

He didn't keep the important promise.

A Forgive him and be generous to him.

He is still young.

A 케니야, 개집 짓는 것 빨리 끝내렴.

B 엄마 걱정 마세요. 거의 끝나가요.

A 네 조카 세바스천이 너랑 영화 구경을 가길 원하고 있다.

B 정말요? 내가 조금 전에 꾸짖었는데요.

중요한 약속을 지키지 않아서요.

A 용서해 주고 너그럽게 대해줘라.

아직 어리잖아.

일상생활

73 It's just my gut feeling.

그저 내 직감이 그래요.

A Something tells me that the Stevens will break up soon.

B You mean they may divorce?

A Yes.

B Why do you think so?

A **It's just my gut feeling.**

A 스티븐 부부가 곧 헤어질 예감이 드는데.

B 이혼할 수도 있다는 말이니?

A 그래.

B 왜 그렇게 생각하니?

A 그저 내 직감이 그래.

일상생활

74 It will come in handy.

상당히 도움이 될 것입니다.

A Do you have any special plans for this summer?

B Yes, I'm going to New York to visit Stuybesant High School and Baruch College.

A Really? I went there a couple of years ago.

B Could you give me some advice?

A Take this book with you when you go to New York. **It'll come in handy.**

B Oh, thank you.

A 이번 여름에 무슨 특별한 계획이라도 있어요?

B 네, 스타이브슨 고교와 버룩대학교를 방문하러 뉴욕에 갈 거에요.

A 정말요? 이삼 년 전에 저도 갔었어요.

B 조언 좀 해주세요.

A 뉴욕에 갈 때 이 책을 갖고 가세요. 상당히 도움이 될 거에요.

B 감사합니다.

일상생활

75 I haven't cracked it yet.

아직 못 알아냈어.

A Hey, buddy, How's it going?

B Oh, good to see you. I', in grave peril. I need your help.

A Okay, what is the problem?

B I spent a whole night trying to find the code but **I haven't cracked it yet.**

A You haven't? Then I can't. You're second to none cracking codes.

A 이봐, 친구. 일은 잘 돼가?

B 야, 마침 잘 만났네. 심각한 문제가 생겼어. 네 도움이 필요해.

A 알았어. 뭐가 문젠데?

B 밤새 암호를 풀어보려고 애썼는데 아직도 못했어.

A 네가 못했다면 나도 못해. 넌 암호 해독엔 최고잖아.

일상생활

76 Beats (the hell out of) me.

난 전혀 모르겠다.

A What's that one about?

B **Beats the hell out of me.**

A Well, it's got Brad Pitt and Johnny Depp in it.

B Did you say Jonny Depp? Then it's got to be a flop.

A Come on, John. You can't brand him as a bad actor just because of one movie.

B I know you're a big fan of his, so don't even try.

A 저건 어떤 내용이지?

B 전혀 모르겠는데.

A 글쎄, 브래드 피트와 자니 뎁이 나오는데.

B 자니 뎁이라고 했니? 그럼 분명 실패작이겠네.

A 그러지 마, 존. 영화 하나 때문에 그를 나쁜 연기자로 낙인찍을 순 없잖아.

B 자니 뎁의 열렬한 팬인 거 아니까 시도도 하지 마.

일상생활

77 I hear you loud and clear.

무슨 말인지 잘 알겠어.

A Mona, would you join me and Cathy for a movie tonight?

B I'd love to. But isn't it weird, me and Cathy? We had a big fight a month ago.

A I know. But it happened a month ago.

B Well.... I'd like to hang around with you but....

A Come on! Don't you wanna make up with her?

B **I hear you loud and clear.**

A 모나, 오늘 나랑 캐시랑 영화 보러 갈래?

B 가고는 싶지만 캐시랑 같이 가면 불편하지 않을까? 한 달 전에 크게 싸웠는데.

A 나도 알아. 하지만 한 달 전 일이잖아.

B 글쎄…. 너랑은 가고 싶지만 그래도 좀….

A 같이 가자! 너도 화해하고 싶지 않아?

B 무슨 말인지는 잘 알겠어.

일상생활

78 I'll go for broke.

모든 것을 걸고 최선을 다하겠다.

A I've decided to invest all my savings in this business venture.

B If it fails, you will go broke. Think twice.

A I'm so certain of succeeding in this business that **I'll go for broke.**

B Well, I'll keep my fingers crossed.

A 나는 그동안 저축한 돈 전부를 이 사업에 투자하기로 마음먹었습니다.

B 실패하면 망하는 것이니 재고해 보세요.

A 이 사업의 성공에 자신이 있기에 모든 것을 걸겠어요.

B 그렇다면 행운을 빌겠습니다.

일상생활

79 Don't get any hopes up.

어떤 희망도 기대하지 마세요.

A Could you do me a favor?.

B Sure, what can I do for you?

A You filmed a lot on my wedding day, right? I wondered if I could look at your videotape because mine has come out all blue.

B OK, but I'm pretty sure I wiped it, so **don't get any hopes up.**

A 저 부탁 하나 할까요?

B 그래요, 뭐죠?

A 제 결혼식 때 식장에서 촬영 많이 하셨죠? 제가 가진 녹화 테이프의 상태가 엉망이라 그러는데요. 당신이 찍은 비디오테이프 좀 볼 수 없을까요?

B 저런, 제 테이프는 이미 확실히 지워 버린 것 같은데요.
(미안하지만) 제게는 기대하지 않는 게 좋을 것 같군요.

일상생활

80 I'm afraid I was taken for a ride.

내가 속은 것 같아요.

A Could you give me a ride home, please?

B Yes, but what happened to your car?

A It broke down again. I think I got a lemon from the used car dealer.

B Maybe. It's not easy to buy a used car without **being taken for a ride**, you know.

A 우리 집까지 차 좀 태워주시겠어요?

B 그래요. 그런데 당신 차에 무슨 문제가 있나요?

A 또 고장 났어요. 결함 있는 중고차 딜러에게서 엉터리 차를 구입한 것 같아요.

B 그럴지도 모르죠. 속지 않고 중고차를 사는 게 쉬운 일이 아니지요.

일상생활

81 It's all been taken care of.

다 처리됐어.

A Did you see the telephone bill?
I think the due day was a few days ago.

B Yes, it was due last Friday. But don't worry.

A What do you mean?

B **It's all been taken care of.**
I already paid it online last week.

A Whew, I am relieved now.

A 전화요금 고지서 봤니?
납부 기한이 며칠이나 지난 것 같던데.

B 응, 지난 금요일이 납부 마감일이었지. 그러나 걱정하지 마.

A 무슨 소리니?

B 납부됐어.
지난주에 온라인으로 지급했거든.

A 후유, 다행이야.

일상생활

82 You're barking up the wrong tree.

넌 잘못 짚었어.

A What're you going to do this afternoon?

B Nothing. What about you?

A Nothing either. I thought you might go out with Brent.

B What's that supposed to mean?
Why would I go out with Brent?

A Isn't something going on with you two?

B Me and Brent? No way.
You're barking up the wrong tree.

A 오늘 오후에 뭐해?

B 아무것도 안 해. 너는?

A 나도 별일 없어. 넌 브렌트를 만나러 외출할 줄 알았는 데.

B 그게 무슨 소리야?
내가 왜 브렌트를 만나?

A 너희 둘 사이에 뭔가 있지 않아?

B 나랑 브렌트랑? 아니.
너 완전히 잘못 짚었어.

일상생활

83 Don't use four-letter words.

나쁜 말을 쓰지 마라.

A Kenny, what do you think of our new vice president?
B He strikes me as a mean SOB.
He uses a lot of **four-letter words**, doesn't he?
A Yes, he does.
B Did you attend the board meeting yesterday?
A Yes I did.

A 케니, 새로운 부사장은 어때?
B 인상이 아주 안 좋아.
말끝마다 욕을 하잖아. 안 그래?
A 맞아.
B 너 어제 이사회에 참석했었니?
A 응. 했어.

일상생활

84 Think nothing of it.

별말씀을요.

A Here is the paper you asked to get done by today.
B It was nice of you to do that for me.
Without your help, I wouldn't be able to submit it to my boss on time. How can I thank you?
A It's no big deal. **Think nothing of it.**
B I really appreciate your help.

A 당신이 오늘까지 해달라고 부탁했던 서류에요.
B 부탁한 일을 해주셔서 감사해요.
당신이 아니었더라면 제시간에 상사에게 제출하지 못할 뻔했어요.
A 별것 아닙니다. 별말씀을요.
B 당신의 도움에 정말 감사드립니다.

일상생활

85 Could you be a little more specific?

좀 더 구체적으로 말씀해 주시겠어요?

A Mr. Kim, your letter is a bit vague.
Could you be a little more specific?
B Well, in what ways, for example?
A Well, it states that you are interested in importing electronic parts, but it doesn't specify which items.
B Oh, I see. Okay, I'll complete the details and send them off to you when I get back to the States.

A 김선생, 편지 내용이 좀 모호하군요.
좀 더 구체적으로 말씀해 주시겠어요?
B 예를 들어 어떤 점들을 말씀하시는 거죠?
A 편지에는 귀사가 전자 부품의 수입에 대해 관심이 있다고 되어있는데, 어떤 품목인지에 대해서는 구체적으로 명시되어 있지 않아서요.
B 아, 알겠습니다. 미국으로 돌아가 세부 사항을 완성해서 보내지요.

일상생활

86 The suspense is killing me.

궁금해서 미치겠어.

A You have to tell me what's going to happen next.

B No way. Just watch the movie and see for yourself.

A **The suspense is killing me.** I have to know now.

B Sorry.

I don't want to ruin the ending for you.

A 이다음에 어떻게 되는지 말 좀 해봐.

B 절대로 안 돼. 그냥 영화 보고 알면 되잖아.

A 궁금해서 죽겠어. 난 지금 알아야겠단 말이야.

B 미안해.

괜히 결말을 말해 줘서 네 영화감상을 망치고 싶지 않아.

일상생활

87 I haven't seen you for ages!

진짜 오랜만이다!

A Look who's here! Jane Johnson!

B Mark! Gosh, **I haven't seen you for ages!**

How are getting along?

A Can't complain. How are you keeping?

B Well, the same old thing.

Anyways, it's great to see you again.

A 이게 누구야! 제인 존슨 아냐?

B 마크! 어머 진짜 오랜만이다.

그동안 어떻게 지냈어?

A 잘 지내지. 너는 잘 지내?

B 글쎄, 똑같지 뭐.

그나저나 다시 만나서 정말 반갑다.

일상생활

88 Don't bother.

그럴 필요 없어.

A Hey, Ian. Where're you headed?

B I'm going to the downstairs to make a copy.

A **Don't bother.**

The copy machine is not working right now.

B What? Are you sure? I'm in a rush to do this.

A Sure. I was just there. Why don't you use a copy machine on the 9th floor?

A 안녕, 이안. 어디가?

B 아래층에 복사하러 가는 길이야.

A 가봤자 헛수고야.

지금은 복사기가 작동이 안돼.

B 뭐야? 확실해? 내가 좀 급해서.

A 확실해. 방금 거기서 오는 길이야.

9층에 있는 복사기를 사용하지 그래?

일상생활

89 Crime doesn't pay.

죄를 지으면 벌을 받기 마련이지.

A I heard that the CEO of ABC Company was sent to jail for insider trading!

B I saw that in the newspaper.
He was sentenced to fifteen years in prison.

A Wow! I guess **crime doesn't pay!**

A ABC사의 사장이 내부자 거래로 구속되었대!

B 나도 신문에서 봤어.
15년형을 선고 받았더라.

A 와! 죄를 지으면 벌을 받기 마련이지!

일상생활

90 Holy cow!

야, 세상에!

A Oh, my gosh! Look over there!

B **Holy cow!** I can't believe my eyes!

A What is it?

B I don't know, but it looks like a UFO.

A 어머나! 저기 좀 봐!

B 세상에! 도저히 내 눈을 믿을 수가 없어!

A 저게 뭐야?

B 모르겠어. 하지만 UFO같이 보이는데.

일상생활

91 Where's the beef?

이게 다야?

A Here is my report. I'm all finished!

B **Where's the beef?**

A What do you mean? I wrote four pages.

B But it's supposed to be a twenty-page paper.

A 여기 제 보고서요. 다 끝났습니다!

B 이게 다야?

A 무슨 말씀이세요? 4페이지나 썼는데.

B 20페이지짜리여야 하잖아.

일상생활

92 Have we met before?

우리 전에 만나지 않았니?

A **Have we met before?**

B No, but I think I've seen you around campus.
My name's Kim.

A I'm Mark.

A 우리 전에 만나지 않았나?

B 아니, 근데 학교에서 본 적이 있는 것 같아.
내 이름은 킴이야.

A 난 마크야.

일상생활
93 Period.

확실해!

A Did you make up your mind about going to Hong Kong?
B Yes. I told Mr. Paulman that I'd accept his proposition.
A **Period?**
B **Period!** I slept on it almost a week.
That's more than enough, I believe.
A Good for you.
I'm sure this will be a once-in-a-lifetime opportunity.
B I hope so.

A 홍콩에 갈지 말지 결정했어?
B 응. 폴먼씨에게 제안을 받아들이겠다고 했어.
A 확실해?
B 확실해! 일주일이나 고민했는걸.
그 정도면 충분히 생각하고도 남은 것 같아.
A 잘됐다.
내게 일생일대의 기회가 될 거야.
B 나도 그랬으면 좋겠어.

일상생활
94 You could have gone to an ATM and got a cash advance.

현금자동지급기에서 현금서비스를 받을 수도 있어.

A I was at a small store that only took cash.
B **You could have gone to an ATM and got a cash advance.**
A If it had been an emergency. But those advances can be expensive, and the interest rates are really high.

A 작은 가게에 갔더니 현금만 받는대.
B 현금자동지급기에서 현금서비스를 받을 수도 있었잖아.
A 급한 일이었으면 그랬겠지. 하지만 현금서비스는 비싼 데다가 이자율이 아주 높아.

일상생활
95 The faucet keeps dripping.

수도꼭지에서 물이 계속 떨어져요.

A **The faucet keeps dripping.**
We're wasting a lot of water.
B I'll get my tools and try to fix the problem.

A 수도꼭지에서 물이 계속 떨어져요.
이건 물 낭비에요.
B 제가 공구를 가지고 와서 고쳐볼게요.

일상생활

96 The table is set for dinner.

저녁상 다 차렸어.

A **The table is set for dinner.**

B Is the ketchup on the table?

A Yes.

A 저녁상 다 차렸어?

B 상 위에 케첩 있니?

A 응.

일상생활

97 After today they expire.

유효기간이 오늘까지야.

A I've got a lot of coupons I have to use, because **after today they expire.**

B One is for peanuts and another for hot sauce. What can you make with all of these things?

A Well, they don't really go together, but I can save them for later.

B Right. And think of all the money you'll save.

A 써야 할 쿠폰이 많이 있어. 유효기간이 오늘까지거든.

B 하나는 땅콩, 또 하나는 핫 소스 쿠폰이네. 이걸 갖고 뭐 해 먹을 수 있지?

A 글쎄, 어울리는 재료는 아니지만 나중을 위해서 아껴두면 되잖아.

B 맞아. 그리고 절약되는 돈을 생각해봐.

일상생활

98 They jack up the prices.

그들은 가격을 올려 팔아요.

A Before we head off, let's make sure we have everything we'll need for the day.

B Don't they have shops there? I'm sure we can pick up anything we forget.

A But **they jack up the prices** at the stores in the park.

B I guess you're right. Hand me that extra bottle of water.

A 가기 전에 오늘 하루 필요한 걸 다 챙겼는지 확인해봐요.

B 거기에 가게 없어요? 잊고 안 챙긴 물건은 사면 돼요.

A 하지만 공원에 있는 가게들은 가격을 올려서 팔아요.

B 당신 말이 맞아요. 물을 더 가져가게 내게 줘요.

일상생활

99 It sure is dismal out today.

오늘은 정말 바깥 날씨가 음산하네.

A How do you like this weather?

B **It sure is dismal out today.**

A 오늘 날씨 어때?

B 오늘은 정말 바깥 날씨가 음산하네.

일상생활 100 There is a slight discount on dented cans.

찌그러진 통조림은 약간 할인이 됩니다.

A This can appears to have a dent in it.

B I'm sorry, sir, but that's all we have in stock. I'm sure the contents are fine.

A Well, I guess I could try. I'll be able to return it and get my money back if there's a problem?

B Of course. And **there is a slight discount on dented cans**, too.

A 이 통조림은 찌그러졌어요.

B 손님, 죄송하지만 이것밖에 없습니다. 내용물은 괜찮을 거예요.

A 그럼 사겠어요. 만일 내용물에 이상이 있으면 반납하고 돈을 되돌려 받을 수 있는 거죠?

B 물론입니다. 그리고 찌그러진 통조림은 약간 할인이 됩니다.

일상생활 101 How did they track me down all the way across the country?

전국 방방곡곡을 뒤져서 어떻게 나를 찾아냈지?

A Did you get your letter from the class reunion committee?

B Mine came last week. **How did they track me down all the way across the country?**

A I don't know how they found me either.

B Well, I guess we'll have to go to our class reunion. There's no way around it.

A 동창회에서 온 편지 받았니?

B 지난주에 왔더라. 전국 방방곡곡을 뒤져서 어떻게 나를 찾아냈을까?

A 그 사람들이 나도 어떻게 찾았는지 모르겠네.

B 음, 동창회에 가야 할 거 같아. 어쩔 수 없지.

일상생활 102 The toilet is blocked up.

화장실이 막혔어요.

A Hey, **your toilet is blocked up.**

B What did you do to it?

A Nothing, it was already like that when I went in.

A 저기요, 화장실이 막혔는데요.

B 어떻게 해서 막혔나요?

A 아무 짓도 안 했어요. 제가 들어갔을 때 이미 막혀 있던데요.

일상생활

103 Is our account overdrawn?

한도를 넘었나요?

A Your transaction was denied.

B **Is our account overdrawn?**

A I don't know.

A 카드가 안 되는데요.

B 한도를 넘었나요?

A 저도 모르겠습니다.

일상생활

104 Are you going to vegetate in front of the TV all day?

하루 종일 텔레비전만 보고 있을 거니?

A **Are you going to vegetate in front of the TV all day?**

B Why not? I've finished my final exam, so I have nothing to do but watch TV. I want to catch up on Ally Mcbeal.

A That program has recently gone down hill.

B You mean the show is boring now?

A 하루 종일 텔레비전만 보고 있을 거니?

B 왜 안돼? 기말고사 끝나고 텔레비전 보는 것밖에는 할 것이 없어. 앨리 맥빌을 볼 거야.

A 요즘에는 내용이 점점 형편없어지는 것 같아.

B 지루하다는 거니?

일상생활

105 I'm tickled to death.

너무 좋아 죽겠다.

A **I'm tickled to death** that you are getting married at last.

B Thank you.

A I hear your bride is coming from Russia. Is that true?

B Yes, I'm dying to see her.

A I'll bet.

A 드디어 당신이 결혼한다니 더할 나위 없이 기쁩니다.

B 감사합니다.

A 듣기론 러시아에서 신부가 온다던데 사실입니까?

B 네. 그녀가 보고 싶어 죽을 지경입니다.

A 그러시겠죠.

일상생활

106 It was a really long day.

정말 힘든 하루였어.

A **It was a really long day.**

B I'm sorry to hear that. Here at home, you can relax.

A 정말 힘든 하루였어.

B 안됐군요. 이제 집에 돌아왔으니 쉬세요.

일상생활

107 She was mugged in an alleyway.

그녀는 골목길에서 강도를 당했대.

A Did you hear about Kate? **She was mugged in an alleyway** last week.

B That's horrible! Was she hurt?

A No, but the man had a knife and demanded her purse. She wasn't going to argue!

A 너 지난주에 케이트가 골목에서 강도를 당한 일을 들었어?

B 저런! 다치지 않았대?

A 응, 칼을 든 강도가 핸드백을 달라고 해서 주저 없이 줬대!

일상생활

108 I got this second-hand.

이거 헌 옷 가게에서 샀어.

A You look stunning in that coat. Where did you buy?

B Does it look good? **I got this second-hand.**

A No way! It doesn't look old at all.

B I had it altered a bit and I think that helped.

A 너 그 코트 입으니까 정말 멋지다. 어디서 샀어?

B 괜찮아 보여? 이거 헌 옷 가게에서 산 거야.

A 말도 안 돼! 전혀 오래된 것 같지 않은데?

B 조금 수선했지. 아마 그래서일 거야.

일상생활

109 I can't wait for it to snow.

눈이 안 오면 견딜 수가 없어.

A **I can't wait for it to snow.**

B Really?

A Yes. Where I grew up there was lots of snow in the winter.

A 눈이 안오면 견딜 수가 없어.

B 정말?

A 응, 내가 자란 곳은 겨울이면 눈이 엄청 많이 내렸거든.

일상생활

110 They startled me.

너무 놀랐으니까.

A Why did you jump back when they all started yelling and screaming?

B Because **they startled me.**

A 사람들이 모두 소리치기 시작했을 때 왜 뒤로 물러났어?

B 너무 놀랐으니까.

일상생활

111 They're all out of style.

(옷들이) 전부 유행이 지났어.

A I need to go shopping. I don't have a thing to wear.

B Oh, not again. Check your closet. You've got tons of clothes.

A **They're all out of style.** I need to update my wardrobe to the latest fashion.

B Well, enjoy your shopping spree but take care not to wear yourself out.

A 나 쇼핑하러 가야 해. 입을 옷이 하나도 없어.

B 어휴, 또 그런다. 네 옷장 좀 봐. 얼마나 입을 옷이 많은데.

A 그 옷들 모두 유행지난 거야. 최신 유행에 맞춰 입고 싶단 말이야.

B 그렇다면 마음껏 쇼핑해. 그래도 지치지는 않게 조심하고.

일상생활

112 I hope it doesn't get too bumpy.

지나치게 난기류가 아니었으면 좋겠네요.

A Could you fasten your seat belt?

B Sorry?

A We have the 'Fasten Seat Belt' sign. We may have some turbulence.

B I get it. **I hope it doesn't get too bumpy.**

A Don't be concerned about it. We will be fine.

A 안전벨트 착용해 주시겠어요?

B 네? 뭐라고요?

A 안전벨트착용 표시등이 동작 중입니다. 기체가 아마 좀 흔들릴 것 같습니다.

B 네 알았어요. 지나치게 난기류가 아니었으면 좋겠네요.

A 너무 걱정하지 마세요. 괜찮을 겁니다.

일상생활

113 Have you thought about being a candy striper?

간호보조원 해보는 게 어떠니?

A I have to choose which volunteer work to do.

B **Have you thought about being a candy striper?**

A No way! I don't want to be stuck around a bunch of sick people.

B Oh, well. I guess I'll give up my dream of you becoming a doctor, then.

A 어떤 봉사활동을 할지 선택해야 돼요.

B 간호보조원 해보는 게 어떠니?

A 싫어요! 아픈 사람들 속에 갇혀 있고 싶지는 않아요.

B 그래. 네게 의사를 기대했던 내 꿈은 포기해야 할 거 같구나.

일상생활

114 You get paid when you volunteer.

봉사활동을 하면 얻는 게 있단다.

A Mom! The school say I have to complete twenty-five volunteer hours before the end of twelfth grade.

B You're just starting ten now. That's plenty of time.

A But all those hours of unpaid work!

B **You get paid when you volunteer**, you get paid in practical experience.

A 엄마! 학교에서 12학년이 끝날 때까지 25시간 봉사활동을 끝마쳐야 한대요.

B 이제 10학년을 시작했으니 시간은 많이 있구나.

A 그런데 그 시간을 다 무급으로 일해야 돼요!

B 봉사활동을 해도 얻는 게 있단다. 세상 경험이라는 거지.

일상생활

115 There are rolls of unexposed film in the bag.

쓰지 않은 필름 몇 통이 가방에 있어요.

A I'm worried about the camera in my bag. Will this machine damage it?

B Is your camera digital or film?

A It's an old film camera, and **there are rolls of unexposed film in the bag**, too.

B If you like, we can hand check the film for you, to make sure it's not harmed by the machine.

A 가방 안에 있는 카메라가 걱정되네요. 이 기계 때문에 망가질까요?

B 디지털 카메라인가요, 필름 카메라인가요?

A 구식 필름 카메라인데 쓰지 않은 필름 몇 통이 가방에 있어요.

B 원하시면 필름을 손으로 확인해볼게요. 기계에 손상되지 않도록요.

일상생활

116 It's a bit pricey.

가격이 좀 비싸다.

A Are you looking for anything in particular?

B How much is the necklace?

A It's 300 bucks.

B **It's a bit pricey.** Will you give a discount?

A Oh, It's already marked down.

B OK, I will take it.

A Would you like it gift-wrapped?

B Sure.

A 뭐 특별하게 찾으시는 것이 있으세요?

B 저 목걸이 얼마에요?

A 300달러입니다.

B 어머, 좀 비싸네요. 할인 안 되나요?

A 죄송합니다. 이미 인하된 가격입니다.

B 할 수 없군요. 주세요.

A 선물용으로 포장해 드릴까요?

B 네.

일상생활

117 I'm a little short on dough.

내가 돈이 좀 부족해서 말이야.

A **I'm a little short on dough.**

B I'll pay it this time, but next time you bring a check book.

A Thanks.

A 내가 돈이 좀 부족해서 말이야.

B 이번엔 내가 낼 테니까 다음 번엔 네가 수표책을 가져와[네가 내라].

A 고마워.

※ dough는 원래 '반죽'을 가리키는 단어지만 구어에서는 '돈'(money)이라는 뜻으로도 사용됩니다.

일상생활

118 I'll write a check for it.

내가 개인 수표를 쓸게.

A Do you have any cash with you?

B No. Sorry.

A **I'll write a check for it.**

A 현찰 좀 있니?

B 없는데. 미안해.

A (그럼) 내가 개인 수표를 쓸게.

※ 미국 사람들은 대부분 신용 카드만큼 개인 수표(personal check)를 씁니다. write a check은 '개인 수표를 발행하다'라는 의미입니다.

일상생활

119 The clock is running out.

시간이 다 되어가고 있거든.

A We're down by five points. Can we pull this out?

B I don't know. **The clock is running out.**

A 우리 5점 뒤지고 있어. 역전시킬 수 있을까?

B 모르겠어. 시간이 다 되어가고 있거든.

※ 'Can we pull this out?'은 'come from behind to win'의 의미로 역전승을 말합니다.

일상생활

120 They link to that other page.

그것들은 다른 페이지로 링크되어 있어.

A Why do these words look different?

B **They link to that other page.** If you click your mouse over them, the other page will be displayed.

A 이 단어들은 왜 달라 보이지?

B 그것들은 다른 페이지로 링크되어 있어. 그 위에 대고 마우스를 클릭하면 다른 페이지가 나올거야.

일상생활

121 Would you like to wear these out?

신고 가시겠어요?

A These shoes are great.

B I'm glad you like them.

Would you like to wear these out?

A Yes, and you can throw away my old shoes.

A 이 신발 너무 맘에 드네요.

B 맘에 드신다니 다행입니다.
신고 가시겠어요?

A 예, 제가 신고 온 신발은 버려주세요.

일상생활

122 I did it on the spur of the moment.

충동적으로 했어.

A Did you think twice before you quit your job at Acme Company?

B No, **I did it on the spur of the moment.**

A Wow - that's a very brave of you.
I could never do that.

A 직장 그만둘 때 신중히 생각한 거야?

B 아니, 충동적으로 했어.

A 와, 용기 한번 대단한데.
난 절대 그렇게 못 할 거야.

일상생활

123 Enough is enough.

그만하면 충분해.

A Jess, do you have any idea for how many hours you stick to the computer?

B It's driving me crazy! I'm almost there.

A That's exactly the same thing as what you said an hour ago.

B It's just a little short of something and I can't find it.

A Hey, **enough is enough.**
Just give a call to the service department, okay?

B Yeah, you're right. **Enough is enough.**

A 제스, 너 지금 그 컴퓨터에 몇 시간째 매달려 있는 거니?

B 정말 돌겠어! 거의 다 고쳤는데.

A 한 시간 전에도 그렇게 말했었잖아.

B 뭔가가 약간 모자라는데 그걸 못 찾겠단 말이야.

A 이봐, 그만하면 충분해.
그냥 서비스센터에 전화해, 응?

B 그래, 네 말이 맞다. 난 할 만큼 했어.

일상생활
124 That's a relief.
안심이네요.

A Can I have your ticket and passport, please?
B Here you go.
I don't really understand the new e-ticket system.
I wasn't sure what to bring.
A You did it correctly.
It has your confirmation number on it.
B **That's a relief.**

A 탑승권과 여권 좀 보여주실래요?
B 여기 있습니다.
새로운 전자티켓 시스템은 잘 이해가 안가더라고요.
뭘 가져오는 건지 잘 모르겠어요.
A 맞게 갖고 오셨습니다.
예약번호가 적혀있으니까요.
B 안심이네요.

일상생활
125 I almost forgot.
깜빡할 뻔 했네요.

A **I almost forgot.** Here is my air miles card.
B Thank you, sir.
I'll make sure you get your mileage points.
A When can I redeem them?
I'd love to get a free flight.
B As of now, you'd only have enough points for a short domestic flight.

A 깜빡할 뻔 했네요. 여기 마일리지 카드요.
B 감사합니다.
마일리지 점수를 틀림없이 적립해드리겠습니다.
A 언제 그걸 쓸 수 있나요?
무료로 비행기 타고 싶어서요.
B 현재로서는 단거리 국내선은 충분히 타실 수 있는 점수를 보유하고 계십니다.

일상생활
126 Can you explain it in plain English?
쉬운 말로 설명 해주실래요?

A I'm not sure if I should upgrade my computer or get a whole new machine.
B It depends on how many expansion slots you computer has.
A **Can you explain it in plain English?**
B Sure.
If there is not enough room to add more hardware, it's not worth it to just upgrade.

A 컴퓨터를 업그레이드 해야 할지 아예 새로 사야 할지 모르겠어요.
B 손님 컴퓨터의 확장슬롯이 얼마나 많은지에 따라 다릅니다.
A 쉬운 말로 설명 좀 해주실래요?
B 그러죠.
하드웨어를 추가할 공간이 충분하지 않으면 업그레이드 할 가치도 없습니다.

일상생활

127 Bear with me, please.

기다려주세요. / 참아주세요.

A May I speak to Kenny?
B Speaking.
A Hi, Kenny. This is Regina calling about the park I ordered last week.
B What was the part number, Regina?
A Daewon-092735.
B OK. **Just bear with me.**

A 케니하고 통화하고 싶은데요.
B 나야.
A 안녕, 케니. 나 레지나인데 지난주에 주문한 부품 때문에 전화해.
B 부품 번호가 뭐였지?
A 대원-092735.
B 알았어, 잠깐만 기다려.

일상생활

128 I always chicken out!

무서워서 무슨 일을 못하겠어!

A I think I'm falling in love.
B With whom?
A A girl in my office. I want to tell her how I feel, but **I always chicken out** when I talk to her.
B What's she like?
A She's smart, Beautiful, and nice.
B You really should ask her out. What are you afraid of?
A My boss. She's his daughter.

A 나 사랑에 빠졌나봐.
B 누구랑?
A 사무실에 있는 사람이야. 내 감정을 얘기하고 싶은데, 무서워서 못하겠어.
B 어떤 사람이길래?
A 그녀는 아주 똑똑하고 예쁘고 착해.
B 그럼, 그녀에게 고백해야겠다. 근데, 뭐가 그렇게 두려운거야?
A 우리 사장님. 그녀가 사장님 딸이거든.

일상생활

129 Is he housebroken?

개가 용변을 잘 가려요?

A Do you have a pet?
B Yes. I have a little puppy. He's like one of the family.
A I see. **Is he housebroken?**
B Yes, he is and he's really well-trained.

A 애완동물 키우세요?
B 네. 작은 강아지를 키워요. 가족이나 다름없죠.
A 그렇군요. 개가 용변 잘 가려요?
B 네, 그럼요. 그리고 아주 말을 잘 들어요.

일상생활
130 No doubt about it. 의심할 여지도 없어.

A Good! Seems like your date went really well.
I thought you guys might get doing well together.
B I saw him in the office this morning,
and we had a little chat about your date.
A I get the feeling that he likes you very much.
No doubt about it.
I'm sure he will call you to ask you out again.
I hope everything goes well.

A 잘됐다! 데이트 정말 좋았나 보네.
둘이 잘 맞을 거라 생각했었지.
B 오늘 아침에 사무실에서 그 사람 만나서, 소개팅에 대해서 좀 얘기했었어.
A 그 사람 네가 아주 마음에 드는 눈치야.
틀림없어, 얘.
확실히 그 사람이 곧 애프터 신청할 거야.
모든 것이 잘 되길 바래.

일상생활
131 You look familiar to me. 낯이 익네요.

A Hi! **You look familiar to me.**
B You, too.
Maybe we've bumped into each other somewhere.
A Oh, wait a moment....
We met at Kelly's birthday party.
B Yes, that's right. I remember now.

A 안녕하세요. 낯이 익네요.
B 저도 그러네요.
어디선가 우연히 봤겠죠.
A 아, 잠깐만요….
캘리 생일 파티 때 만났네요.
B 네, 맞아요. 이제 기억이 나네요.

일상생활
132 Don't get your hopes up too high. 너무 기대 많이 하지 마.

A Have you made your Christmas list?
B As a mater of fact, I haven't gotten around to it yet.
A Well, I look forward to getting something wonderful from you again this year.
B OK, but **don't get your hopes up too high.**

A 너 크리스마스 선물 리스트 만들었어?
B 사실, 아직 손도 못 댔어.
A 음, 나 올해에도 너한테 어떤 근사한 것을 받을지 기대되는데.
B 알았다구, 그래도 너무 큰 기대는 하지 마.

일상생활

133 Loosen up!

맘 편안히 가져!

A Hey, Sophie, you look nervous. Are you all right?

B Just the person I wanted to see.
You know I'm not comfortable being with a bunch of strangers.

A Oh, don't tell me you are too shy to talk to anyone.
Just **loosen up** and be yourself! You will be fine.

B Thanks. I'll try, schmoozing around.

A 소피, 왜 그렇게 긴장하고 있어? 괜찮아?

B 너 마침 잘 왔다.
너 나 모르는 사람들 많은 데 있으면 불편해 하는 것 알잖아.

A 야, 네가 부끄러워서 사람들한테 말 못하는 건 아니지?
그냥 맘 편안하게 갖고 너답게 행동해. 괜찮을 거야.

B 고마워. 어울려 볼게.

일상생활

134 Today is not my day.

오늘 일진이 별로 안 좋아.

Today is not my day. I left home earlier than usual, so I decided to take my car instead of the subway.
On the way to work I made a wrong turn and I got stuck in traffic for more than an hour.
That really stressed me out and put me in a rotten mood. When I finally arrived at work, my boss, of course, got angry and didn't want to listen to my excuses.

오늘 일진이 사나워. 평소보다 좀 일찍 집을 나와서 지하철을 안 타고 차를 가지고 갔거든.
출근하는데 방향을 잘못 바꾸는 바람에 한 시간 넘게 교통체증 때문에 오도 가도 못했어.
그거 때문에 스트레스 많이 받고 기분이 나쁘더라구.
겨우 출근했는데 당연히 상사가 화가 나서 내 변명은 들으려고 하지도 않는 거야.

일상생활

135 Christmas is just around the corner.

크리스마스가 바로 코앞에 다가왔네.

A Do you have any plans for this weekend?

B I need to go shopping for christmas presents.

A Right. **Christmas is just around the corner.**
Can I tag along with you?

B Be my guest.
Let's hit all the big department stores and malls.

A 너 이번 주말에 무슨 계획 있어?

B 크리스마스 선물 사러 가야해.

A 맞다. 크리스마스가 코앞에 다가왔지?
나 따라가도 돼?

B 같이 가자.
우리 큰 백화점이나 대형 매장은 전부 들르자.

일상생활
136 Would you get a grip?

좀 진정하지 그래?

A I don't know why I let you convince me to come here. I hate parties.

B **Would you get a grip** on yourself? This is going to be a blast!

A Well, I don't know. I'm just not that into parties.

B Come on, don't be a party poorer. Just enjoy it as if you belong here.

A 도대체 왜 네 꼬임에 넘어가서 여길 왔는지 모르겠다.
나 진짜 파티 싫은데.

B 좀 진정하지 그래?
이 파티 진짜 재밌을 거야!

A 글쎄, 잘 모르겠다. 난 파티에 별로 관심이 없어.

B 제발 파티 좀 망치지마.
그냥 네 집이다 생각하고 즐겨.

일상생활
137 It really takes the cake.

진짜 대단하다 .

A What a great party! **It really takes the cake.** Thanks for inviting me here, Susan.

B Likewise. Having you is such a great pleasure for me. Thanks for coming.

A Well, now that I've seen you. I have to hit the road. I have to get an early start tomorrow.

B Already? I wish you could stay longer. We have tons of things to catch up on.

A 진짜 멋진 파티인데! 진짜 대단하다.
초대해 줘서 고마워, 수잔.

B 나도 마찬가지야. 너랑 같이 있으면 너무 즐거워. 와줘서 고마워.

A 그나저나 너 봤으니까 이제 집에 가야겠다.
내일 일찍 일어나야 하거든.

B 벌써? 조금만 더 있다가 가.
우리 아직도 할 얘기 많이 있잖아.

일상생활
138 Time certainly flies.

시간 정말 빨리 간다.

A It's almost the end of the year already.

B Wow, **Time certainly flies.** I don't feel like I've accomplished anything this year.

A Looking back, I can't say it was a real productive year for me either.

B Let's talk it over at the year-end bash. Tomorrow night, all right?

A 벌써 올해가 다 지나가네.

B 우와, 시간 정말 빨리 간다.
올해 아무것도 해놓은 게 없는 것 같아.

A 돌아보니, 나에게도 그다지 생산성 있는 해는 아니었던 것 같다.

B 우리 송년파티하면서 얘기해보자.
내일 밤 괜찮아?

일상생활

139 Can I have a rain check?

다음 기회로 미루면 안 될까?

A Hey, Jess. Will you be free this Saturday.

B **Can I have a rain check?**

I have a blind date this Saturday.

A Wow, awesome. Who fixed you up with the guy?

B My friend, Michael.

I hope he has picked Mr. right for me this time.

A 제스, 이번 주 토요일에 시간돼? 나 콘서트 티켓 있는데.

B 우리 다음번으로 미루면 안 될까? 나 이번 주 토요일에 소개팅이 있거든.

A 진짜? 좋겠다. 누가 주선한 거야?

B 내 친구 마이클.

이번에는 제대로 된 남편감을 소개해 줬으면 좋겠어.

일상생활

140 Stop putting me on.

농담 그만 해.

A Hi, you must be Jess. I'm Joshua.

So, finally we get to see each other.

B It's great to meet you at last. How are you?

A I am thrilled. Actually I'm a little flusterd. I didn't expect such a beautiful girl like you to show up.

B **Stop putting me on.**

But thanks, It's very good of you to say so.

A 안녕하세요, 제스 맞죠? 저 조슈아예요.

마침내 만나게 되네요.

B 드디어 만나서 너무 반가워요. 안녕하세요?

A 저 기분 너무 좋아요. 솔직히 말하면 약간 떨리네요. 이렇게 아름다운 분이 나오실 줄 몰랐거든요.

B 농담 그만하세요.

그래도 그렇게 말씀해 주시니 고마워요.

일상생활

141 Live a little.

걱정하지 말고 즐겨!

A You want a refill, Jesse?

B No thanks, I've had enough already. I'm a bit tipsy.

A Come on.

This is supposed to be a New Year's party!

Live a little, huh?

B Well I'm not really a big drinker,

but I guess just one more for the road won't kill me.

A 한 잔 더 마실래, 제시?

B 아니 괜찮아. 이미 많이 마셨어. 약간 취기가 있네.

A 이봐,

지금 송년회잖아!

걱정 말고 한 잔 더해.

B 글쎄, 나 술은 잘 못 마시지만

딱 한 잔 더 한다고 죽기야 하겠어.

일상생활 142 Wake up and smell the coffee! 정신 좀 차려!

A I think I'm going to ask Paul out tomorrow.
B What do you mean? Paul has a girlfriend already.
A Yeah, but who knows when they might break up?
B Girl, **Wake up and smell the coffee!** They are crazy about each other and Paul will never leave her.

A 나 내일 폴한테 데이트 신청할까봐.
B 무슨 소리야. 폴 여자 친구 있잖아.
A 알아. 그래도 걔네들 언제 헤어질지 누가 알아?
B 야, 정신 좀 차려! 걔네들 서로한테 얼마나 빠져있는데. 그리고 폴은 절대 그 여자 안 떠나.

일상생활 143 I'll try make time. 시간을 한 번 내볼게.

A Can you find time to meet tonight?
We have some things to go over.
B I'm pretty tied up today,
but if it's an emergency **I'll try make time.**
A It's about the Anderson firm we've been working on.
We were planning on meeting at 7.
B Oh, I think I'll be able to make it. See you then.

A 오늘 밤에 만날 시간 좀 있어요?
검토해야할 일들이 있는데.
B 오늘 좀 바쁜데,
그래도 긴급한 일이면 시간을 낼게요.
A 우리가 처리중인 앤더슨 회사에 관한 일이에요.
7시에 미팅하기로 했거든요.
B 어, 갈 수 있을 것 같아요. 그럼 그때 봅시다.

일상생활 144 Let's start moving stuff in. 어서 짐을 들입시다.

A That was a good lunch. I needed a break.
B **Let's start moving stuff in.**
A Okay!

A 점심 맛있었어요. 좀 쉬고 싶었거든요.
B 어서 짐을 들입시다.
A 알았어요!

일상생활 145 Don't pick on your brother. 동생 괴롭히지 마.

A Mom, Brian's hitting me!
B Brian, **don't pick on your brother.**

A 엄마, 브라이언이 절 때려요!
B 브라이언, 동생 괴롭히지 마.

일상생활
146 I'll heat up some left-overs.
남은 음식 있는데 데워 줄게요.

A I'm pretty hungry.
Have you made anything for dinner?
B No, not yet. **I'll heat up some left-overs.**

A 나 배고파 죽겠어.
저녁 준비했어?
B 아직요, 남은 음식이 있는데 데워 줄게요.

일상생활
147 Would Saturday work better?
그럼 토요일은 어때?

A I'm busy Friday.
B **Would Saturday work better?**
A I'll be out of town this weekend.

A 난 금요일에 바빠
B 그럼 토요일은 어때?
A 이번 주말엔 시내에 없어.

일상생활
148 Get off my back!
그만 좀 해!

A You need to finish your work soon.
B **Get off my back!** I'm working as hard as I can.
A You don't have to get angry at me.

A 너 일 얼른 끝내야 해.
B 그만 좀 해! 최대한 열심히 하고 있단 말야.
A 나한테 화낼 필요는 없잖아.

일상생활
149 School was OK today.
오늘 학교에서 그냥 그랬어요.

A **School was OK today.**
The teacher told me that I was making good progress.
B That's excellent! I'm proud of you.

A 오늘 학교에서 그냥 그랬어요.
선생님이 나보고 많이 좋아졌대요.
B 잘했어! 네가 자랑스럽구나.

일상생활
150 It looks cozy.
참 안락해 보인다.

A What do you think of our place?
B **It looks cozy.**
A We thinks so, too.

A 우리 집 어때?
B 참 안락해 보인다.
A 우리 생각도 그래.

일상생활

151 The toilet won't flush. 변기가 물이 안 내려가네.

A Oh,no! **The toilet won't flush.**
B We'll have to take the lid off the tank to see inside.
Maybe we can solve this problem.

A 아. 이런! 변기 물이 안 내려가네.
B 그럼 수조 뚜껑을 열고 안을 들여다 보자.
우리가 고칠 수 있을지도 모르니까.

일상생활

152 Let's put some tunes on. 음악을 틀자.

A I want people to dance! **Let's put some tunes on.**
B I've got a great CD full of dance music.
Let's put that one on.

A 사람들이 춤을 추었으면 좋겠어! 음악을 틀자.
B 댄스 음악이 가득한 굉장한 CD가 있어.
그걸 틀자.

일상생활

153 We'll go cold turkey on January 1st. 1월 1일부터 (담배를) 딱 끊을 거야.

A I'm finally going to quit smoking.
B I'm going to cut down on smoking and try to drink less, too.
A Perfect. We can help motivate and support each other.
B Right, but let's not start until after the New Year's Eve party. **We'll go cold turkey on January 1st.**

A 드디어 담배를 끊기로 했어.
B 나도 담배를 줄이고 술도 덜 마시려고.
A 좋아. 우리 서로 동기를 부여하고 용기를 주면서 도와주자.
B 그래. 하지만 새해전야 파티까지는 하지 말자. 1월 1일부터 딱 끊자고.

일상생활

154 It is nice to get away from it all. 일상생활을 벗어나니 좋다.

A It feels great to get out into nature and breathe some fresh air.
B **It** sure **is nice to** be out of the office and **get away from it all.**
A I can't wait to get out and lose myself in nature.
B Me, too. But, first let's find a place to park the car.
It looks like this lot is full.

A 자연으로 나와서 신선한 공기를 마시니까 기분이 아주 좋아.
B 사무실을 벗어나 일상생활을 털어버리니 정말 좋구나.
A 밖에 나와 자연에 묻히는 걸 얼마나 기다렸는데.
B 나도 그래. 그런데 주차할 곳부터 찾아보자.
여기는 주차장이 꽉 찬 거 같아.

일상생활

155 Cost me an arm and a leg.

돈 좀 들였어요.

A Ta-dah! It's the max Murdoch action figure.

B Where did you get that?

All the stores have been out of stock for weeks.

A I bought it on the Internet.

Cost me an arm and a leg.

B Well, Billy will be thrilled come Christmas morning.

A 짜잔! 맥스 머도크 전투 인형이요.

B 어디서 샀어요?

가게마다 품절된 지 몇 주 됐는데.

A 인터넷으로 샀죠.

돈 좀 들였어요.

B 그렇군요, 크리스마스날 아침에 빌리가 감격하겠어요.

일상생활

156 I just clip coupons from the newspaper.

신문에서 쿠폰을 잘랐어요.

A Do you have one of our preferred costumer coupon cards?

B No. **I just clip coupons from the newspaper.**

What are the benefits of having a card?

A You get all the discounts automatically.

All I do is swipe the card at the register and your total is automatically adjusted.

A 우리 점포의 우대고객 쿠폰카드를 가지고 계신가요?

B 아니요. 신문에서 자른 쿠폰이 있어요.

카드가 있으면 어떤 혜택이 있나요?

A 자동으로 할인 받을 수 있습니다.

카드를 금전등록기에 긁기만 하면 손님이 쓰신 총액이 자동적으로 할인 적용됩니다.

일상생활

157 Have a seat.

앉으세요.

A I have an appointment with Tony for three.

It's for highlights.

B I see. He's running a bit behind today

Michael is available.

A No thanks. I'll wait.

I dont' trust anyone else with my hair.

B I understand. **Have a seat** and Tony will be with you as soon as he can.

A 3시에 토니 미용사에게 예약했습니다.

하이라이트를 하려고요.

B 네. 토니가 오늘 일이 좀 밀려 있는데 마이클은 시간이 괜찮습니다.

A 아니에요. 기다릴게요.

제 머리를 아무나 믿고 맡길 수 없잖아요.

B 알겠습니다. 앉으세요.

토니는 가능한 한 빨리 올 거예요.

일상생활
158 I've socked away about $30 thousand.
3만 달러를 모았어요.

A You seem to have a good steady job, so it's not like you're going to be suddenly unemployed anytime soon.
B And I have some savings, too. Over the last few years **I've socked away about $30 thousand.**
A Excellent. That could be a nice size down payment.

A 안정적인 좋은 직장을 갖고 계시니 당분간 갑작스런 실업의 우려는 없겠군요.
B 그리고 저축해놓은 돈도 있어요. 지난 몇 년 동안 3만 달러를 모았죠.
A 아주 좋습니다. 계약금도 어느 정도 내실 수 있겠네요.

일상생활
159 Just don't go overboard.
적당히 해둬.

A Do you think I'd look good with highlights?
The stylist at the salon said I should get them.
B Highlights? What are those?
A It's where you just dye some of your hair a lighter color.
B OK. **Just don't go overboard.**
You don't want them to be too obvious.

A 하이라이트를 하면 괜찮아 보일까?
미용사가 하라고 해서.
B 하이라이트? 그게 뭐야?
A 머리 일부를 더 밝은 색으로 염색하는 거야.
B 좋은데. 적당히 해.
너무 튀는 건 안 좋아.

일상생활
160 I never actually keep any of them.
그것들을 실제로 한 번도 지킨 적이 없어.

A Have you made any resolutions for the coming year?
B I've made three New Year's resolutions every year, but **I never actually keep any of them.**
A So, your resolution is to not make any more resolutions?
B No. This year I'm making a fourth:
To keep the other three resolutions.

A 내년 결심을 정했니?
B 해마다 세 가지씩 새해 결심을 정했는데 실제로 한 번도 지킨 적이 없어.
A 그럼, 너의 새해 결심은 더 이상 다른 결심을 하지 않겠다는 거야?

일상생활

161 This one is pressing.

이건 매우 급합니다

A How soon would you like to have them done?

B well, **this one is pressing**, but the other one can wait.

A When is this one due?

B At the latest, by February, 28

A 언제까지 그것들을 완료시키면 되겠습니까?

B 음, 이건 아주 급합니다만 다른 것들은 여유가 있어요.

A 언제가 마감일입니까?

B 늦어도 2월 28일까지입니다.

일상생활

162 It's been a full day.

꼬박 하루 걸렸어요

A So, we cleaned the bathroom, vacuumed the carpets, swept and mopped the floors, and washed the dishes.

Did I miss anything?

B We also did the laundry. Separated, washed, dried and folded it.

A **It's been a full day.**

Let's take a quick break and then have dinner.

A 자, 화장실 청소를 했고, 진공청소기로 카펫도 밀었고, 바닥을 쓸고 닦았고, 설거지도 했어요.

빠진 거 있어요?

B 빨래도 했잖소. 색깔 별로 분류해서 세탁하고 건조한 후 갰어요.

A 꼬박 하루 걸렸네요.

일상생활

163 It totally slipped my mind.

완전히 잊고 있었네.

A Are you all set for the potluck party tomorrow night?

B **It totally slipped my mind.**

I could just bring a slad, or a jelly mold.

A That'll be sort of embarrassing.

Can't you whip up something nice?

A 내일 밤에 있을 음식지참 파티에 갈 준비는 다 했니?

B 완전히 잊고 있었네.

그냥 샐러드나 젤리를 가져가면 어떨까.

A 그건 좀 창피할거야.

잽싸게 맛있는 거 만들면 안 될까?

B 그래. 이 요리책에서 빠르고 쉽게 하는 요리를 찾아봐야겠다.

일상생활

164 My family is as poor as church mice.

우리 가족은 찢어지게 가난해.

A One day I'll bo telling you "My ship's come in."
I'm going to be rich.
B Do you have a rich old uncle?
Are you planning on inheriting the family fortune?
A No, everyone in **my family is as poor as church mice.**
B In that case, you better make plans to win the lottery.

A 언젠간 너한테 "나 부자 됐어"라고 말할 거야.
난 부자가 될 거니까.
B 나이 드신 부자 삼촌이라도 있어?
가족 유산 물려받을 계획이라도 있니?
A 아니, 우리 가족은 다 찢어지게 가난해.
B 그렇다면 복권에 당첨될 계획을 세우는 게 낫겠네.

일상생활

165 My husband and I are empty nesters.

아이들 없이 남편과 저만 있어요.

A What kind of home were you thinking about?
B Well, **my husband and I are empty nesters.**
A So, you're looking for something smaller and easier to manage.
B And it should be a bungalow, not a two-story.
We've both got bad knees.

A 어떤 집을 생각하고 있었나요?
B 글쎄요, 저희 내외만 살 거라서요.
A 그렇다면, 크기가 작고 관리하기 쉬운 집을 찾고 있으시군요.
B 그리고 이층집 말고 베란다가 있는 단층집으로요.
우리 둘 다 무릎이 불편하거든요

일상생활

166 I can't say offhand.

당장은 말씀드릴 수가 없군요.

A How soon do you think you can make the shipment?
B I'd say somewhere around the first of next month.
A Do you know if it'll be a direct shipment?
B Well. **I can't say offhand.**
I'll have to check.

A 선적을 얼마나 빨리 해 주실 수 있겠습니까?
B 다음달 1일쯤 될 것입니다.
A 직항으로 선적을 하나요?
B 글쎄요. 당장은 말씀드릴 수가 없군요.
확인해 봐야겠습니다.

일상생활

167 That's typical. 그럴 줄 알았다.

A **That's typical** of human resources.

B Well, I am also from ICM.

I represent the programming division.

A Anyway, nice to meet you. I remember now being told that I would have company.

B I believe I have previously worked with you on a project.

A Really?

A 인사관리부에서 그럴 줄 알았어요.

B 실은 저도 ICM 소속입니다.

전 프로그래밍 사업부 소속이죠.

A 어쨌든 반가워요. 일행이 있을 거라던 말이 이제야 기억나네요.

B 전에 우리 어느 프로젝트에서 같이 일한 적이 있는 것 같아요.

A 그래요?

일상생활

168 How arrogant! 저런 건방진!

A The principal said that foreign teachers and instructors are not educators.

B **How arrogant** the principal is!

A He thinks they're only "teaching machines or work horses." What the hell is the difference between an educator and a teaching machine?

B I guess an educator deserves retirement pay and a pension, but the teaching machine can be fired anytime.

A 교장이 외국인 선생과 강사들은 교육자가 아니라고 했네.

B 저런 건방진 사람이 있나!

A 외국인과 강사들은 단지 '가르치는 기계나 일꾼'이라고 생각하나 봐. 교육자와 가르치는 기계의 차이가 도대체 뭐야?

B 교육자는 퇴직금과 연금을 받을 자격이 있고 가르치는 기계는 언제든지 해고될 수 있는 것 아니겠어.

일상생활

169 Give me a hug! 날 안아주렴!

A Aunt Sandra! Hi!

B **Give me a hug!**

A Hi, uncle Herbie!

A 샌드라 숙모! 안녕하세요!

B 날 안아주렴!

A 안녕하세요, 허비 삼촌!

일상생활

170 It's kind of a bittersweet thing.

시원섭섭합니다.

A I'm leaving this school next month.
B Are you? How long have you been working here?
A Thirty years.
B That long? What are your feelings about leaving a workplace after such a long time?
A **It's kind of a bittersweet thing.**

A 다음 달에 이 학교를 떠납니다.
B 그래요? 근무한 지 얼마나 되셨는데요.
A 30년이오.
B 그렇게나 오래요? 그렇게나 오랜 세월이 지난 후 직장을 떠나는 심정이 어떠세요?
A 시원섭섭하죠.

일상생활

171 That's a cheap shot.

치사한 행동입니다.

A Did you see the TV debate between the two men running for congress in our district?
B No. I missed it. How did it go?
A They didn't debate polices. They just exchanged **cheap shots** about each other's personal life.
B They did?
A Yes. They spent the whole hour hitting each other below the belt.

A 우리 선거구에서 국회에 출마한 두 사람이 TV 토론하는 것 봤니?
B 아니, 못 봤는데. 어땠는데?
A 정책 토론은 하지 않더군. 단지 서로의 사생활을 가지고 치사한 공방만 하더군.
B 그랬어?
A 그래. 치사한 말을 주고받는데 온 시간을 할애하더라고.

일상생활

172 Shake a leg!

서둘러!

A Hey, kido! It's almost 8:00.
You've gotta really hurry up.
B Okay, mom. I'm doing it as fast as I can.
A What keeps you so long?
I told you to prepare everything for class last night.
B Mom, bare with me. I didn't sleep well last night.
A **Shake a leg**, or you're gonna miss the bus.
B Yes yes. I'm coming down.

A 꼬맹아! 벌써 여덟 시야.
어서 서둘러라.
B 네, 엄마. 빨리 하고 있어요.
A 왜 이렇게 오래 걸리니?
수업 준비는 어젯밤에 다 해놓으라고 그랬잖아.
B 좀 봐주세요, 엄마. 어젯밤에 잠을 설쳤단 말이에요.
A 빨리 해라. 이러다간 버스를 놓치겠다.
B 네. 지금 내려가요.

일상생활 173 It's OK to brag a little bit here. 여기서는 자랑을 좀 해도 돼.

A OK. Next, it's asking here about my past work experience. What should I include?

B Write your past jobs, starting with the most recent.

A I guess I should put my job titles, too. Anything else?

B Any special responsibilities or projects you completed. And **it's OK to brag a little bit here.**

A 자, 다음은 과거 경력을 묻고 있네. 어떤 걸 써야 하지?

B 가장 최근 것부터 시작해서 과거의 직업을 쓰면 돼.

A 그럼 직책도 써야겠구나. 또 포함시킬 게 있니?

B 네가 완수했던 특별과업이나 프로젝트도 써. 경력란에는 자랑 좀 해도 돼.

일상생활 174 Just make sure you don't get caught. 들키지 않도록 조심해.

A See? I've hidden the microphone under my hat.

B What? Are you sure that's legal? Aren't you breaking copyright, or something?

A Don't worry. Lots of people do it. It's called a "bootleg."

B Well, **just make sure you don't get caught.**

A 보여? 모자 아래 마이크를 숨겨왔어.

B 뭐? 그거 법적으로 문제없는 거니? 저작권 같은 것을 어기는 거 아니야?

A 걱정 마. 많이들 이렇게 해. 이런 복제품을 "해적판"이라고 하는 거야.

B 음, 들키지 않도록 조심해

일상생활 175 Do you mind if I tag along? 나도 따라가도 될까?

A I'm going to run down to the store to pick up a few items. Is there anything you need?

B You're going shopping? **Do you mind if I tag along?** I need to look for shoes.

A Oh, in that case, we can go and do some serious shopping.

B Sure. We'll make an afternoon of it.

A 물건 좀 사려고 백화점에 갈 건데 너 필요한 거 뭐 있니?

B 쇼핑하러 가는 거야? 나도 따라가도 될까? 신발을 좀 봐야 해서.

A 아, 그럼 가서 본격적으로 쇼핑을 하면 되겠다.

B 좋아. 쇼핑하면서 오후를 보내자.

일상생활

176 She gave me a hard time about it.

나를 힘들게 하더라고.

A I need to get home before my wife gets upset again.

B She doesn't like it when you come home late?

A I was late one time last month, and **she gave me a hard time about it** for weeks!

A 집사람이 또 화내기 전에 집에 가는 편이 좋겠어.

B 집에 늦게 오면 싫어해?

A 지난달에 한 번 늦게 귀가했더니 몇 주 동안이나 나를 힘들게 하더라고!

일상생활

177 That's sort of hard to say.

뭐라 말하기 어렵네요.

A What do you consider to be your greatest weakness as an employee?

B **That's sort of hard to say.**
I guess I tend to work too hard.

A That can be a problem.
It puts a lot of pressure on your co-workers.

B That's why I started reading books about how to relax.

A 사원으로서 귀하의 가장 큰 단점이라고 생각되는 것은 무엇인가요?

B 뭐라 말하기 어렵네요.
너무 열심히 일하는 거라고 할까요?

A 그것도 문제가 될 수 있겠군요.
동료들에게 많은 압박을 주니까요.

B 여유롭게 사는 방법이 실린 책을 읽기 시작한 것도 그 때문이에요.

일상생활

178 Get your priorities in order.

우선순위를 정해.

A I have so many things to do but I don't know where to begin.

B You've taken on too many projects again. You always spread yourself too thin.

A I know. I keep digging myself into a deeper hole by continuing to do it.

B Just **get your priorities in order** and know your limits.

A 할 일이 너무 많은데 어디서부터 시작해야 할지 모르겠어.

B 너 또 일 너무 많이 맡았구나. 넌 항상 네가 할 수 있는 것보다 너무 많은 일을 한꺼번에 맡는 것 같아.

A 나도 알아. 계속 그러면서 내 상황을 악화시키는 것 말이야.

B 일단 일의 우선순위를 정하고 네 한계를 인정해.

CHAPTER

02

스포츠와 건강

스포츠와 건강

1 My stomach is in knots.

속이 울렁거려요.

A Five minutes to showtime, Emily. Are you ready to dominate the stage?

B I don't know. **My stomach is in knots.** I don't think I can perform the song like I rehearsed.

A Take a deep breath There's no need to be nervous. You're one of the most talented singers that I've trained in my whole career.

A 공연 시작 시간 5분 전이야, 에밀리. 무대를 지배할 준비 됐지?

B 모르겠어요. 속이 울렁거려요. 연습할 때처럼 노래를 부르지 못 할 것 같아요.

A 깊게 호흡해 봐. 긴장할 필요 없어. 너는 내가 평생 가르쳤던 가장 재능 있는 가수들 중에 하나야.

스포츠와 건강

2 Better safe than sorry.

미리 조심하는 것이 더 나아요.

A Hey, you look terrible. You've come down with the flu, haven't you?

B Yeah. I think I have to go home and go to bed. This sucks-I really wanted to go to the concert tonight.

A See? I told you to get a flu shot like I did. **Better safe than sorry.**

A 얘, 너 상태가 아주 안 좋아 보여. 너 독감 걸린 거지, 맞지?

B 응. 집에 가서 자야 될 것 같아. 짜증나, 오늘 밤 콘서트에 진짜 가고 싶었는데 말이지.

A 그거 봐! 나처럼 독감 예방 주사 맞으라고 했잖아. 미리 조심하는 게 낫다고.

스포츠와 건강

3 I was a bench warmer.

나는 후보 선수였어요.

A You're such a huge sports fan, Mike. Did you play a lot as a kid?

B **I was a bench warmer.** I once went a whole season without touching the ball!

A Coaches put too much emphasis on winning. Kids should play just for fun.

A 마이크, 정말 스포츠 광팬이군요. 어렸을 때 공 많이 찼어요?

B 후보 선수였어요. 공 한번 만져 보지도 못하고 한 시즌을 보낸 적도 있다니까요!

A 코치들은 우승을 지나치게 강조해요. 아이들은 시합도 재미로 해야 하는데 말이에요.

스포츠와 건강

4 I think it's just a minor sprain.

그냥 살짝 접지른 것 같아요.

A So your file says you slipped on the stairs and twisted your ankle?

B That's correct. **I think it's just a minor sprain.**

A Even so, you need an X-ray. Your ankle might be broken.

A 차트에는 계단에서 미끄러져서 발목을 접질렸다고 쓰여있는데 맞나요?

B 네 맞아요. 그냥 살짝 접지른 것 같아요.

A 그래도 X선 촬영을 해봐야 합니다. 발목이 부러졌을 수도 있으니까요.

스포츠와 건강

5 That was slop.

우연의 일치였어.

A That was a nice shot.

B No, **That was slop.**

A 샷 죽이는데.

B 아니야, 우연이었어.

※ pool(포켓볼)을 칠 때 slop이란 말은 '우연(an accident)'이란 의미입니다.

스포츠와 건강

6 I can bench-press 105 pounds.

난 벤치 프레스 105파운드는 할 수 있어.

A **I can bench-press 105 pounds.** I could probably beat you up.

B You're a weakling! I can bench-press twice that weight.

A 난 벤치 프레스 105파운드는 할 수 있어. 넌 상대가 안 되지.

B 약골께서 무슨 말씀! 난 너보다 두 배 더 무거운 걸 들 수 있어.

※ bench-press는 '의자에 누워서 역기를 들어올리는 운동'을 말하는 것으로 아래 예문에서는 동사로 쓰였습니다.

스포츠와 건강

7 I'm working on my biceps.

이두박근 운동 중이야.

A What are you doing now?

B **I'm working on my biceps.** Soon, I'll have huge, muscular arms.

A 지금 뭐 해?

B 이두박근 운동 중이야. 조만간 엄청난 근육질 팔이 될 거야.

※ work on~은 '~ 운동 중이다'의 의미. 그리고 biceps는 '이두박근'을 가리킨다.

스포츠와 건강

8 Bull's-eye!

명중이다!

A I'm not very good at darts.
B **Bull's-eye!**
A That's my first bull's-eye!

A 나는 다트를 잘 못해.
B 명중이다!
A 태어나서 처음이야!

※ Bull's-eye는 표적의 한가운데 부분, 즉 점수가 가장 높은 부분에 명중되었음을 말합니다.

스포츠와 건강

9 I got the double.

나 더블이야.

A **I got the double!**
B That's the second time in this game! Keep it up!

A 나 더블이야!
B 벌써 두 번째네! 계속 살려봐!

※ 다트 표적(dartboard)에는 double이 있고 triple이 있는데 표적 바깥 부분에 얇게 그어진 선을 맞히면 double이 됩니다. 점수는 두 배.

스포츠와 건강

10 Nice scratch!

자~알 했다!

A **Nice scratch!**
B Well, I gave it my best try.
A Don't hit it so hard next time.

A 자~알 했다!
B 글쎄, 난 최선을 다해 친 건데.
A 다음번에는 그렇게 세게 치지 마.

※ Nice scratch!는 상대편이 잘못하여 내 공을 포켓에 넣는 실수를 했을 때 던지는 비꼬는 식의 멘트(a sarcastic comment).

스포츠와 건강

11 They get a corner kick.

코너킥을 얻었어.

A What's happening?
B **They get a corner kick.**

A 어떻게 됐어?
B 코너킥을 얻었어.

※ 코너에서 차는 볼을 corner kick이라고 한다.

스포츠와 건강

12 Hold your horses.

좀 천천히 가.

A It's so lovely to have a stroll in the park.

B Is it so? Then who is the person I asked a hundred times to go out and walk?

A Come on! I'm not a fitness-freak as you are.

B You really need to work out, though.

A By the way, **hold your horses.** Why are you walking so fast?

B Let's speed up a little bit. It's fun.

A 공원을 산책하는 건 정말 상쾌해.

B 그래? 나가서 좀 걷자고 해도 꼼짝하지 않던 게 누구더라?

A 이봐! 난 너처럼 운동광이 아니야.

B 넌 정말 운동이 꼭 필요해.

A 그런데, 좀 천천히 가.
너 왜 그렇게 빨리 걷는 거야?

B 조금만 빨리 걷자. 재밌잖아.

스포츠와 건강

13 I want everyone to see how I've stayed in shape.

내가 몸매 유지를 얼마나 잘했는지 모두에게 보여주고 싶어.

A I'm thinking of wearing my graduation tuxedo to the reunion.

B It's twenty years old! Why in the world would you do that?

A It still fits, sort of. **I want everyone to see how I've stayed in shape.**

B I can see what you're saying, but I still think it's one of your top ten worst ideas of all time.

A 졸업식 때 입었던 턱시도를 입고 동창회에 갈까 생각 중이야.

B 20년 전 옷이야!
도대체 왜 그걸 입으려는 거야?

A 아직도 대충 맞아. 내가 몸매 유지를 얼마나 잘했는지 보여주고 싶어.

B 무슨 말인지 알겠는데, 그건 아주 안 좋은 생각 같아.

스포츠와 건강

14 Take it on an empty stomach.

공복에 드세요.

A Here's your prescription. You should take two tablets, three times a day.

B Before meals or after meals?

A **Take it on an empty stomach.**

A 여기 처방전입니다.
두 알씩 하루 세 번 드세요.

B 식전에요, 식후에요?

A 공복에 드세요.

스포츠와 건강

15 We had to learn CPR.

심폐소생술을 알아야 돼.

A What experience did they require you to have to be a lifeguard?

B **We had to learn CPR.**

A 인명구조원이 되려면 어떤 경력이 있어야 돼?

B 심폐소생술을 알아야 돼.

스포츠와 건강

16 I have an upset stomach.

배탈 났어.

A Are you feeling okay?

B Not really. **I have an upset stomach.**

A You should avoid spicy foods for a while.

A 몸 좀 괜찮아?

B 아니. 배탈 났어.

A 매운 음식은 한동안 피해야겠다.

스포츠와 건강

17 I've been recuperating well.

몸조리를 잘 하고 있었어.

A Hey! I haven't seen you in ages. How is it going?

B Not bad. I was quite sick last month.

A I'm sorry to hear that. How do you feel now?

B Much better. **I've been recuperating well.**

A 정말 오랜만이네. 어떻게 지내?

B 그럭저럭. 지난달에 많이 아팠거든.

A 그랬구나. 지금은 좀 어때?

B 훨씬 좋아졌어. 몸조리를 잘 하고 있었어.

스포츠와 건강

18 What are your symptoms?

증상이 어떤데?

A I think I'm sick. I feel errible.

B **What are your symptoms?**

A I have a stuffed-up nose and a sore throat.

B You may want to try a decongestant.

A 아무래도 아픈 것 같아. 몸이 너무 안 좋아.

B 증상이 어떤데?

A 코도 막혔고 목도 아파.

B 소염제를 먹어야겠네.

스포츠와 건강

19 There's going to be a pinch hitter.

대타가 나올 거야.

A **There's going to be a pinch hitter.**

B What's that?

A A substitute batter.

A 대타가 나올 거야?

B 그게 뭔데?

A 교체 타자라는 말이지.

스포츠와 건강

20 I think I'm starting to get the hang of this.

이제 요령이 생기는 거 같아.

A **I think I'm starting to get the hang of this.**

B You're a fast learner. You'll be.... Hey! That guy almost crashed into me!

A Well, there are five of us, two adults and three kids. And we need ticktets that cover the entrance fees and unlimited redes.

B Let me double-check.

A 이제 요령이 생기는 거 같아.

B 아주 빨리 배우는구나. 너는…. 야! 저 사람 나랑 부딪힐 뻔했어!

A 저 사람은 자기가 먼저 갈 권리가 있다고 생각했나봐.

B 저 사람이 잘못했어. 항상 아래쪽에 더 가까이 있는 사람한테 우선 통행권이 있어.

스포츠와 건강

21 This slope has a ski lift.

이 슬로프에는 스키 리프트가 있습니다

A **This slope has a ski lift.** It'll be easy to get to the top.

B That's good, because I don't want to climb this slope. I'm exhausted.

A 이 슬로프에는 스키 리프트가 있습니다. 꼭대기까지 올라가기가 아주 쉽죠.

B 잘 됐네요, 꼭대기까지 기어 올라가고 싶진 않으니까요. 전 완전히 지쳤어요.

스포츠와 건강

22 The bases are loaded.

만루야.

A **The bases are loaded.**

B If this batter hits a home run, it'll be a grand slam.

A 만루야.

B 이 타자가 홈런을 치면 만루 홈런이네.

스포츠와 건강

23 I think I'm under the weather.

몸이 좋지 않은 것 같아.

A You don't look very well, Kenny.

B **I think I'm under the weather.**

A Really? I hope it's not the flu.

B I don't know, but I have a mild fever.

A Do you?

In that case, why don't you all in sick today?

B I think I will.

A 케니, 안색이 안 좋아 보이는데.

B 몸이 안 좋은 것 같아.

A 그래? 독감은 아니겠지.

B 모르겠어. 그런데 열이 좀 있네.

A 그래?

그럼, 아파서 출근 못 한다고 전화하는 게 어때?

B 그래야겠네.

스포츠와 건강

24 Who are you rooting for?

어느 편을 응원하고 있습니까?

A **Who are you rooting for?**

You seem to be egging both teams on.

B That's exactly what I'm doing.

A Why?

B Because neither is my hometown team.

A Oh, I see. What is your hometown team?

B New York Yankees.

A 너 누구 응원하니?

둘 다 응원하는 것 같은데.

B 맞아. 둘 다 응원하고 있어.

A 왜 그러니?

B 둘 다 우리 고향 팀이 아니라서 말이지.

A 이해가 가네. 고향 팀은 어디니?

B 뉴욕 양키스야.

스포츠와 건강

25 He must think he's going to be the next Tiger Woods!

제2의 타이거 우즈가 될 거라 생각하나 보네!

A I haven't seen David around lately.

Where is he these days?

B He goes to the golf course for lessons every single night. He's really dedicated.

A **He must think he's going to be the next Tiger Woods!**

A 데이비드 본 지 오래됐네.

요즘 뭐해?

B 매일 밤 골프레슨 받으러 다녀.

진짜 열심이야.

A 제2의 타이거 우즈가 될 거라 생각하나 보네!

스포츠와 건강

26 The game ended in a draw.

경기가 무승부로 끝났거든.

A What was the final score of the game?Did your team win?

B No, but the other team didn't win either. **The game ended in a draw.**

A Well, that's better than losing, I suppose!

A 경기 결과가 어땠어? 네 팀이 이겼어?

B 아니, 하지만 상대편도 못 이겼어. 경기가 무승부로 끝났거든.

A 지는 것보단 낫지 뭐!

스포츠와 건강

27 The game went into extra innings.

게임이 연장전에 들어갔거든.

A You were late getting home from the baseball game last night.

B **The game went into extra innings** because the score was tied at the end of the ninth.

A So, who won?

A 어제 야구 경기에서 늦게 돌아왔더라.

B 9회 말에 동점이 돼서 게임이 연장전에 들어갔거든.

A 그래서 누가 이겼어?

스포츠와 건강

28 I need to take some blood.

채혈을 해야 돼요.

A Hold still, please. **I need to take some blood.**

B I hate needles. Is there any way you could do this without sticking that thing in me?

A Don't worry. It just feels like a pinch. See? We're already done.

B Wow. I hardly felt that at all. You have a really soft touch, nurse.

A 가만 계세요. 채혈을 해야 돼요.

B 바늘이 너무 끔찍한데 그걸 찌르지 않고 채혈할 수 있는 방법은 없나요?

A 걱정 마세요. 그냥 따끔할 뿐이에요. 보이죠? 벌써 다했어요.

B 우와. 전혀 느낌이 없었어요. 선생님, 안 아프게 잘 해주시네요.

스포츠와 건강

29 All that junk will rot their teeth.

그런 정크푸드 때문에 이가 썩어요.

A Let's bring a nice healthy bag lunch for the kids.

B But the kids will want hot dogs and drinks.

A Cotton candy and candy apples and popcorn.... **All that junk will rot their teeth.**

B I'll pack lunch, but we should allow the kids one treat each.

A 아이들에게 영양가 있는 도시락을 가져다 줍시다.

B 하지만 아이들은 핫도그와 음료수를 먹고 싶어할 거에요.

A 솜사탕, 사과엿, 팝콘…. 그런 정크푸드 때문에 이가 썩는 거에요.

B 점심을 쌀게요. 그렇지만 아이들이 좋아하는 것 한 가지씩은 사먹게 하죠.

스포츠와 건강

30 I don't have an athletic bone in my body.

난 운동신경이 없어.

A Did you see Tim run the 100 meters? He was so fast!

B Wow. But I guess ti's easy for him, because he has such long legs.

A You should give credit where credit's due. You know that he also trains a lot.

B I know. I guess I'm just a bit jealous. **I don't have an athletic bone in my body.**

A 팀이 100미터 달리기하는 거 봤니? 정말 빠르더라!

B 와, 하지만 그 애한테는 쉬웠을 거야. 다리가 정말 길잖아.

A 칭찬할 일은 칭찬해야지. 팀은 훈련도 많이 했어.

B 알아, 샘나서 그런 거야. 난 운동신경이 없거든.

스포츠와 건강

31 The symptoms don't go away.

증상이 나아지지 않는다.

A How is your blood pressure?

B I am getting much better. The diet I'm on is doing wonders for it.

A If you stick to the diet, you can stop taking the medication in another few weeks.

B That's good to hear. I will keep in mind whatever you tell me to do.

A But if **the symptoms don't go away** after three weeks, come back.

A 요즘은 혈압이 어때요?

B 점점 좋아지고 있어요. 식이요법 중인데 놀랄 만큼 효과가 있네요.

A 음식 조절을 꾸준히 잘 하면 몇 주 후에는 약을 안 먹어도 됩니다.

B 듣던 중 반가운 소식이군요. 선생님 말씀 명심하겠습니다.

A 3주 후에도 증상이 나아지지 않으면 다시 오십시오.

스포츠와 건강

32 None of them are in good shape.

몸매 좋은 사람은 아무도 없어요.

A Matt is a great trainer. And look at him! He's got huge muscles.

B But look at his clients. **None of them are in good shape.**

A I see what you mean. It's possible that Matt is not very good at explaining how to exercise.

B Right. A good personal trainer has to be a good teacher, too.

A 매트는 아주 좋은 코치에요. 보세요! 근육도 대단하잖아요.

B 그런데 그가 지도하는 회원들 좀 봐요. 몸매 좋은 사람은 아무도 없네요.

A 무슨 말인지 알겠어요. 매트는 운동 방법을 설명하는 데는 서툴지 모르겠군요.

B 맞아요. 좋은 코치가 되려면 가르치는 것도 잘해야 되니까요.

스포츠와 건강

33 I'm highly motivated.

의욕이 넘쳐요.

A You will have to come into the gym about four times a week. Can you promise to come?

B **I'm highly motivated**, so I'll come here every day, except Sundays.

A That is not a good idea, actually. Getting enough rest is just as important as getting enough exercise.

A 일주일에 네 번 정도는 체육관에 오셔야 합니다. 꼭 오실 수 있죠?

B 운동이 하도 하고 싶어서 일요일 빼고는 매일 여기에 올 거예요.

A 사실 매일 오는 게 좋은 생각은 아니에요. 충분한 휴식을 갖는 것도 충분한 운동만큼 중요하거든요.

스포츠와 건강

34 They were knocked out of the tournament.

그들은 대회에서 탈락했습니다.

A Jennifer's team didn't do very well in the tournament.

B They didn't win the championship?

A They weren't even close. **They were knocked out of the tournament** in the first round.

A 제니퍼네 팀이 대회에서 잘 못했어.

B 우승을 못했어?

A 근처도 못 갔어.
대회 1회전에서 탈락했어.

스포츠와 건강

35 It's possible to get into shape.

몸매 관리가 가능해요.

A I think that Janet should be my personal trainer. She seems perfect for me.

B Did you know that before she was a trainer, she was really overweight?

A I know. So, now she really understands what it takes to lose weight.

B Right. She's living proof that **it's possible to get into shape.**

A 자넷이 제 개인코치를 맡아야할 것 같아요. 저한테 딱 맞는 것 같거든요.

B 자넷이 코치가 되기 전에 아주 뚱뚱했던 거 아세요?

A 알아요. 그럼 체중감량이 얼마나 힘든 일인지 정말 잘 아시겠네요.

B 맞아요. 몸매관리가 가능하다는 걸 보여주는 좋은 본보기죠.

스포츠와 건강

36 You have a potbelly.

배가 많이 나왔군요.

A Hey, man, what brings you in here?

B I decided to work out.

A You should. You look like you are getting fatter. Wow, **you have a potbelly!**

B Are you pulling my leg?

A 야, 너 여기에 웬일이야?

B 운동하기로 결심했어.

A 갈수록 더 뚱뚱해지니까 당연히 그래야겠지. 어머, 배 나온 것 좀 봐!

B 너 지금 나 놀리는 거야?

스포츠와 건강

37 I think you're really athletic.

만능 스포츠맨이신 것 같네요.

A **I think you're really athletic.**

B Yes. I'm a fitness buff. I love all kinds of sports. What about you?

A Well. I don't like sports that are too strenuous. I sometimes use a hula-hoop. I used to go bowling, but I'm a bit rusty now.

B Okay. Why don't we go bowling sometime?

A 정말 운동 좋아하시는 것 같네요.

B 네. 전 헬스 광이에요. 모든 종류의 스포츠를 다 좋아하죠. 그 쪽은 어떠세요?

A 저는 너무 과격한 운동은 좋아하지 않아요. 가끔 훌라후프 정도 하고요. 예전엔 볼링도 좀 쳤는데, 예전 같지 않아요.

B 그렇군요. 언제 한번 볼링장에 같이 가는 거 어때요?

스포츠와 건강

38 I want to watch my weight.

체중 조절을 하고 싶어.

A I'm planning on losing some weight this year. What about you?

B **I want to watch my weight, too.** I'm planning on joining a gym.

A I'm sure you can stick to it.

B Out with the old and in with the new. So long, old me. Say hello to the new me!

A 올해는 살을 좀 빼야겠어. 넌 어떠니?

B 나도 체중 조절을 하려고. 체육관에 등록할 계획이야.

A 넌 반드시 해낼 수 있을 거야.

B 오래된 건 버리고 새 것을 맞이하려고. 예전의 나는 안녕. 새로운 내가 돼야지!

스포츠와 건강

39 I never realized how physically draining it was.

체력 소모가 그렇게 많은지 몰랐어.

A Now that we're out here, I have to admit it's harder than it looks.

B What's the hardest part of snowboarding?

A **I never realized how physically draining it was.** And my hands hout, too.

B Sure, because you spend a lot of time trying to break your falls with your hands.

A 막상 여기 나와 보니까 보기보다 어렵다는 걸 알겠구나.

B 스노보드 타면서 어떤 게 가장 어려우세요?

A 체력 소모가 그렇게 많은지 몰랐어. 손도 다쳤단다.

B 그렇죠, 넘어지지 않으려고 손을 사용하실 때가 많으니까요.

스포츠와 건강

40 I've finally got the hang of kicking.

발차기 요령을 드디어 터득했어.

A I think **I've finally got the hang of kicking.**

B Good. Now move your arms, one at a time, like windmils.

A This sure takes a lot of energy, and I can't really move that fast at all.

B It's the same for everyone when they're just learning.

A 발차기 요령을 드디어 터득한 거 같아.

B 좋아. 이제 풍차가 도는 것처럼 한 번에 한 팔씩 움직여.

A 확실히 힘이 너무 들어서 그렇게 빨리는 못 나가겠어.

B 누구나 배울 때는 똑같아.

스포츠와 건강

41 You'll get soaking wet.

흠뻑 젖을 거예요.

A You can't wear that jacket to snowboard in. **You'll get soaking wet.**

B Why? This is the jacket I use for skiing. It's nice and warm.

A But you need a jacket that's long enough for you to sit on.

B Right! Snowboarders spend a lot of time sitting in the snow adjusting their bindings.

A 스노보드 탈 때 저 재킷을 입으면 안 돼요. 다 젖을 거예요.

B 왜?
스키 탈 때 입었던 건데 따뜻하고 괜찮단다.

A 그렇지만 눈에 앉아있어도 괜찮은 긴 재킷이 필요해요.

B 그렇지! 스노보드 타는 사람들은 바인딩을 조절하느라 눈 위에 앉아 있는 시간이 많구나.

스포츠와 건강

42 You have to avoid slamming into other people.

다른 사람과 부딪치지 않도록 해야 해.

A So, I point my skis downhill and just let myself slide along?

B No. **You have to** be able to slow down and **avoid slamming into other people.**

A OK. So, to stop I stick my poles in the ground really quickly?

B No! Point the tips of your skis together and dig the edges into the snow.

A 그럼, 스키를 아래쪽으로 향하게 하고 그냥 미끄러져 내려가면 돼?

B 아니. 속도를 줄일 수 있어야 다른 사람과 부딪치지 않아.

A 알겠어. 그럼 멈추려면 스키 폴을 땅에다 잽싸게 꽂으면 되니?

B 안 돼! 스키앞 쪽 끝을 함께 모으고 날 부분을 눈 속으로 넣어야지.

스포츠와 건강

43 Bank it off the wall.

쿠션을 이용해서 쳐봐.

A **Bank it off the wall.**

B I'm no good at banking my shots.

A 쿠션을 이용해서 쳐봐.

B 나는 쿠션엔 약한데.

CHAPTER 03

직장

직장

1 I'm not decent.

저는 옷을 제대로 안 입었어요.

A I need to use your stapler. Can I come in?

B Hold on a second! **I'm not decent** right now.

A All right. Just bring it to my room when you're ready, okay?

A 스테이플러를 써야 하는데요. 들어가도 돼요?

B 잠깐만요! 저는 지금 옷을 제대로 안 입었어요.

A 알겠어요. 준비되면 제 방으로 가져다줘요, 알았죠?

직장

2 I'll see what I can do

제가 알아볼게요.

A Ms. Webb's office, this is Jake. How can I help you?

B Hey, it's me, Mike. I'd like to talk to Ms. Webb about a project idea I had. Can you fit me into her schedule today?

A Hmm, she's very busy. But **I'll see what I can do.** Let me call you back in a few minutes.

A 웹씨 사무실입니다, 저는 제이크입니다. 무엇을 도와드릴까요?

B 안녕, 나야, 마이크, 웹씨랑 내가 갖고 있는 프로젝트 아이디어에 대해서 이야기 나누고 싶어서. 오늘 시간 좀 마련해줄 수 있어?

A 음, 웹씨가 너무 바쁘시긴 하네요. 제가 알아볼게요. 조금 있다가 다시 전화해 드릴게요.

직장

3 It was meant to be.

그럴 운명이었어요.

A Hey, I'm sorry to hear that you didn't get the job in that company. Are you okay? You really wanted to work there.

B Yeah, I'm pretty disappointed. That position was so perfect for me, and it opened up right when I left my other job. I really thought **it was meant to be.**

A Aw, keep your chin up! I know you're a smart person. You'll get a job soon. Okay?

A 이봐, 네가 그 회사에 취업하지 못 해서 유감이야. 괜찮니? 거기에서 정말 일하고 싶어 했잖아.

B 네, 매우 실망했어요. 그 자리는 저에게 진짜 완벽했고, 그리고 하던 일을 그만두었을 때 바로 자리가 생겼어요. 저는 정말 그럴 운명이었다고 생각했죠.

A 저런, 기운 내! 네가 똑똑한 사람인 것을 내가 알아. 곧 취업할 거야. 알겠지?

직장

4 What nerve!

참 뻔뻔하네요!

A Why did Mike look angry this morning? Did something happen at the meeting?

B Yeah-Jenny criticized him for being just one minute late to it.

A **What nerve!** She was 10 minutes late to a meeting we had last week.

A 오늘 아침에 마이크가 왜 화나 보였죠? 회의에서 무슨 일 있었나요?

B 네, 마이크가 딱 1분 늦었는데 제니가 뭐라 했거든요.

A 참 뻔뻔하네요! 그녀는 지난주 회의에 10분이나 늦었는걸요.

직장

5 I blurred their faces out.

그들의 얼굴을 모자이크 처리했어요.

A Are you going to post the picture of you that I took? You know there are some strangers behind you in it, right?

B I know. Don't worry, **I blurred their faces out.**

A Oh! That's OK, then. As long as you can't recognize them.

A 내가 찍은 당신 사진 올릴 거예요? 사진 속에 낯선 사람들이 뒤에 있다는 거 알고 있죠?

B 알아요. 걱정 마요. 얼굴을 다 모자이크 처리했어요.

A 아! 그럼 됐어요. 알아보지만 못하면 되니까요.

직장

6 I'm really excited.

정말 설레네요.

A I just heard you'll be relocating to the head office in Seoul. Congratulations!

B Thanks. **I'm really excited.** But they'd like me to start in just a month, and there's an important project I haven't finished.

A Don't worry. We'll help you finish it as quickly as possible.

A 방금 들었는데 서울에 있는 본사로 옮긴다면서요. 축하해요!

B 고마워요. 정말 설레네요. 그런데 회사에서 바로 한 달 후에 근무를 시작했으면 하는데 제가 끝나지 못한 중요한 프로젝트가 하나 있어요.

A 걱정 말아요. 우리가 가능한 한 빨리 올 수 있게 도와줄게요.

직장 7 I'll take care of this right away. 즉시 처리할게요.

A I would like to change my presentation topic for the conference this weekend. I hope it is not too late to change.

B Well, I'll have to find out about it, but I am positive it is still possible.

A Thank you. And I hope so, too.

B Yes it is possible and **I'll take care of this right away.**

A Thank you very much.

A 이번 주말 학회에서 발표할 발표 제목을 수정하고 싶습니다. 너무 늦지 않았겠지요?

B 글쎄요. 알아봐야겠지만 아마도 가능하리라 생각합니다.

A 감사합니다. 그랬으면 좋겠네요.

B 네, 가능하고요.
즉시 알아봐서 처리할게요.

A 감사합니다.

직장 8 How should I phrase it so it sounds good? 어떻게 써야 그럴듯해 보일까?

A It's sort of hard to explain all of the things I did at my old jobs.

B The trick is to use really active verbs. Never say, "I did this and that." It sounds weak.

A **How should I phrase it so it sounds good?**

B Use word like "completed," supervised," and "organized."

A 예전에 했던 일들을 전부 설명하기가 좀 까다롭네.

B 능동적인 동사를 사용하는 게 요령이야.
"이거 했다, 저거 했다" 같은 말은 약해 보이니 쓰지 마.

A 그럼 어떻게 써야 그럴듯해 보일까?

B "완수했다", "지도했다", "조직했다"와 같은 단어를 써 봐.

직장 9 Let's put it in writing and sign it. 그것을 문서화해서 서명합시다.

A Now I think we've been able to come to an agreement.

B Yes, all the problems have been ironed out, as far as we can see.

A Right. So **let's put it in writing and sign it.**

A 이젠 계약을 해도 될 것 같습니다.

B 그렇군요. 저희가 보기에도 모든 문제점들이 조정된 것 같습니다.

A 맞습니다. 그렇다면 문서화해서 서명을 합시다.

직장

10 She's living on borrowed time.

지금까지만 해도 오래 버틴 거야.

A Mary has made so many mistakes.

B She can't last much longer.

She's living on borrowed time.

A If it weren't for her personality,

She'd have been canned a long time ago

A 메리는 실수가 많은데 아직도 회사에 남아있는 것이 신기해!

B 아마 오래가지 못할걸.
지금까지만 해도 오래 버틴 거야.

A 성격마저 좋지 않았다면 오래 전에 해고 되었을 거야.

직장

11 We just can't assume full responsibility for it.

우리가 전적으로 책임을 다 질 수는 없다.

A We've just got to settle this claim somehow.

B I understand your position, Mr. Smith. But, I'm sorry, **we just can't assume full responsibility for it.**

A Then that'd leave me no choice but to take legal action.

A 어떻게든 이 클레임을 해결해 줘야겠습니다.

B 스미스씨의 입장은 이해합니다만, 우리가 그에 대한 책임을 전부 질 수는 없습니다.

A 그렇다면 법적 조치를 취할 수밖에 없겠네요.

직장

12 James should be dismissed for his poor record-keeping.

기록 보관을 제대로 못해서 제임스를 해고시켜야 겠어.

A **James should be dismissed for his poor record-keeping.** He's made a mess of things!

B That's too bad. I really like him!

A I do too, but he's been warned repeatedly.

A 기록 보관을 제대로 못해서 제임스를 해고시켜야 겠어.
일을 아주 엉망으로 만들었어!

B 안됐다. 난 그 사람 진짜 좋은데.

A 나도 좋아하지만 여러 번 경고했다고.

직장 13 How long is your commute? 출퇴근 시간이 얼마나 걸려?

A I wish I lived closer to work. I spend too much time driving to and from the office.

B **How long is you commute?**

A It's ninety minutes each way.
That's a three hours lost every day!

A 회사에서 조금 더 가까운 데 살았으면 좋겠어. 출퇴근하는 데 시간이 너무 많이 걸려.

B 출퇴근 시간이 얼마나 걸리는데?

A 편도 1시간 반 걸려.
매일 3시간씩이 날아간다고!

직장 14 We have a performance-based pay system. 우리는 성과급체제야.

A At my company, our pay is determined by seniority.

B Our company is different; **we have a performance-based pay system.**

A I like that idea better. I work really hard, but I'm not compensated enough!

A 우리 회사는 근속 연수에 따라 급여가 지급돼.

B 우리 회사는 달라.
우리는 성과급체제야.

A 그게 더 낫다. 난 진짜 열심히 일하는데 충분한 보상을 못 받아.

직장 15 Here goes nothing. (잘 안 되겠지만) 한 번 해보는 거야.

A Are you ready for the presentation?
I hear the VP will be sitting in.

B I'm so nervous. But there's no looking back now.

A Right. Just think to yourself, **"Here goes nothing!"**

A 발표 준비 다 됐어요?
부사장님께서 참석하신대요.

B 너무 떨려요. 하지만 이제 돌이킬 수 없어요.

A 맞아요. 그냥 "별 거 아니야!"라고 생각해요.

직장 16 Are you willing to relocate? 파견 나가실 의향이 있습니까?

A Our headquarters are herein New York, but this position is based in Hong Kong. **Are you willing to relocate?**

B I'm interested in hearing about your relocation package.

A 저희 본사는 이곳 뉴욕에 있지만 이 업무는 홍콩 지사에서 하시게 됩니다. 파견 나가실 의향이 있습니까?

B 파견 근무시 제공되는 혜택에 대해 듣고 싶습니다.

직장

17 What can you bring to the company?

회사에 어떤 기여를 할 수 있죠?

A **What can you bring to the company?**

B From my previous jobs, I gained experience in working in a variety of environments. I feel confident that I can handle any situation that might arise in the workplace.

A 회사에 어떤 기여를 할 수 있죠?

B 저는 여러 직장에서 다양한 상황별 업무 경험을 쌓았습니다. 직장에서 발생하는 어떤 상황에도 대처할 자신이 있습니다.

직장

18 What is your educational background?

학력이 어떻게 됩니까?

A **What is your educational background?**

B I majored in electrical engineering. Also, I worked for two years as a research assistant in the Math department.

A 학력이 어떻게 됩니까?

B 전기공학을 전공했습니다. 또한 수학과에서 2년간 연구조교로도 일했습니다.

직장

19 He needs to be given a written warning.

서면경고를 줘야겠어.

A Did you see the complaint that James made about Charlie?

B I did. That kind of behavior at work can't be tolerated. What should we do?

A **He needs to be given a written warning.**
This is a serious situation!

A 제임스가 찰리에 대해 제기한 문제들을 봤어?

B 응. 그런 행동은 직장에서 허용될 수 없어.
어떻게 해야할까?

A 서면경고를 줘야겠어.
이건 심각한 상황이라고!

직장

20 I'm the low man on the totem pole.

저는 말단 직원입니다.

A I hate **being the low man on the totem pole.**
I always get the worst tasks in the office!

B We were all in your position once.
I'm sure you'll be promoted soon.

A I hope so. I', tired of doing all the thankless jobs!

A 저는 말단인 게 정말 싫어요. 사무실에서 제일 하찮은 일만 맡긴다고요!

B 우리도 다 너 같았던 때가 있었어.
금방 승진될 거야.

A 그러면 좋겠어요. 하찮은 일 하는 데 지쳤어요.

직장
21 Our boss is falling asleep at the wheel.
우리 상사는 일을 게을리 하고 있어.

A **Our boss is falling asleep at the wheel.**
B What's wrong with him? He should show a little more responsibility for his work.
A We really need someone in charge who stays on top of things better.
B Well, we can't really advise him to be more careful. After all be is our boss.

A 우리 상사 또 일을 게을리 하고 있어.
B 그 사람 왜 그래? 자기 일에 좀 더 책임감을 보여야 하잖아.
A 우리에겐 정말 제대로 일 처리 잘하는 상사가 필요해.
B 글쎄, 그렇다고 우리가 좀 더 조심하라고 충고할 순 없잖아. 그래도 우리 상관인데.

직장
22 Let me briefly go over.
간단하게 요약해 드리겠습니다.

A How was the meeting with our American buyer?
B It went well. **Let me briefly go over** what was covered in the last meeting.
A Why don't we do it over lunch?
B That sounds fine. It'll give me some time to get organized.
A I'll see you around 12:00.

A 미국 바이어들과 회의가 잘 됐나요?
B 잘됐어요. 지난 회의에서 다룬 내용을 간단하게 요약해 드리겠습니다.
A 점심 먹으면서 하는 것이 어떨까요?
B 좋아요. 그럼 그때까지 정리할 시간이 좀 있겠네요.
A 그럼 12시쯤에 보도록 하죠.

직장
23 Time to go back to the salt mines.
다시 돌아가 일할 시간이다.

A What time is it?
B Oh, it's already ten to one.
A Yeah? Lunch is over.
Time to go back to the salt mines.
B Are you prepared for the marketing meeting this afternoon?
A Almost there. Just a couple of numbers to check out.

A 지금 몇 시야?
B 아, 벌써 1시 10분 전이네
A 그래? 점심시간이 끝났군.
다시 돌아가 일할 시간이야.
B 오늘 오후에 있을 마케팅 회의 준비는 끝났어?
A 거의. 숫자 몇 개만 확인하면 돼.

직장

24 I'm open to that.

그것에 대해선 상의할 용의가 있습니다.

A I have an importer in New York who's hot for your new model. He says he'll start with 500 sets a month.

B Oh, that's good. What are we looking at price-wise?

A He says you need to come down a ways from your original asking price.

B Well, **I'm open to that**, but the question is how far.

A 귀사의 새 모델에 관심이 많은 뉴욕의 수입업자를 알고 있어요. 우선 한 달에 500세트로 거래를 시작하고 싶다고 하더군요.

B 좋네요. 가격은 어떻게 하고요?

A 귀사가 요구하는 가격에서 좀 할인해 줬으면 합니다.

B 음 그 점은 상의해 볼 용의가 있습니다만, 얼마냐가 문제죠.

직장

25 We are short-handed.

일손이 모자란다.

A Are you finished with the market analysis report, Gilbert?

B I am working on it now. It'll take a couple of more hours.

A What? Oh, no. You need to speed things up.

B Stop pushing me, please. **We are just short-handed.** I am doing what I can.

A 길버트, 시장 분석 보고서 끝냈어?

B 지금 하는 중이야. 한두 시간 더 걸릴 거야.

A 뭐? 안 돼. 그럴 시간이 없어.

B 그만 좀 재촉해. 우리 일손이 부족하잖아.
난 지금 최선을 다하고 있단 말이야.

직장

26 As soon as we get the green light from upstairs.

상부로부터 정식허가가 나오는 대로요.

A When do you think we can sew up the deal?

B **As soon as we get the green light from upstairs.**

A Well, when do you figure that will be?

B The way things look now, it may be a little while yet.

A 언제쯤 이 거래를 확정지을 수 있을 것 같습니까?

B 상부로부터 정식허가가 나오는 대로요.

A 그래요. 그게 언제쯤 될 것 같아요?

B 현재의 상황으로는 시간이 조금 걸리겠는데요.

직장 27 We must go into it fully before deciding.

결정 전에 충분히 검토해야 합니다.

A Do you think you can give me a definite answer on our offer later today?

B I'm afraid I can't. I need a chance to take it up with the board of directors.

A Can't you make a decision on your own?

B No, not without the board's approval. **We must go into it fully before deciding.**

A 저희 오퍼에 대한 분명한 답변을 오늘 오후에 해 주실 수 있습니까?

B 힘들겠는데요. 이사진과 그 문제를 이야기해 볼 필요가 있어서요.

A 혼자서는 결정을 못 내리시나요?

B 예, 이사진의 승인 없이는 안 돼요. 결정전에 충분히 검토해야 해요.

직장 28 Don't pass the buck to me.

내게 책임을 미루지 마라.

A Who drove and wrecked my car?

B I did, Kenny. But the accident wouldn't have happened if Regina hadn't rushed me while I was giving her a ride to her friend's home.

C **Don't pass the buck to me**, Michael. I didn't tell you to speed.

A Ok. It's my fault. Forget it! Get out of my sight!

A 누가 내 차를 몰고 나가서 망가뜨렸지?

B 내가 그랬어, 케니야. 그렇지만 레지나를 자기 친구 집에 데려다 줄 때 재촉하지만 않았어도 사고가 나진 않았을거야.

C 마이클! 내게 덮어씌우지 마. 난 과속으로 달리란 말은 안 했어.

A 알았어. 내 잘못이야. 신경 끄고 내 눈앞에서 사라져!

직장 29 Our company is cutting jobs.

우리 회사는 감원하고 있어요.

A Please take a seat.

B Sure.

A As you know due to the economic downturn **our company is cutting jobs.** I am sorry to say this, but we have to lay you off.

B I got it. How about my severance pay?

A We will definitely pay you; so don't be concerned about it.

A 앉으세요.

B 네.

A 당신도 알다시피 경기침체로 인해 회사에서는 정리해고를 하고 있어요. 이런 말씀을 드려서 죄송하지만 당신을 일시해고해야만 합니다.

B 알겠습니다. 그러면 저의 퇴직금은 어떻게 되나요?

A 확실하게 지급할 겁니다. 그러니 그 문제에 대해 걱정하지 마세요.

직장

30 She's in the driver's seat.

그녀가 책임자이다.

A Did you hear that Mr. Sanders got in an accident?
B What? When did that happen? Is he hurt?
A This morning on the way to this office.
He seems to be in serious condition.
B Who's gonna be in charge of this company now?
A Now that Mr. Sanders is not available, **Mrs. Bender must be in the driver's seat.**

A 미스터 샌더스에게 교통사고가 났다는 소식 들었어?
B 뭐? 언제? 많이 다쳤대?
A 오늘 아침 출근길에.
상태가 심각한가 봐.
B 그럼 이제 누가 우리 회사의 책임자가 되는거지?
A 샌더스씨가 없으니 벤더가 책임자겠지.

직장

31 Guilty as charged.

제가 맡고 있어요.

A Are you the volunteer coordinator?
I'm here to volunteer, but I don't know where to go.
B **Guilty as charged.** My name is Gail.
A Glad to meet you. So, you're a volunteer, too.
B Actually, the title means I coordinate the volunteers.
But, it's a paid position.

A 자원봉사 책임자이신가요?
봉사활동 하러 왔는데 어디로 가야할지 몰라서요.
B 제가 맡고 있어요. 제 이름은 게일입니다.
A 만나서 반갑습니다. 그럼 선생님도 자원봉사자이시군요.
B 사실 자원봉사자들을 책임지고 있는 일이긴 한데요, 유급직입니다.

직장

32 Opinion is divide.

의견이 분분하다.

A Did you see the minutes of the last board meeting?
Has the board made a decision?
B Almost. They've all agreed to merge the company's subsidiaries in the US. But **opinion is divided** on which offer to take.
A How much longer do you think it'll take?

A 지난번 이사회 회의록 봤어?
이사회에서 결론은 났어?
B 거의. 미국 내의 자회사를 합병하자는 데 모두 합의했어.
하지만 어느 쪽 제안을 받아들일지에 대해서는 의견이 분분해.
A 결론이 날 때까지 앞으로 얼마나 걸릴 거라고 생각해?

직장

33 I'll keep my eyes open for you.

앞으로 눈여겨 지켜보겠다.

A My secretary got married and quit. She was a very efficient secretary.

B Really? You must miss her very much.

A I sure do. Can you recommend anyone?

B Not at the moment
but **I'll keep my eyes open for you.**

A 내 비서가 결혼을 하고는 사직했어요. 아주 유능한 비서 였는데.

B 정말요? 당신, 그녀를 몹시 그리워하겠는데요.

A 그럼요. 누구 추천할 사람 없어요?

B 당장은 없지만,
앞으로 눈여겨보도록 할게요.

직장

34 He may not be pulling his weight.

그는 제 몫을 하는 것 같지 않아.

A Hiring Tom for our department doesn't seem to be working out.

B Well, **he may not be pulling his weight** just yet, but he's still new. Give him a little more time.

A Well, he'd better get his act together soon.

B Have a little more patience. I'm sure he will be alright.

A 톰을 우리 부서에 뽑은 건 잘 못한 일 같아.

B 뭐, 아직 제 몫을 하는 것 같지 않지만, 신입이잖아. 조금만 시간을 더 줘.

A 글쎄, 빨리 자리를 잡는 것이 좋을 텐데.

B 좀 기다려봐. 좋아질 거야.

직장

35 Your input shed a great deal of light on our work.

당신의 생각이 우리 일을 이해하는 데 도움이 됐어요.

I'm e-mailing you to let you know that I appreciate how helpful you've been to us on this project. **Your input shed a great deal of light on our work** and thanks to you we've finally worked out a good deal with our client and everything is falling into place. I'm going to throw a party next week and we would love for you to drop by and join our celebrations. Thank you again for everything.

당신이 이번 일에 얼마나 큰 도움이 되었는지 감사드리기 위해서 이메일을 보냅니다. 당신의 아이디어는 우리 일을 이해하는 데 정말 많은 도움이 되었고 덕분에 거래처와 좋은 계약을 성사시킬 수 있었습니다. 모든 일이 다 잘 되고 있어요. 제가 다음 주에 파티를 열 계획인데, 오셔서 함께 축하해 주시면 좋겠습니다. 다시 한 번 여러 가지로 감사드립니다.

직장

36 I will get caught up with everything.

모든 일을 마무리 지을 수 있을 거야.

How have you been? I'm terribly sorry for the late reply. I have been under tremendous pressure with the workload, not to mention the fact that I was already behind schedule. But don't worry. Eventually **I will get caught up with everything.** I can't find time to meet you at the moment but as soon as things get better let's hook up and have a good time. Take care.

잘 지냈어? 답장 늦게 보내서 정말 미안해. 나 요즘 너무 일이 많아서 스트레스를 너무 받고 있어. 그런데다 이미 일도 많이 밀려 있고. 그래도 걱정하지 마. 결국은 다 잘 처리할 수 있을 거야. 지금은 널 만날 시간이 없지만 상황이 나아지는 대로 우리 만나서 좋은 시간 갖자. 잘 있어.

직장

37 I've got to tie up a few loose ends.

나 남은 일 좀 마무리할게.

A Working overtime again?
Do you realize it's already 11:00?

B Already? Gosh, I feel like I have no social life outside of work these days.

A Wrap it up and let's have a cold one.
Mike and Angela are at the bar already.

B Why don't you go ahead? **I've got to tie up a few loose ends** and then I'll catch up with you guys a little later.

A 또 야근하고 있어?
지금 벌써 11시인 것 알아?

B 벌써? 이런, 요즘 일 외에 다른 사회생활은 전혀 없는 것 같아.

A 일 그만 마무리 짓고 시원한 맥주나 마시러 가자.
마이크하고 앤젤라는 벌써 바에 가 있어.

B 먼저 가 있을래? 난 남은 일만 좀 마무리하고 조금 이따 거기로 갈게.

직장

38 We're not in the red yet.

아직 적자는 아니야.

A How's our revenue for this month?

B Well, **we're not in the red yet** but I don't see much reason to be optimistic.

A We should be doing much better than this.

B Perhaps, but we're not through yet.
We'll come up with something to turn things around.

A 우리 이번 달 수익이 어떻게 돼?

B 아직 적자는 아닌데 낙관적이지는 않아.

A 지금보단 훨씬 더 잘해야만 하는데.

B 하지만 아직 끝나지 않았잖아.
뭔가 개선방안을 생각해 낼 거야.

직장

39 Things are all under control.

일이 계획대로 잘 진행되고 있어요.

A Is there anything I can help you with?
I habe a little time on my hands.

B Perfect! I was just going to ask you to take this equipment down to the meeting.

A Got it. Looks like **things are all under control**, doesn't it?

B Yep, I just hope everything goes smoothly.

A 내가 도울 일 좀 없어?
나 시간 좀 있어.

B 잘 됐다. 안 그래도 지금 너한테 이 장비 좀 아래 회의 장소에 갖다 놔 달라고 하려고 했어.

A 알았어. 일이 계획대로 잘 진행되는 것 같지, 안 그래?

B 응, 모든 일이 순조롭게 진행되길 바랄 뿐이야.

직장

40 Our department might be downsized soon.

우리 부서는 곧 축소될지도 모릅니다.

As I reported, **our department might be downsized soon.** Our business is going south and we are barely managing to get by. I'm guessing more than 30% of our employees might get the axe. I hope you can find a way to bail us out of this mess. I am definitely not looking forward to being the bad guy who has to let good people go.

보고 드렸듯이, 우리 부서는 곧 축소될지도 모르겠습니다. 사업이 하향세라 간신히 버티고 있습니다. 아마도 30% 이상의 직원들을 해고해야 할 것 같습니다. 이 위기에서 벗어날 방법을 찾아주셨으면 합니다. 전 죄 없는 사람들을 내보내야 하는 악역이 되고 싶지 않습니다.

직장

41 I'm in over my head on this one.

이 일이 내 능력 밖인 것 같아.

A There's no way I can meet the deadline.
I'm in over my head on this one.

B Our clients will hit the ceiling if you don't get it done on time.

A I will see what I can do.
But to be honest I'm not very optimistic.

B I understand you've had your hands full with too much work, but let's try to work it out together.

A 절대 마감시간 못 지킬 것 같아. 이 일 내 능력 밖이야.

B 너 이 일 제시간에 안 끝내면 우리 고객이 난리가 날 거야.

A 내가 어떻게든 해 볼게.
그래도 솔직히 낙관적이진 않아.

B 네가 지금 일이 너무 많은 것 알고 있지만 그래도 우리 함께 일을 풀어나가도록 노력해 보자.

직장

42 We're going to have to face the music.

우리가 대가를 치러야 할 거야.

A Why the long face? Something wrong?

B I've just got stuck with the Anderson account. No one seems to know how to figure out what to do with it.

A Well, perhaps everyone feels that you can take care of these kinds of things the best.

B Maybe, but sooner or later **we're going to have to face the music.**

A 얼굴 표정이 왜 그래? 뭐가 잘못 됐어?

B 앤더슨 회사와 문제가 생겼어. 아무도 이것을 어떻게 처리해야 할지 모르는 것 같아.

A 아마도 모두들 네가 이 일을 처리하는 데 최고라고 생각하나 보지.

B 그럴지도 모르지. 그렇지만 조만간에 우리가 대가를 치러야 할 거야.

직장

43 I was trapped at work.

꼼짝 못하고 일만 했어.

A How come you didn't show up at my party last night?

B Sorry, **I was trapped at work** all last weekend.

A Well, you missed out on a great party although we all ended up getting plastered.

B Maybe it's best that I didn't go then.
I'm a bit behind in my work.

A 너 왜 어젯밤 파티에 안왔어?

B 미안해. 나 지난 주말 내내 꼼짝 못하고 일만 했어.

A 너 진짜 재밌는 파티 놓친거야. 결국엔 우리 다 취해서 뻗어버리긴 했지만.

B 그럼 안간게 잘한 걸지도 모르겠다. 일이 좀 밀려서 말이야.

직장

44 Things are really going downhill.

일이 정말 안 좋게 돌아간다.

A How's it going with your new boss?

B **Things are really going downhill.**
All he does these days is complain and yell at us.

A Maybe he thinks that's the way to manage employees.

B Maybe, but he'd better lighten up soon.
We've all had enough.

A 너 새로운 상사와 좀 어때?

B 일이 정말 안 좋게 돌아가. 그 사람 요즘 하는 일이라곤 우리한테 불평하고 소리치는 게 다야.

A 아마도 그게 사람들 관리하는 방법이라고 생각하나 보지.

B 그럴지도 모르지. 그렇지만 그 사람 이제 좀 덜 그러는 게 좋을 거야. 우리 모두 많이 참았거든.

CHAPTER 04

인간관계 – 사람의 성격

인간관계-사람의 성격

1 Let it go.

이쯤 해두다, 잊어버리다.

A Hey, you look a little frustrated. Are you okay?

B I just had a big fight with Jenny. We've been dating for a month now and it's our first fight.

A Don't be so upset about it. All couples fight. Just **let it go.**

A 좀 심기가 불편해 보이는데, 괜찮아요?

B 방금 제니랑 크게 다퉈서요. 만난 지 한 달째인데 처음 크게 싸우게 됐네요.

A 너무 속상해하지 말아요. 커플들은 다 싸우잖아요. 그냥 잊어버려요.

인간관계-사람의 성격

2 I'm bad with names.

나는 이름을 잘 기억하지 못합니다.

A Do you remember that student who studied in the States for a couple of years?

B Yeah, I think so. What was his name again?

A That's what I wanted to ask you! **I'm bad with names.** All I can remember is his face.

A 2년 동안 미국에서 공부했다던 학생 기억나요?

B 네, 기억날 것 같아요. 이름이 뭐였죠?

A 그게 내가 묻고 싶은 거예요. 나는 이름을 잘 기억하지 못하거든요. 얼굴만 기억이 나요.

인간관계-사람의 성격

3 We're in the same boat.

우리 한 배를 탔어.

A Adrian, can you tell me where you are with your work?

B Okay. I have only a couple of more modules to cover.

A Wow, You're really fast. I'd better speed up to keep up with you.

B Take your time. Your portion is way more complicated than mine.

A But it's better we're on the same track as partners.

B **We're in the same boat** and I'll help you whenever you need me.

A 애드리안, 네 일 진도 얼마나 나갔어?

B 한두 부분만 더 하면 돼.

A 와, 너 진짜 빠르다. 너랑 진도를 맞추려면 서둘러야겠어.

B 천천히 해. 네 부분이 내 것보다 훨씬 복잡하잖아.

A 하지만 우린 파트너니까 진도를 맞추는 게 좋아.

B 우린 한 배를 탔으니까 필요할 때면 언제든 내가 널 도울게.

인간관계-사람의 성격

4 She's aged very well.

그 연세로 안 보이셔.

A It was a pleasure to meet your mother last week. What a lovely lady!
B Thanks. Actually, today is her 80th birthday.
A I had no idea she was 80! **She's aged very well.**

A 지난주에 네 어머니 만나서 너무 좋았어. 정말 좋은 분이신 것 같아.
B 고마워. 실은 오늘이 어머니 팔순 생신이야.
A 팔순이나 되셨다고는 생각도 못했어! 그 연세로 안 보이셔.

인간관계-사람의 성격

5 He's the black sheep of the family.

그 애는 가족의 애물단지야.

A I heard from John last week. Apparently he's in India studying Hinduism.
B Yeah, his parents can't understand why he has spent so much time there.
A Well, **he always was the black sheep of the family.**

A 지난주에 존이랑 얘기했어. 인도에서 힌두교 공부 중이라더라.
B 그래. 그 애 부모님도 그 애가 왜 거기서 그렇게 오래 지내는지 이해 못 하셔.
A 그 애는 항상 가족의 애물단지잖아.

인간관계-사람의 성격

6 Where do you see yourself in five years?

5년 뒤 당신은 어떤 모습일 것 같습니까?

A **Where do you see yourself in five years?**
B I would like to keep growing in a company that challenges me.
A Excellent. We are looking for employees with a long term commitment to the company.

A 5년 뒤 당신은 어떤 모습일 것 같습니까?
B 제 능력을 시험할 수 있는 회사에서 성장해 나가고 싶습니다.
A 좋습니다. 저희는 장기간 근무할 직원을 찾고 있습니다.

인간관계-사람의 성격

7 I wouldn't give her the time of day.

걔랑 상대 안 할 거야.

A After the way Sarah talked about me yesterday, **I wouldn't give her the time of day!**
B She must have said some terrible things about you.
A You have no idea! And they were all untrue!

A 어제 사라가 나에 대해 그런 식으로 말하다니. 걔랑 상대 안 할거야!
B 너에 대해 아주 나쁜 말을 한 모양이구나!
A 말도 마! 게다가 모두 다 거짓말이야!

인간관계-사람의 성격

8 There's some bad blood between us.

불화가 좀 있었어.

A Do you have any siblings?
B Yes, I have a brother, but we're not close.
A Why not? Did you have some trouble in the past?
B Yeah, **there's some bad blood between us.**

A 넌 형제가 있어?
B 응. 오빠가 있는데 가깝지는 않아.
A 왜? 예전에 좀 문제가 있었어?
B 응. 불화가 좀 있었어.

인간관계-사람의 성격

9 I could set you up on a blind date

내가 소개팅을 주선해 줄 수 있을 것 같아.

A **I could set you up on a blind date.** I have several eligible friends.
B That would be great! Why didn't you mention that before?
A I didn't realize you were looking for a relationship!

A 내가 소개팅 주선해 줄 수 있을 것 같아. 괜찮은 친구가 여럿 있거든.
B 그럼 좋지! 전에는 왜 얘기 안 했는데?
A 네가 만날 사람 찾고 있는지 몰랐지!

인간관계-사람의 성격

10 We don't see eye to eye.

의견이 맞지 않아.

A I just had a marathon meeting with Mr. Kim.
B Oh, really? What was the problem?
A It's our hiring policy. He and **I just don't see eye to eye** on our benefits package.

A 지금까지 미스터 김과 마라톤 회의를 했어.
B 그래? 뭐가 문제였는데?
A 고용방침 때문이야. 복리후생제도에 대해 의견이 맞지 않아.

인간관계-사람의 성격

11 My wife takes care of the bills.

돈은 집사람이 관리해.

A Oh no, my credit card is maxed out again.
B I don't know how you survive. You are terrible with money.
A Thank goodness **my wife takes care of the bills.**

A 이런, 신용카드 한도가 또 초과됐네.
B 네가 어떻게 버티는지 모르겠다. 돈 관리 정말 못한다.
A 돈을 집사람이 관리해서 정말 다행이야.

인간관계-사람의 성격

12 He's finally coming of age.

이제 철이 들었어.

A I'm so proud of my son. He recently started his own business.

B Is that so? It seems like just yesterday he was in college.

A **He's finally coming of age.**

A 내 아들이 정말 자랑스러워. 최근에 자기 사업을 시작했거든.

B 그래? 대학 다닐 때가 엊그제 같은데 말이야.

A 이제 철이 들었어.

인간관계-사람의 성격

13 He's the breadwinner.

그가 혼자 벌어.

A John was complaining that it's been hard to make ends meet.

B Yeah, since his wife had a baby, **he's been the breadwinner.**

A These days, it's hard to make ends meet with only one income.

A 존이 생활비 맞추기가 어렵다고 불평하더라.

B 그러게, 부인이 아이를 낳은 후로 그가 혼자 벌잖아.

A 요즘은 한 사람 수입으로 생활하기가 쉽지 않지.

인간관계-사람의 성격

14 He's sort of a loner.

그는 혼자 있어.

A Who's that guy?

B He's in our class, but **he's sort of a loner.**

A We should go say "Hi!" to him.

A 쟤 누구야?

B 우리 반인데 보통 혼자 있는 편이야.

A 우리 쟤한테 인사하자.

※ loner는 혼자 지내는 것을 좋아하는 사람을 가리킵니다. 이 표현은 "He tends to keep to himself."와 같은 의미입니다.

인간관계-사람의 성격

15 I was in a mood.

기분이 그냥 그래서.

A Why didn't you talk to anyone at the party?

B Oh, **I was in a mood.**

A 왜 파티에서 아무하고도 말 안했니?

B 아, 기분이 그냥 그래서.

인간관계-사람의 성격

16 He's a jolly guy.

걔는 기분 좋은 친구야.

A I like Gus. **He's a jolly guy.**

B I think so, too.

A 나는 거스가 좋아. 걔는 기분 좋은 친구야.

B 나도 그렇게 생각해.

※ 누군가 jolly하는 말은 같이 있으면 happy하고 cheerful하다는 의미입니다. (=He's a happy fellow.)

인간관계-사람의 성격

17 He has got a short temper.

그는 화를 잘 내거든.

A Why did you say I should be careful around the boss?

B **He has got a short temper.**

A Thanks for the warning.

A 내가 왜 사장 앞에서 조심해야 한다는 거지?

B 화를 잘 내거든.

A 알려줘서 고마워.

인간관계-사람의 성격

18 I am in bad condition.

컨디션이 안 좋아.

A I don't feel well. I have a headache.

B I am very tired today. **I am in bad condition.**

C I am upset because I failed my exam yesterday.

A 몸이 안 좋아. 두통이 있어.

B 오늘 너무 피곤하네. 컨디션이 안 좋아.

C 어제 시험을 망쳐서 기분이 안 좋아.

인간관계-사람의 성격

19 I like him, but he's so naive.

그 사람이 좋긴 한데 너무 순진하단 말야.

A **I like him, but he's so naive.**

B Yes. He's got a lot to learn.

A 그 사람 좋긴 한데 너무 순진하단 말야.

B 그래. 걔는 많이 배워야 돼.

인간관계-사람의 성격

20 He's very family-oriented.

아주 가정적인 사람이야.

A My husband is taking the kids to the zoo today.

B Wow, he's a really dedicated father.

A Yes, he's great. **He's very family-oriented.**

A 남편이 오늘 애들 데리고 동물원에 가.

B 와, 정말 헌신적인 아버지네.

A 응, 최고야. 아주 가정적인 사람이야.

인간관계-사람의 성격

21 You look kind of low.

기분이 우울해 보여요.

A What's wrong? **You look kind of low.**

B Does it show that much?

A Yes, because your eyes are puffy.

B Actually I was crying. My grandmother's death made me upset.

A Perk up!

A 무슨 일 있으세요? 기분이 안 좋으신가 봐요.

B 그렇게 보이세요?

A 네, 눈이 부은 것 같아요.

B 실은 울었거든요. 할머니의 부음 때문에 기분이 안 좋아요.

A 힘내세요!

인간관계-사람의 성격

22 You'll be hearing from my lawyer.

당신을 고소하겠소.

A What do you mean you owe me nothing?
You must pay me the security deposit back.

B I'm not going to pay you back, because you've done a lot of damage to my property.

A That's not true. That was normal wear and tear.

B No, it's not.

A OK, if you don't may me $10,000 within a week, **you'll be hearing from my lawyer.**

A 저에게 줄 돈이 하나도 없다니 무슨 소리에요?
보증금을 돌려주셔야 하잖아요.

B 내 재산을 많이 파손시켰으니 보증금을 돌려 줄 수 없습니다.

A 그건 사실이 아니에요. 정상적으로 닳은 거잖아요.

B 아니요, 그렇지 않아요.

A 좋아요. 일주일 내로 1만 달러를 갚지 않으면 고소하겠어요.

인간관계-사람의 성격

23 Both of us bring home the bacon.

저희는 맞벌이 부부입니다.

A Kenny, what do you do for a living?

B I am a junior high school teacher.

A Does your wife work, too?

B Yes, we are a two-paycheck couple. **Both of us must bring home the bacon** to make the mortgage payments on our house.

A 케니씨, 직업이 어떻게 되세요?

B 저는 중학교 교사입니다.

A 부인도 일하시나요?

B 네, 저희는 맞벌이 부부입니다. 주택 대출금을 납부하기 위해서 둘 다 일해야 하거든요.

인간관계-사람의 성격

24 Between you and me.

아무에게도 말하지 마라.

A In fact, I'm the only reason we made this sale. I worked night and day on this project.

B Did anyone else help you?

A Well, **between you and me**, right now no one else is qualified here.

B Really? I thought they were all qualified when I hired them.

A 사실 나 때문에 이 제품이 성공리에 판매된거지 뭐. 내가 밤낮으로 일했거든.

B 널 도와준 사람은 아무도 없었고?

A 이거 아무한테도 말하지 마. 지금 여기 아무도 자격을 갖춘 사람이 없어.

B 정말? 내가 그 사람들 뽑았을 때는 모두 적임자라고 생각했었는데.

인간관계-사람의 성격

25 You're way off base.

네 생각은 완전히 틀렸어.

A Regina says she is engaged to marry.

B Really? Who is the lucky guy?

A I thought you were.

B No, I am not. If you thought I was going to marry her, **you were way off base.**

A But you love her, don't you?

B I like her very much, but I'm not in love with her.

A 레지나가 약혼했다고 그러던데.

B 그래? 행운아가 누구야?

A 난 너로 생각했는데.

B 아니, 난 아냐. 내가 그 여자랑 결혼할 걸로 알았다면 크게 잘못 안 거야.

A 그렇지만, 넌 그녀를 사랑하잖아.

B 매우 좋아하지만, 사랑에 빠져 있지는 않지.

인간관계-사람의 성격

26 Could you fix me up with her?

내게 그녀를 소개해주시겠어요?

A Does your sister have a boy friend?

B Why? Are you attracted to her?

A If she hasn't got any boy friend, **could you fix me up with her?** Actually I have a crush on her.

B I am not sure if you are her type. But I will ask her when she is available.

A Thanks man.

A 네 여동생 남자 친구 있니?

B 왜? 그녀에게 관심 있어?

A 남자 친구 없으면 소개해줄래? 실은 나 그녀에게 반했어.

B 네가 그녀 타입인지는 모르겠다. 언제 시간이 나는지 물어볼게.

A 고마워. 친구.

인간관계-사람의 성격

27 He's full of beans.

그는 매우 신이 나 있다.

A Didn't Andrew make it? I haven't seen him recently.
B Andrew? He went on a trip to Japan. I bumped into him going to the airport this morning.
A Really? He must be having some fun now.
B Sure. He deserves it. He studied really hard this year.
A Yeah. **All kids are full of beans** after final exams.
B Definitely. Look back on us. We used to be the same.

A 앤드루는 안 왔나? 요즘 통 못 보겠네.
B 앤드루? 일본으로 여행 갔잖아. 오늘 아침에 우연히 봤는데 공항으로 가는 길이던데.
A 정말? 지금 한참 즐겁겠네.
B 그럼. 당연히 그래야지. 올해 정말 열심히 공부했잖아.
A 맞아. 애들이 기말고사 끝내고 신나는 건 당연하지.
B 그렇지. 우리 때를 생각해 봐. 우리도 그랬어.

인간관계-사람의 성격

28 He's such a brat.

그는 아주 버르장머리가 없어.

A I was with my sister's kid yesterday. **He's such a brat.**
B Don't be so judgmental. Maybe he's just stubborn. You know, hardheaded.
A You're right. Besides, I'm sure it's just a phase. He'll grow out of it.

A 어제 조카와 함께 지냈는데, 그 녀석 아주 버르장머리가 없어.
B 그렇게 판단하지 마. 어쩌면 그저 고집이 센 걸지도 모르니까. 똥고집 있잖아.
A 네 말이 맞아. 게다가, 딱 그럴 시기인 것 같아. 크면 괜찮아지겠지.

인간관계-사람의 성격

29 It's like I'm rubbing their noses in it.

내가 그 애들의 기분을 상하게 할 것 같아.

A I'll take you to a nice coffee shop.
B Just promise me that we won't go to that place on Third.
A But I thought you loved it there.
B I do, but some of my friends work there. They don't have boyfriends, so if I show up with you, **it's like I'm rubbing their noses in it.**

A 분위기 좋은 커피숍에 가자.
B 3번가에 있는 그 커피숍에는 가지 않겠다고 약속해줘.
A 너 거기 정말 좋아하잖아.
B 좋아하긴 하는데 친구들이 거기서 일해. 그 애들은 남자친구가 없어서 내가 너랑 가면 기분 나빠할 거 같아.

인간관계-사람의 성격

30 I'm here to sub for him.

그 사람 대신 (일하러) 나왔어요.

A Can I help you?

B Hi. My name is Kenny. My friend NBC is sick, so **I'm here to sub for him.**

A What? NBC studio?

B Oh, sorry. NBC stands for Nam Bong-chul, not the NBC studio in Manhattan.

A Oh, I see. It's so nice of you to stand in for NBC. He is not very ill, is he?

B No. A good day's rest should bring him back to work tomorrow.

A 도와 드릴까요?

B 안녕하세요? 저는 케니라고 합니다. 제 친구 NBC가 아파서 제가 대신 일하러 나왔습니다.

A 뭐라고요? NBC 스튜디오라고요?

B 미안합니다. NBC는 맨해튼에 있는 NBC 스튜디오가 아니라 남봉철을 뜻합니다.

A 아, 알겠어요. NBC를 대신해 일하러 나왔다니 반갑군요. 그 친구 많이 아픈 건 아니죠?

B 아니요. 하루 푹 쉬면 내일 일하러 나올 수 있을 겁니다.

인간관계-사람의 성격

31 You're such a bleeding-heart.

너는 마음이 너무 여려.

A What took you so long to come home? You're supposed to be home like an hour ago.

B Sorry, mom. I came home on foot.

A You walked home? What happened?

B I saw a pauper and his poor little girl at the subway station. They looked so abject and I accidentally gave them all the money I had.

A Oh, **you're such a bleeding-heart**, sweetheart.

B You wouldn't have passed over them either.

A 왜 이렇게 오래 걸렸어? 평소보다 한 시간이나 늦게 왔잖아.

B 죄송해요, 엄마. 집까지 걸어오느라 그랬어요.

A 집까지 걸어왔어? 왜?

B 지하철역에서 한 걸인과 어린 딸을 봤는데 너무나 가엾어 그냥 제가 가진 돈을 다 줘버렸거든요.

A 넌 마음이 너무 여려 탈이야.

B 엄마도 보셨다면 아마 그냥 지나칠 수 없었을 거예요.

인간관계-사람의성격

32 I don't want to put you out.

너한테 부담 주기 싫어.

A Heading home? Do you want me to give you a ride?

B Thanks, but **I don't want to put you out.**

A It's okay. I'm going past your place anyway. Besides, I could use some good company.

B Thanks, I owe you a big one.

A 집에 가? 내가 차로 데려다 줄까?

B 고마워, 그렇지만 너한테 부담을 주기 싫은데.

A 괜찮아 어차피 너희 집 지나는 길인데 뭐. 게다가 너 있으면 지루하지 않아서 좋지.

B 고마워 이번에 크게 빚졌네.

인간관계-사람의성격

33 I'm no one's doormat anymore.

사람들한테 더 이상 고분고분 하지 않을 거야.

A Wow. Was that Bill you were gust talking with on the phone? I can't believe what you said to him.

B I surprised myself, too. But my resolution is to be tougher with co-workers. **I'm no one's doormat anymore!**

A You might want to take it slow. Remember, baby steps.

A 와. 너랑 전화통화 한 사람 빌이었니? 네가 그 사람한테 그렇게 말하다니 말도 안돼.

B 나도 내 자신한테 놀랐어. 내 결심은 직장동료에게 좀 더 강하게 하기야. 사람들한테 더 이상 고분고분하지 않을거야!

A 천천히 신중하게 해. 조금씩 바꿔가는 것도 잊지 말고.

인간관계-사람의성격

34 What would you do in my shoes?

당신이 내 입장이라면 어떻게 하겠습니까?

A What do you think I am. a swindler or something?

B Don't raise your voice. I didn't call you a swindler.

A Why do you treat me like that?

B **What would you do in my shoes?** Put yourself in my place.

A I don't get it. What's the point?

A 당신은 나를 사기꾼쯤으로 생각하고 있지?

B 언성을 높이지 마세요. 나는 당신을 사기꾼이라고 하지 않았습니다.

A 왜 날 사기꾼처럼 대하지?

B 당신이 내 입장이라면 어떻게 하겠습니까? 입장을 바꿔놓고 봅시다.

A 무슨 소리인지 모르겠네. 요점이 뭐야?

인간관계-사람의성격

35 He's so full of himself.

걔는 자기가 가장 잘난 줄 알지.

A What is mark's problem?

B **He's so full of himself.**

A 마크는 뭐가 문제야?

B 걔는 자기가 가장 잘난 줄 알지.

인간관계-사람의성격

36 I think he is crass.

내 생각에 걔는 무식해.

A Is Jim mean?

B No. **I think he is crass.**

A That might explain it.

A 짐이 좀 못됐지?

B 아니. 내 생각에 걔는 멍청해.

A 그 말이 맞겠다.

인간관계-사람의성격

37 He really pissed me off.

걔가 날 진짜 열받게 했어.

A When he said that my girlfirend was ugly, **he really pissed me off.**

B I understand. What a mean thing to say!

A 걔가 내 여자친구가 못생겼다고 했을 때 나 진짜 열받았어.

B 이해된다. 어떻게 그런 말을 할 수가!

인간관계-사람의성격

38 Philately is a relaxing hobby.

우표 수집은 마음을 편안하게 해주는 취미지요.

A I need to relieve all the stress in my life. What would you recommend?

B **Philately is a relaxing hobby.** So is RC car driving.

A 일상에서 받는 스트레스를 모두 풀어야겠어요. 추천할 만한 것이 있나요?

B 우표 수집은 마음을 편안하게 해주는 취미지요. 무선조종 자동차 운전도 그렇고요.

인간관계-사람의성격

39 I was sort of jealous.

난 좀 질투가 났어

A When he received that important job and I didn't, **I was sort of jealous.**

B You shouldn't feel that way. You're a good person, even if you didn't receive the job.

A 그 사람은 번듯한 직장을 잡았는데 나는 그러지 못했을 때, 좀 질투가 났지.

B 그렇게 생각하지 마. 그 직장에 들어가지 못 했어도 넌 아주 훌륭한 사람이야.

인간관계-사람의 성격

40 I have a soft spot for people like her.

나는 그녀 같은 사람에게 약해.

A How do you get along with Susan so well?
She seems to be so moody.

B True. But she had a really bad childhood and I can't help but care for her.

A Well, I don't know how you do it.
She drives me crazy.

B I guess **I just have a soft spot for people like her.**

A 너 어떻게 수잔이랑 그렇게 잘 지내? 걔 너무 변덕스러운 것 같은데.

B 맞아. 그렇지만 그 애 아주 힘든 유년기를 보냈거든. 그래서 내가 그 애를 돌봐줄 수 밖에 없어.

A 글쎄, 네가 어떻게 그렇게 할 수 있는지 모르겠다.
난 걔 때문에 미치겠던데.

B 내가 그런 사람들에게 약한 것 같아.

인간관계-사람의 성격

41 She is such a know-it-all.

쟤 정말 잘난 척 심해.

A Look! There goes Kevin and Sue.

B I wonder why Kevin goes out with Sue.
She is so annoying.

A You're right. **She is such a know-it-all** and always looks down on everyone.

B I don't understand what Kevin sees in her.

A 저것 봐! 케빈하고 수 지나간다.

B 난 케빈이 왜 수하고 사귀는지 모르겠어.
수 정말 짜증 나.

A 맞아. 쟤 정말 잘난 척 끝내주고 항상 모든 사람을 무시해.

B 케빈이 저 애 뭘 보고 좋아하는지 정말 이해가 안가.

인간관계-사람의 성격

42 We are not meant to be together.

우리는 서로 잘 맞는 상대가 아니야.

Hi, thanks for understanding how I feel about things. I should have come clean about everything a lot earlier. Like I said before, it's nothing you did wrong. It's just that as time went on I realized that **we were just not meant to be together.** I'm sorry to let you down by saying this but I'm sure you will be better off without me. Anyway, I hope we can still be good friends.

안녕, 내 마음을 이해해 줘서 고마워. 내가 진작에 모든 것을 다 털어놓았어야 했는데. 전에도 얘기했듯이 넌 잘못한 게 아무것도 없어. 그냥 우리가 시간이 지나면서 우리가 서로 잘 맞는 상대가 아니라는 것을 깨달았어. 미안해. 이렇게 말하고 널 실망시켜서. 그렇지만 나 없으면 넌 더 잘 살 거야. 어쨌든 우리가 계속 좋은 친구로 남았으면 좋겠다.

인간관계-사람의 성격

43 We have one thing in common.

우린 한 가지 공통점이 있네.

A So, Jess. I've heard that you are a writer. What are you writing about?

B Well, I write mostly about food, you know, recipes, restaurants and all that jazz. What do you do, Joshua?

A I'm a movie critic. I write for a weekly movie magazine.

B Funny that **we have one thing in common**; cutting down people around us.

A 그래서 제스, 듣기로는 작가라고 하던데, 어떤 글을 쓰시죠?

B 글쎄요, 전 거의 음식에 대해 써요. 그러니까 요리법이나 식당 등에 관해서요. 조슈아는 무슨 일을 하세요?

A 전 영화 평론가예요. 주간 영화 잡지에 글을 싣고 있어요.

B 재밌게도 우리 한 가지 공통점이 있네요. 주변 사람들 깎아내리는 일을 한다는 거요.

인간관계-사람의 성격

44 They were like fish out of water.

그들은 잘 어울리지 못했다.

The costume party we went to turned out to be a blast. I chose to be Elvis Presley, wearing tight white jeans and white boots. It was a little awkward at first, but I soon got comfortable after mingling with people. In fact, I think the people who forgot to wear costumes were the real **fish out of water.** Funny, huh?

우리가 갔던 가장 파티 정말 재미있었어. 난 엘비스 프레슬리처럼 꽉 끼는 하얀색 바지에 하얀색 부츠차림으로 갔지. 처음엔 좀 어색했는데 사람들이랑 어울리면서 곧 괜찮아졌어. 사실, 잊어버리고 70년대 복장을 안 입은 사람들이 오히려 물 떠난 물고기같이 어색했던 것 같아. 웃기지?

인간관계-사람의 성격

45 We are not speaking the same language.

우린 서로 말이 안 통해요.

A Let's wrap up this meeting. It's just going nowhere.

B You're right. We're all getting worn-out and I don't even think **we are speaking the same language** anymore.

A Why don't we meet up another time after we calm down and clear our heads?

B I guess we should.

A 이 회의 마무리 합시다. 도대체 결론이 나지 않네.

B 맞아요. 모두 점점 지쳐서 이젠 말도 통하지 않는 것 같아요.

A 좀 진정하고 머리나 식힌 후에 다시 모이는 게 어때?

B 그래야 할 것 같아요.

인간관계-사람의 성격

46 He must have pigged out a lot.

걔 진짜 많이 먹고 살았나 보다.

A Get a load of the guy over there. He looks kind of familiar to me.

B Who? Andrew Chan? Boy, he's gained so much weigh. What's up with him?

A He sure has. **He must have pigged out a lot.** But he still looks cute, though.

B Uh oh. He is coming this way! We should say hi.

A 저기 저 남자 좀 봐. 저 남자 어디서 많이 본 것 같은데.

B 누구? 앤드류 찬? 맙소사, 정말 살쪘네. 도대체 무슨 일이지?

A 진짜 그러네. 정말 많이 먹고 살았나 봐.
그래도 아직 잘생겼네.

B 이런. 지금 여기로 온다. 우리 인사해야겠다.

인간관계-사람의 성격

47 Are you seeing anyone these days?

너 요새 사귀는 사람 있어?

A Hey, Jess. **Are you seeing anyone these days?**

B Not that I recall. No. Why do you ask?

A I know someone who would get along with you perfectly. He is caring and funny, not to mention that he's drop-dead gorgeous.

B Sound like a lady's man, but it wouldn't hurt to meet him. Set me up with him. I'm pretty mush free next week.

A 제스 너 요새 사귀는 사람 있어?

B 내가 아는 한 없어. 왜 물어봐?

A 너한테 완벽하게 어울릴 만한 사람을 알거든. 그 사람 자상하고 재밌어. 물론 엄청 잘 생기기도 했고.

B 여자 꽤나 만나고 다닐 남자 같다. 그래도 만나본다고 나쁘진 않겠지. 소개시켜 줘봐. 나 다음 주엔 꽤 한가해.

인간관계-사람의 성격

48 She's got a lot of willpower.

그 애는 의지력이 아주 강해.

A The key to sticking to a resolution is having a support network.

B It'll be easier to follow through on my plans if I have a group of friends helping me out.

A Right, because you can encourage one another.

B Perfect. I'll ask Betty to help me.
She's got a lot of willpower.

A 결심을 지키는데 중요한 것은 도와주는 사람들이 주변에 있냐는 거야.

B 나를 도와주는 친구들이 있으면 계획을 끝가지 지키는 게 더 쉬울 거야.

A 맞아, 서로 격려해줄 수 있으니까.

B 좋아. 베티에게 도움을 청해야겠어.
그 애는 의지력이 아주 강하거든.

인간관계-사람의 성격

49 It's hard to stay motivated.

평정심을 유지하기가 어려워.

A Have you kept your resolution to lose weight?

B Not really. I was very motivated for the first couple of days, but….

A I know. **It's hard to stay motivated**, but if you keep at it, you'll see result.

B I hope so. Nowdays, every time I look in a mirror I feel guilty.

A 체중 감량 결심은 잘 지켜지고 있니?

B 그렇지마는 않아. 처음 며칠간은 결심이 대단했는데….

A 알아. 처음 결심을 유지하긴 어렵지만 하다 보면 효과가 나타날 거야.

B 그랬으면 좋겠어. 요즘 거울을 볼 때마다 죄책감이 들거든.

인간관계-사람의 성격

50 I'd like to take you out to lunch for all the help you've given me.

저를 도와주신 감사의 표시로 점심을 대접하고 싶은데요.

A **I'd like to take you out to lunch for all the help you've given me.**

B You don't have to do that. But thanks.

A 저를 도와주신 감사의 표시로 점심을 대접하고 싶은데요.

B 그럴 필요까지는 없어요. 어쨌든 고마워요.

인간관계-사람의 성격

51 Did you bump into him recently?

최근에 그와 우연히 만났니?

A Do you remember Mike Smith from high school? He just got married.

B Mike Smith? I haven't heard that name in ages. **Did you bump into him recently?**

A Not really. I stumbled across his blog last night.

B I guess blogs are the new way of staying in touch.

A 고등학교 동창인 마이크 스미스 기억나? 결혼했더라.

B 마이크 스미스? 그 이름은 들어본 지 꽤 됐는데. 최근에 우연히 만난 거야?

A 그런 건 아니고 어젯밤에 그 애 블로그를 우연히 발견했어.

B 블로그가 연락을 유지하는 새로운 수단인 거 같아.

인간관계-사람의 성격

52 I'm actually head over heels in love with you.

실은 너한테 푹 빠졌어.

A I know I'm supposed to play it cool, but **I'm actually head over heels in love with you.**

B Really? Then, I can admit I'm really into you, too.

A So, what is it that you like about me the most? My good looks, right?

B Actually…. You remind me of the expression, "Love is blind."

A 냉정해야 되는 건 알지만, 실은 너에게 푹 빠졌어.

B 정말? 그럼, 나도 너한테 관심이 많다는 거 고백할게.

A 근데 나의 어떤 점이 가장 좋아? 잘생긴 얼굴?

B 실은…. 너를 보면서 생각나는 말이 있어. "사랑은 맹목적이다"라는 말.

인간관계-사람의 성격

53 You could hang out with them there.

여기서 그분들과 놀아 드리는 게 어떨까요.

A It's my first time volunteering.

B Some of the residents are already in the Day Room, watching TV. If you like, **you could hang out with them there.**

A I just watch TV with them?

B If they want, but a lot of them love card games.

A 봉사활동은 처음 해봐요.

B 여기 사는 어르신들이 휴게실에서 TV를 보고 계세요. 괜찮으면 가서 그분들과 놀아드리는 게 어떨까요.

A 그분들과 TV만 같이 보면 되나요?

B 그분들이 원하시면요. 하지만 대부분 카드게임을 좋아하세요.

인간관계-사람의 성격

54 He's gone too far.

그 사람 너무했군요.

A I hear that Michael Bang is in jail. Is that true?

B Yes, it's true.

A What did he do this time?

B He stole the test paper and the entire hard drive before beginning of midterm.

A He did? **He's gone too far.**

B He sure has.

A 마이클 방이 감옥에 갔다는데 사실이니?

B 응, 사실이야.

A 이번엔 또 무슨 일을 저질렀니?

B 중간고사 시작 전에 시험지와 하드 드라이브 전체를 훔쳤다는군.

A 그랬다고? 너무 심했군.

B 그러게 말이야.

인간관계-사람의 성격

55 I am done with him.

그 사람과는 완전히 끝났어요.

A Why do you have a long face?

B I no longer see her.

A You mean you have split with her?

B Yes, **I am done with her.**

A That's too bad.

B Where is my new better half?

A 침울해 보이는데 무슨 일 있니?

B 나 그녀를 더 이상 만나지 않기로 했어.

A 그녀와 완전히 결별했다는 거야?

B 응, 그녀와는 이제 끝났어.

A 저런. 안됐구나.

B 새로운 나의 반쪽은 그 어디에 있을까?

PART 2

특별한 장소에서의 생활영어

CHAPTER

05

영화관

영화관 1

tear-jerker.

눈물을 흘리게 하는 영화나 이야기

A Do you like sad movies? If so, ther's one I'd like to invite you to.

B Well, sometimes i'm not in the mood to see a **tear-jerker**, because they can be so depressing. But these days, that sounds good.

A Okay! Does Friday work for you?

A 슬픈 영화 좋아해요? 좋아하면, 같이 보러 가자고 할 영화가 있거든요.

B 음, 가끔 감상적인 영화를 볼 기분이 아닐 때가 있긴 해요. 우울해지니까요. 그런데 요즘은 괜찮거든요.

A 좋아요! 금요일 시간 괜찮겠어요?

영화관 2

What a tearjerker!

정말 슬픈 영화야!

A **What a tearjerker!**

That film told an emotionally moving story.

B Yeah. It was a very sad movie.

A 너무 슬픈 영화야!

영화 정말 감동적이다.

B 그래. 아주 슬픈 영화였어.

영화관 3

This flash movie is hilarious.

이 플래시 무비 정말 재미있다.

A **This flash movie is hilarious.**

B Are those hard to make?

A The Flash program makes it easy.

A 이 플래시 무비 정말 재미있다.

B 그런 거 만들기 힘드니?

A 플래시 프로그램만 있으면 만들기 쉬워.

영화관 4

That was a surprising plot twist.

반전이 정말 놀랍더라.

A When the main character found out that his brother was really a spy, **that was a surprising plot twist.**

B I agree. I was surprised that that happened.

A 주인공이 자기 형이 스파이인 걸 알았을 때 반전이 정말 놀랍더라.

B 맞아. 나도 그 장면에서 놀랐어.

영화관

5 That movie was for the birds.

그 영화는 정말 형편없었다.

A Did you have a nice weekend?

B Almost, except the terrible movie I saw Saturday night.

A Uh-uh. How terrible was it?

B In a nut shell, **it was strictly for the birds.**

A That bad, huh? What did your boyfriend say?

B He was barely awake through the whole movie.

A 좋은 주말 보냈어?

B 대충, 토요일 밤에 봤던 끔찍한 영화만 빼면.

A 이런. 얼마나 끔찍했는데?

B 한 마디로 말하자면, 정말 형편없었어.

A 그렇게 나빴어? 네 남자친구는 뭐래?

B 영화 내내 거의 졸던데.

영화관

6 It's being called the sleeper hit of the year.

이게 올해 예상외의 흥행작이래.

A Hey, let's check out this one.
It's being called the sleeper hit of the year.

B I've never heard of it.

A You only pay attention to movies with multimillion-dollar advertising campaigns.

B But that's park of the fun. There are the teasers and then the trailers and then the movie!

A 야, 이것 좀 봐.
올해 예상외로 흥행하고 있는 영화래.

B 처음 듣는데.

A 넌 수백 만 달러를 들여 광고하는 영화에만 관심이 있더라.

B 그것도 영화의 재미야. 광고 보고, 예고편 보고, 그 다음 영화 보는 거!

CHAPTER 06

주점

주점 1 I already feel a little tipsy. 나 벌써 좀 취한 거 같아.

A I've only had one drink but **I already feel a little tipsy.**

B You're a cheap date. Besides, I told you not to drink on an empty stomach.

A You're right. The alcohol went right to my head.
I need to sit down.

B And you need to pace yourself.
Don't have more than one drink an hour.

A 술을 한 잔 밖에 안 마셨는데 벌써 좀 취한 거 같아.

B 너 빨리 취하는구나. 게다가 내가 빈 속에 술 마시지 말라고 했잖아.

A 네 말이 맞아. 술 마시니 정신이 없네.
좀 앉아야겠어.

B 술 마시는 속도를 알아서 조절해야지. 한 시간에 한 잔 이상 마시지 마.

주점 2 You're three sheets to the wind. 너 고주망태가 됐어.

A You look like **you're three sheets to the wind.**

B What did you say?

A I said you look drunk.
Your face is all red and you're slurring your words.

B You're right. I think I've had one too many. Can you call me a cab?

A 너 고주망태가 된 거 같아.

B 뭐라고?

A 너 취한 거 같다고 했어. 얼굴이 전부 벌겋고 말도 꼬이잖아.

B 맞아. 너무 많이 마신 거 같아. 택시 좀 불러 줄래?

주점 3 Would you like to see a wine list? 와인 메뉴 보시겠어요?

A **Would you like to see a wine list?**

B Could you please recommend some good wines?

A 와인 메뉴 보시겠어요?

B 좋은 와인 좀 추천해주시겠어요?

주점

4 We really tied one on.

우리 정말 과음했어.

A I'm still hung over from the New Year's Eve party. How about you?

B I'm about 80% recovered. **We really tied one on.**

A Tell me about it. I have never been that sick before in my life.

B Me neither. Oh well. It was worth it, though. It was the perfect way to bring in the new year.

A 새해전야파티 때의 숙취가 아직도 있어. 넌 어때?

B 난 거의 깼어. 우리 정말 과음했어.

A 그러게 말이야. 이렇게 아픈 적은 처음이야.

B 나도 그래. 그래도 보람은 있었어. 새해를 맞는 방법으로는 최고였거든.

주점

5 I would love a cocktail to take the edge off.

피로가 풀리도록 칵테일 한 잔 주세요.

A Can I get you something from the bar before dinner?

B Well, **I would love a cocktail to take the edge off.** It was a tough day at the office.

A A dry martini would certainly help you relax.

B Sounds perfect.
Ask the bartender to throw in a couple of extra olives.

A 저녁 식사 전에 바에서 뭐 좀 갖다 드릴까요?

B 피로가 풀리도록 칵테일 한 잔 주세요. 회사일이 힘들었거든요.

A 산뜻한 마티니 한 잔이면 분명 편안해지실 거예요.

B 좋아요.
바텐더에게 올리브 몇 개만 좀 더 넣어달라고 해주세요.

주점

6 Should we order another round?

한 잔씩 더 할까?

A **Should we order another round?** You know, one for the road?

B Sure. Isn't it your turn to buy?

A It's yours. The booze here tastes a little watered down. I'm hardly even buzzed.

B I agree. So that's two double shots of Jack with two beer chasers.

A 한 잔씩 더 할까? 마지막 딱 한잔 어때?

B 그래. 네가 살 차례 아니야?

A 네 차례야. 여기 술에 물을 좀 탔는지 취하지도 않아.

B 맞아. 그럼 더블샷을 넣은 잭 두 잔에다가 입가심으로 마시는 맥주를 두 잔 더 시키자.

주점 7 Let's have just one more round, Okay?

한 잔만 더 하시죠?

A Oh it's getting very late, I should go now.

B **Let's have just one more round, okay?**

A I would, but I don't have enough money to cover it.

B Don't worry, it'll be my treat.

A 야, 이거 시간이 너무 늦어 지금 가야겠는데요.

B 한 잔만 더 하시죠?

A 그러고 싶지만 감당할 돈이 충분히 없는데요.

B 걱정하지 마세요. 제가 냅니다.

주점 8 Do you stock alcohol?

술 있어요?

A **Do you stock alcohol?**

B Sure, but we don't sell hard alcohol.

A So, you have beer and wine? Is that it?

B And wine coolers, too. Those are like wine flavored soft drinks. But they have some alcohol in them.

A 술 있어요?

B 물론이죠. 하지만 도수 높은 술은 팔지 않습니다.

A 그럼 맥주와 와인이 있겠네요? 그렇죠?

B 와인쿨러도 있습니다. 와인 맛이 나는 음료수인데 알코올도 좀 들어 있어요.

주점 9 a bartender sometimes offers drinks to people on the house.

바텐더가 가끔은 사람들에게 술을 무료로 줍니다.

A I don't see why we are out in this noisy place with all this smoke. We could be home relaxing together!

B I heard that this bar is fabulous. You know **a cool bartender sometimes offers drinks to people on the house.**

A Really? But I guess we'd better not have any more drinks. I feel a bit tipsy.

A 왜 우리가 이렇게 담배 연기가 가득하고 시끄러운 곳에 왔는지 모르겠어. 집에서 함께 쉴 수 있었는데도 말이야.

B 이 술집이 굉장하다고 들었어. 바텐더가 사람들에게 가끔 공짜로 술을 준대.

A 정말? 하지만 더 이상 술을 안 마시는 것이 좋겠어. 나 좀 취했거든.

주점

10 I drank so much I blacked out.

술을 너무 많이 마셔서 필름이 끊겼어요.

A I think you had too much to drink.
B Yeah. Last night was a little crazy.
A Do you remember what you did?
B No. **I drank so much I blacked out.**

A 너 너무 많이 마신 것 같던데.
B 응. 어젯밤에 장난 아니었어.
A 네가 무슨 짓을 했는지는 기억나니?
B 아니. 너무 많이 마셔서 필름이 끊겼거든.

주점

11 Why don't we go for another round?

우리 2차 갈까요?

A It's getting boring here. **Why don't we go for another round?**
B Good idea. I saw a fancy singing room nearby.
A Shouldn't we call to book a table first? The place might be full on a night like this.
B Good thinking! I'll call right now.

A 여기 지루해진다. 우리 2차 갈까?
B 좋은 생각이야. 나 이 근처서 근사한 노래방 봤었는데.
A 전화해서 미리 예약해야 하는 거 아니야? 오늘 밤 같은 날은 자리가 다 찼을지 몰라.
B 그래! 내가 지금 전화할게.

주점

12 Leave out the rum and just give me the coke.

럼주 빼고 콜라만 주세요.

A Would you like a complimentary beverage as we wait, sir?
B Sure. I'd love a rum and coke, please. Not too much ice.
A Only non-alcoholic beverages are free of charge. There is a fee for alcoholic drinks.
B In that case, **leave out the rum and just give me the coke.**

A 손님, 기다리시는 동안 서비스 음료 좀 드릴까요?
B 좋습니다. 콜라 넣은 럼주 한 잔 주세요. 얼음은 많이 주지 마시고요.
A 무알코올 음료만 무료이고, 알코올 음료는 돈을 내셔야 합니다.
B 그렇다면 럼주는 빼고 콜라만 주세요.

CHAPTER 07

파티

파티

1 decked out.

잘 차려입은

A You went to the gala with your friends, right? How was it?

B Fabulous! People were all **decked out** in gowns and tuxedos, and expensive food and champagne were everywhere. It was so fancy.

A Sounds like you guys had a great time. Please let me know if you ever have an extra ticket to an event like that!

A 친구들과 축하 행사에 갔죠, 그렇죠? 어땠어요?

B 멋졌어요! 사람들이 다 드레스와 턱시도를 잘 차려입었고, 비싼 음식과 샴페인이 도처에 있었죠. 아주 고급스러웠어요.

A 즐거운 시간을 보냈던 것 같네요! 그런 행사를 위한 여분의 표가 있으면 알려 줘요.

파티

2 Don't mind if I do.

그러죠, 그거 좋지.

A Hey, look who's here. Thanks for coming to the party. Do you want some beer?

B **Don't mind if I do.** Happy birthday, dude. Wow, what a big bunch of people!

A I just invited everyone on my Facebook friends list. Talk to you later.

A 이봐, 이게 누구야! 파티 와줘서 고마워. 맥주 마실래?

B 응, 그래. 생일 축하해! 와, 사람 정말 많구나!

A 페이스북에 '친구'로 등록된 사람들 모두 다 초대했어. 이따가 얘기하자.

파티

3 Let's hit the dance floor.

춤추러 나가자.

A **Let's hit the dance floor.**

B I don't know how to dance.

A That's okay. I'll show you how.

A 춤추러 나가자.

B 어떻게 춤추는지 모르는데.

A 괜찮아. 내가 어떻게 하는지 보여줄게.

파티 4 What if someone tries to talk with me?

누가 나한테 말 걸려고 하면 어쩌지?

A There are a million people here I don't remember.
What if someone tries to talk with me?

B That's why everyone is wearing these name-tags.

A Right. I can just read the nametag.

B Hey, do you recognize that guy? I think it's Tom, but he's put on a lot of weight.

A 이름이 기억 안 나는 사람들이 여기 너무 많아.
누가 나한테 말 걸려고 하면 어쩌지?

B 그래서 다들 이 이름표를 달고 있는 거야.

A 그렇구나. 이름표를 읽기만 하면 되겠네.

B 야, 저 남자 알아보겠어? 톰인 거 같은데 살이 많이 쪘네.

파티 5 Just bring yourself.

그냥 몸만 와.

Hi, this is Susan Brown who happened to meet you at Carl's promotion party last week. I jumped for joy when I heard that you went to the same high school as me. No wonder you looked familiar to me. Well, my husband and I are going to throw a party at our place this Saturday and I would love for you to come to our party. **Just bring yourself.** We will love to see you. E-mail me back if you're interested. Take it easy.

안녕, 나 지난 주 칼의 승진 파티에서 우연히 만났던 수잔 브라운이야. 나 네가 나랑 같은 고등학교 출신이란 걸 들었을 때 진짜 기뻤어. 어쩐지 네가 낯이 익더라. 그나저나 이번 주 토요일에 남편하고 나하고 우리 집에서 파티를 열 예정인데 너도 왔으면 좋겠어. 그냥 몸만 오면 돼. 우린 너 꼭 보고 싶어. 만약에 관심 있으면 이메일로 알려줘. 잘 있어.

파티 6 Look at the expression on his face.

쟤 얼굴 표정 좀 봐.

A I'm sure this is him.
This time it's not going to bo another false alarm.

B Turn out the lights. As soon as he turns them on, we'll yell "Surprise!"

A "Surprise!" I bet you didn't expect this, did you, Tom?

B Wow! **Look at the expression on his face.**
He looks like he's about to fall over.

A 이제 그 애가 확실해.
이번엔 틀림없을 거야.

B 불을 꺼. 주인공이 불을 켜면 바로 "서프라이즈!"라고 함께 소리치자.

A "서프라이즈!" 깜짝 파티는 생각도 못 했을 거야, 그렇지 톰?

B 와! 쟤 얼굴 표정 좀 봐.
놀라서 쓰러지려고 해.

파티

7 So far only fifteen have RSVP'd.

지금까지 15명만 연락이 왔어.

A How many people are you expecting to show up at the party?

B I invited twenty people, but **so far only fifteen have RSVP'd.**

A I'm sure more people will end up coming, and some people will bring dates.

B In that case, you should get a cake big enough for twenty-five people.

A 파티에 몇 명이 올 거라고 예상하니?

B 20명을 초대했는데 지금까지 15명만 연락이 왔어.

A 결국엔 사람이 더 많이 올 거야. 게다가 애인을 데려오는 사람도 있을 거고.

B 그럼 25명은 족히 먹을 수 있는 큰 케이크를 사야겠네.

파티

8 Everyone gets dressed up in costumes.

모두들 정장을 차려입다.

A There's a midnight showing of The Rocky Horror Picture Show. Want to go?

B Are you serious? That's the movie where **everyone** in the audience **gets dressed up in costumes.**

A Sure. It's lots of fun.

B Doesn't sound like fun to me.

A 심야 영화로 '록키 호러 픽쳐 쇼'를 하는데, 보러 갈래?

B 진심이니? 관객들 모두 정장을 하고 보는 영화야.

A 물론이야. 아주 재미있어.

B 나는 재미없을 것 같다.

파티

9 This is a rockin' party!

이 파티 끝내주는데!

A **This is a rockin' party!**

B I'm so glad you came.
You're my favorite person here.

A Thanks for all the beer.

A 이 파티 끝내주는데!

B 네가 와서 너무 좋다.
넌 여기서 내가 제일 좋아하는 사람이야.

A 맥주 고맙다, 야.

파티 10 You look really sharp in that suit!

너 그 정장 입으니 너무 잘 어울린다.

A **You look really sharp in that suit!**

B Thanks. You look like a million bucks as well.

A Well, thanks for saying that.

I was a bit worried this might be too loud.

B Not at all! It's just eye-catching enough.

A 너 그 정장 입으니까 너무 잘 어울린다!

B 고마워 너도 정말 멋진데.

A 그렇게 말해줘서 고마워.

나는 좀 야하지 않나 걱정했거든.

B 천만에! 근사하기만 한데 뭐.

파티 11 I'll light the candles.

내가 촛불을 켤게.

A **I'll light the candles** and put them on the cake.

B Then I'll turn off the electric lights, so that the cake will look very bright.

A 내가 촛불을 켜서 케이크에 꽂을게.

B 그러면 나는 전깃불을 끌게.

그래야 케이크가 빛나니까.

파티 12 Things got a little out of hand at the party.

파티가 약간 걷잡을 수 없이 돌아갔어.

I'm just wondering if you got home safely last night. **Things got a little out of hand at the party** and I guess I was a little too drunk to see you off after the third round. But what's the point of going to a year-end party without getting loaded, right? Anyway, I hope you had a great time and you're all ready for a brand new year.

네가 어젯밤에 집에 잘 갔는지 궁금하다. 파티가 약간 격해져서, 3차 이후 너무 취해서 널 배웅할 수 없었어. 그래도 송년회 때 좀 취하기도 하고 그러는 거 아니겠어? 어쨌든, 어제 좋은 시간이었기를 바라고, 새해 잘 맞길 바란다.

파티 13 What are you all dressed up for? 무슨 일로 정장을 다 차려입었어?

A **What are you all dressed up for?**
B I have a formal party to attedn tonight.
It's our company promotion party.
A You should try this necklace then.
It would go with your dress nicely.
B Wow, it does. Thanks a lot.

A 무슨 일로 다 차려 입었어?
B 오늘 밤에 정장차림 파티가 있거든.
우리 회사 홍보파티야.
A 그럼 이 목걸이 한번 해봐.
네 드레스랑 잘 어울릴거야.
B 진짜 그러네. 정말 고마워.

파티 14 He had a whale of a time at the party! 그는 파티에서 최고의 시간을 보냈지!

A Did John enjoy the reunion party on Saturday?
B **He had a whale of a time!**
He met all of his old friends and they talked for hours.
A I'm glad he enjoyed himself.
I know he was worried that it might be boring.

A 존이 토요일 동창회에서 좋은 시간 보냈대?
B 최고의 시간을 보냈지!
예전 친구들 모두 만나서 오랜 시간 얘기했어.
A 즐거웠다니 다행이다.
혹시 지루할까봐 걱정하던데.

파티 15 Let's put the lights on the tree first 우선 트리에 조명부터 달자.

A Help me with the decorations.
Let's put the lights on the tree first.
B Wow. How did the lights get tangled like this?
It looks like a giant ball of yarn.
A You start untangling the lights and I'll get the ornaments out of the box.
B Ask Mom for help.
She can get the strings of popcorn ready.

A 장식 좀 도와줘.
우선 트리에 조명부터 달자.
B 저런, 조명 줄이 어쩌다 이렇게 엉켰어?
큰 실 뭉치 같잖아.
A 넌 엉킨 줄부터 풀어. 난 장신구를 상자에서 꺼낼게.
B 엄마한테 도와달라고 하자.
팝콘을 실에다 쉽게 다실 수 있어.

파티

16 She must have crashed the party.

저 여자 파티초대도 안 받았는데 그냥 왔나봐.

A Thank you so much for coming to my party.
Are you having fun?

B Oh, yes. Big time! It's a great party. Oh, no. Look who just walked in, Mary Jane Smith. Did you invite her as well?

A Are you kidding me?
She must have crashed the party. What a gut!

B I know. Talking to her is like pulling teeth.
Anyway, I gotta go. Catch you latter.

A 파티에 와 줘서 너무 고마워.
파티 재미있어?

B 그럼, 너무 재미있어! 정말 대단한 파티인데. 이런, 저기 지금 방금 들어온 애 봐. 메리 제인 스미스다. 너 저 애도 초대했어?

A 장난하니?
저 애 초대도 안 했는데 그냥 왔나봐. 뻔뻔하기도 해라.

B 글쎄 말이야. 걔랑 얘기하는 건 곤욕이라니까.
어쨌거나 나 가야겠다. 다음에 보자.

CHAPTER

08

식당

식당

1 It's on the house.

무료로 드리는 거예요.

A Excuse me. I didn't order a drink. What's this orange juice?

B Oh, **it's on the house.** It's our way of thanking you for being a regular.

A Thanks a lot. By the way, this shaker's out of pepper. Could you refill it?

A 실례합니다. 저는 음료를 주문하지 않았는데요. 이 오렌지 주스는 뭔가요?

B 오, 무료로 드리는 거예요. 단골 손님에게 감사의 뜻으로요.

A 정말 고마워요. 그런데 이 통에 후추가 다 떨어졌네요. 다시 채워 주겠어요?

식당

2 Still or sparkling?

물로 드릴까요? 아니면 탄산수로 드릴까요?

A Ok, I'll have a pepperoni pizza and the seafood spaghetti. And can I have some water, please?

B Sure. **Still or sparkling?**

A Um... Sparkling, please. And where is your bathroom?

A 네, 페퍼로니 피자와 해산물 스파게티로 할게요. 그리고 물 좀 가져다주겠어요?

B 물론이죠. 물로 드릴까요? 아니면 탄산수로 드릴까요?

A 음… 탄산수로 주세요. 그리고 화장실은 어디에 있어요?

식당

3 There are so many no-shows.

예약해 놓고 오지 않는 손님들이 너무 많다.

A How's your new job at the restaurant? Getting the hang of it yet?

B Sort of. It's tough to stay on top of all the reservations. And **there are so many no-shows.**

A Really? I always assumed people had the common courtesy to call and cancel.

A 새로 시작한 식당 일은 어때요? 일은 다 파악했어요?

B 어느 정도는요. 예약 관련 업무가 힘들어요. 예약해 놓고 오지 않는 손님들도 너무 많고요.

A 정말이요? 사람들이 전화해서 취소하는 기본 예절 정도는 있다고 늘 생각했었는데요.

식당

4 a combo meal.

세트 메뉴

A Hi. Give me just one second to look at the menu.... OK, I'd like a number seven.

B Absolutely, sir. Just the sandwich?

C Oh, no-**a combo meal**, please. But for my drink, could I get bottled water instead of soda?

A 안녕하세요. 메뉴를 볼 시간을 잠시 주세요…. 좋아요, 7번으로 할게요.

B 그러시죠, 손님, 샌드위치만 드릴까요?

C 아, 아니요, 세트로 주세요. 저기 음료수 말인데요. 탄산음료 대신에 생수로 주시겠어요?

식당

5 How is everything?

뭐 더 필요한 게 있으신가요?

A **How is everything, sir?**

B My steak is a little undercooked. Could you take it back to the kitchen?

A I'm sorry. I'll have the cook put it back on the grille for a few more minute.

A 더 필요한 게 있으신가요?

B 제 스테이크가 약간 덜 익었어요. 더 익혀주시겠어요?

A 죄송합니다. 더 익혀달라고 하겠습니다.

식당

6 I'm about to burst.

배가 터질 것 같아요.

A Can I get you anything else? Would you like to see the dessert menu?

B No, thank you. **I'm about to burst.** I couldn't eat another bite. But, I'll have a cup of coffee, please.

A Certainly. I'll brew a fresh pot and bring you out a cup as soon as it's ready.

A 뭐 다른 걸 가져다 드릴까요? 디저트 메뉴 보시겠어요?

B 아, 됐어요. 배가 터질 것 같아요. 더는 한 입도 못 먹겠어요.

A 알겠습니다. 커피가 준비되는 대로 가져다 드릴게요.

식당 7 You are very fussy about what you eat. 입이 매우 까다롭군.

A You don't seem to be enjoying your meal.
B No, I'm not.
A I guess **you are very fussy about what you eat**, aren't you?
B Yes, I am.
A No wonder you are so skinny.
I have a great appetite. I eat like a pig.
B No wonder you are overweight.

A 입맛이 없나 보구나.
B 아냐.
A 너 입이 까다롭지, 그렇지 않니?
B 그래.
A 그러니까 네가 그렇게 말랐지. 난 식욕이 왕성해서 아주 잘 먹지.
B 그러니까 살이 쪘지.

식당 8 Is anyone saving room for dessert? 디저트 먹을 사람?

A **Is anyone saving room for dessert?**
B No, I'm stuffed. I can't eat another bite.

A 디저트 먹을 사람?
B 아니, 난 배불러. 한입도 더 못 먹겠다고.

식당 9 Can I get some extra coleslaw? 콜슬로 좀 더 주실래요?

A Will that be all?
B **Can I get some extra coleslaw?**
A Yes, but it cost extra.

A 이제 다 주문하셨나요?
B 콜슬로를 좀 더 주실래요?
A 예, 그런데 돈을 더 내셔야 해요.

※ 콜슬로와 콘샐러드(corn salad)는 패스트푸드점에서 인기있는 사이드 메뉴.

식당 10 I think the bill is wrong. 계산서가 잘못 나왔어요.

A Waiter, **I think the bill is wrong.** We didn't order an appetizer platter.
B Oh, I'm terribly sorry. I'll fix that right away.

A 이봐요, 계산이 잘못 나왔어요. 우린 전채 요리는 주문하지 않았어요.
B 아, 정말 죄송합니다. 바로 고쳐드리겠습니다.

식당
11 I'll bring you a doggy bag.
포장해 드리겠습니다.

A Are you finished with your meal, ma'am?

B Yes, can I get the leftovers wrapped up?

A **I'll bring you a doggy bag, ma'am.**

A 식사 다 하셨습니까, 손님?
B 네. 남은 것 싸주실 수 있나요?
A 포장해 드리겠습니다, 손님.

식당
12 Can we get separate checks?
계산서는 따로 끊어주시겠어요?

A Will that be all for your orders?

B **Can we also get separate checks?**

A Sure.

A 주문하신 것은 이게 다죠?
B 계산서는 따로 끊어주시겠어요?
A 알겠습니다.

식당
13 You can dice the onions.
양파 좀 잘게 썰어.

A Can I help with dinner?

B Sure. **You can dice the onions.**

A 저녁 만드는 데 내가 뭐 도와줄까?
B 그래. 양파 좀 잘게 썰어.

식당
14 I had my fill. I'm stuffed.
많이 먹어서 배가 터질 지경입니다.

A We have plenty of chicken soup. Eat your fill.

B I will.

-Later-

A Would you like more chicken soup?

B No, thank you. **I had my fill. I'm stuffed.**

A 치킨수프가 많이 있으니까 실컷 먹어.
B 그렇게 할게.
–얼마 뒤–
A 치킨수프 더 먹을래?
B 아니. 잔뜩 먹어서 배가 터질 지경이야.

식당

15 What do you feel like eating?

뭐 먹고 싶어요?

A Well, Jess. Shall we continue talking over dinner? **What do you feel like eating?**

B Well, I know a great Italian restaurant just around the corner. Are you okay with Italian?

A A place nearby sounds great since I'm starving now, not to mention the fact that Italian food is one of my favorites.

A 근데요 제스, 우리 저녁 먹으면서 얘기하는 것이 어떨까요? 뭐 먹고 싶어요?

B 음, 제가 여기 바로 옆에 좋은 이탈리아 식당을 알거든요? 이탈리아 음식 괜찮아요?

A 바로 옆이라니 너무 좋은데요. 이탈리아 음식은 제가 좋아하는 음식 중에 하나이기도 하지만 제가 지금 배가 엄청 고프거든요.

식당

16 It's maybe just a bit beyond my means.

이거 내가 사기엔 좀 비싼 것 같아.

A This is a perfect Christmas present for my mom.

B Are you sure you can afford it? It looks quite pricey.

A **It's maybe just a bit beyond my means** but this will make her so happy.

B If you say so, but don't be surprised if she returns it just like late year.

A 이거 우리 엄마 크리스마스 선물로 딱인데.

B 살 수 있겠어? 많이 비싸 보이는데.

A 내가 사기엔 좀 비싸긴 하지만 엄마가 받으시면 많이 좋아하실 것 같아.

B 네가 그렇게 말한다면야, 근데 작년처럼 선물 물리셔도 놀라지 마라.

식당

17 I love drumsticks.

닭다리를 아주 좋아해.

A Wait! How can I get a whole chicken into this little pan?

B We're just cooking boneless, skinless chicken breasts. I've already cut them into strips.

A **I love drumsticks....** Hey why no skin?

B Drumsticks are dark meat, but for this dish we only use white meat.

A 잠깐만! 이 작은 프라이팬에 치킨을 통째로 어떻게 올리지?

B 뼈를 바르고 껍질을 벗긴 닭가슴살만 요리할 거야. 이미 조각으로 잘라 놓았어.

A 난 닭다리를 아주 좋아하는데…. 왜 껍질은 안 되는 거니?

B 닭다리는 색이 검잖아. 이 요리에는 흰 살코기만 사용돼.

식당

18 How hot is the kung pao chicken?

쿵파오 치킨 맵니?

A **How hot is the kung pao chicken?**

B Not too spicy.

A 쿵파오 치킨이 맵니?

B 그리 맵지 않아.

식당

19 Your eyes may be bigger than your stomach.

너 식탐이 많은 것 같다.

A What's good here, Jess?

B Well, last time I came here I tried the pasta and pizza. They tasted as good as I expected.

A It won't hurt to follow what the expert is saying.
Why don't we get 2 pizzas and 2 pastas?
Oh, and a salad.

B Joshua, **Your eyes may be bigger than your stomach.**
You might need a doggy bag.

A 여기 뭐 잘해요 제스?

B 글쎄요, 전에 여기 왔을 때 파스타하고 피자를 먹어봤는데요, 예상한 대로 맛있었어요.

A 전문가 말씀을 들어야겠죠.
우리 피자 2개 파스타 2개 시킬까요?
아, 샐러드도요.

B 조슈아, 너무 많이 시키는 것 같아요.
나중에 남은 음식 싸달라고 해야 될지도 모르겠어요.

식당

20 We'd like another bowl of rice, please.

한 그릇 더 주세요.

A Have you eaten all of the rice?

B Yes, and **we'd like another bowl of rice, please.**

A 밥 다 드셨어요?

B 네, 한 그릇 더 주세요.

식당

21 I usually go with spaghetti.

난 보통 스파게티를 주문해.

A **I usually go with spaghetti.**

B I know, but maybe you should try something else.

A 난 보통 스파게티를 주문해.

B 아는데, 이번엔 다른 거 먹어봐.

식당

22 Under what name, please?

어떤 분 성함으로 할까요?

A Chez Michel. Good afternoon.

B Hello. I would like to make a reservation for tomorrow-lunch for six people. Do you have any quiet rooms? It's a business lunch.

A Yes, of course. We can reserve one of our private rooms for your group. **Under what name, please?**

B Jack Frost, for six.

A Very good. We'll see you then. Goodbye, Mr. Frost.

B Goodbye.

A 체즈 마이클입니다. 안녕하세요.

B 안녕하세요. 여섯 사람용 점심 예약을 하려고 합니다. 조용한 방 가능할까요?
비즈니스차 식사하는 겁니다.

A 물론이죠. 개인실을 예약해 드리겠습니다. 어떤 분 성함으로 할까요?

B 잭 프로스트로 여섯 명요.

A 좋아요. 그때 뵙겠습니다. 안녕히 계세요. 프로스트씨.

B 안녕히 계세요.

식당

23 Put it on my account, please.

외상으로 달아놓으세요.

A What do I owe you?

B $723.

A **Put it on my account, please.**

B Sorry, I can't.

A OK. Is financing available?

B Yes, it is.

A 얼마를 내야 하죠?

B 723달러요.

A 외상으로 달아주세요.

B 미안하지만 안 되겠는데요.

A 좋아요. 월부로 가능합니까?

B 네, 가능합니다.

식당

24 Can I take your order?

주문하시겠습니까?

A **Can I take your order?**

B I'd like the cheeseburger combo, with a salad instead of French fries, please.

A Do you want everything on your burger?

B Hold the onions, please.

A 주문하시겠습니까?

B 치즈버거 콤보 주시고요. 감자튀김 대신 샐러드로 주세요.

A 버거에 토핑 다 넣어드릴까요?

B 양파만 빼주세요.

CHAPTER

09

학교

학교

1 I need to drop a class.

수업을 취소해야 돼.

A This line hasn't moved in hours.

B I just hope I can get to the front before the end of the day. The Records Office closes at six.

A I'm here to pay tor my classes. What about you?

B **I need to drop a class.**

It conflicted with another one.

A 몇 시간째 줄이 움직이질 않네.

B 일과 끝나기 전에 앞에까지 갈 수 있어야 할 텐데.
학적과는 6시에 문을 닫거든.

A 나는 등록금 내러 여기 왔는데, 너는 왜 왔니?

B 수강 신청 하나를 취소해야 돼서, 다른 수업과 겹치거든.

학교

2 It's an honors level class.

그건 우등생들이 듣는 수업이야.

A Have you heard of Professor Wilson's Asian History class?

B **It's an honors level class.**

Only the top history students can get in.

A I asked Dr. Wilson and he said I could audit the class if I wanted to.

B Wow. You won't get any credit, but you'll learn a lot.

A 윌슨 교수님의 아시아 역사 수업에 대해 들어본 적 있니?

B 우등생들이 듣는 수업이잖아.
최고의 역사학도들만 들어 갈 수 있어.

A 윌슨 교수님께 여쭤봤는데 내가 원하면 청강할 수 있다고 하셨어.

B 우와. 학점은 못 따도 배울 게 많이 있을 거야.

학교

3 I brown-bagged it today.

나 오늘 도시락 싸왔어.

A Hey, do you want to go get some lunch?

I want to try the new restaurant next door.

B Sorry, **I brown-bagged it today.** Maybe we can do it tomorrow.

A Sounds good to me.

A 점심이나 먹으러 갈래?
옆에 새로 생긴 레스토랑에 가보고 싶은데.

B 미안, 난 오늘 도시락 싸왔어.
내일 가자.

A 그래, 좋아.

학교

4 He flunked out at the end of last semester!

지난 학기 말에 학교에서 제적당했어!

A I haven't seen Will around campus lately. Is he still enrolled here?

B Didn't you hear? **He flunked out at the end of last semester!**

A I guess he spent too much time partying, and not enough time studying.

A 학교에서 윌을 못 본 지 오래됐네. 걔 아직 여기 다녀?

B 못 들었어? 지난 학기 말에 학교에서 제적당했어.

A 공부는 얼마 안 하고 너무 파티만 했나 보구나.

학교

5 I pulled an all-nighter studying for the test!

시험 공부하느라 밤 샜어.

A Wow-you look terrible this morning! Are you okay?

B I'm exhausted. **I pulled an all-nighter studying for the test!**

A I hope you have enough energy to stay awake.

A 야, 너 오늘 아침 진짜 안 좋아 보인다. 괜찮은 거야?

B 피곤해 죽겠어. 시험 공부하느라 밤을 샜어.

A 시험 보는 동안 깨어있을 체력이 남아 있길 바라.

학교

6 Have you thought about joining a sorority?

여성 동아리에 가입하는 거 생각해봤어?

A I feel like all I do is study. I have no social life.

B **Have you thought about joining a sorority?** it's like a campus club only for girls.

A But I've heard it's hard to get in

B Well.... they don't let just anyone in, but once you're in, it's for life.

A 내가 하는 건 공부뿐인 것 같아. 사회생활이 없어.

B 여성 동아리에 가입하는 거 생각해봤어? 여학생들만을 위한 교내 클럽 같은 거야.

A 그런데 거기 들어가기가 힘들다고 들었어.

B 글쎄…. 아무나 들어가진 못하겠지만 일단 들어가면 평생회원이 되지.

학교 7 I'm on the verge of flunking out of school.

퇴학당하게 생겼어.

A **I'm on the verge of flunking out of school.**

B How did you let it get to this point?

A I don't know. Once my grades started slipping, I just stopped caring.

B Well, you need to resolve to do better. Or, you'll be a dropout.

A 퇴학당하게 생겼어.

B 어쩌다 이 지경이 됐니?

A 모르겠어. 점수가 한 번 내려가기 시작하니까 신경도 안 썼어.

B 그럼 성적 올릴 결심을 해야지. 안 그러면 낙제할 거야.

학교 8 All my hard work finally paid off.

열심히 공부한 성과가 드디어 나왔어.

A **All my hard work finally paid off.** Check out my latest grades!

B Wow. You've really jumped to the head of the class. Congratulations.

A Thanks. Now I can finally take a break and relax a little bit. I've earned it.

B Not too much, though. You don't want to slide back into your old bad habits.

A 열심히 공부한 성과가 드디어 나왔어.
이번 점수를 봐!

B 우와. 정말 반의 상위권으로 올랐구나.
축하해.

A 고마워. 이제 드디어 좀 쉬면서 편히 지낼 수 있겠다. 그만큼 했으니까.

B 그래도 너무 많이 쉬지는 마. 자칫하면 이전의 나쁜 습관으로 다시 빠질 거야.

학교 9 I'm living off campus this year.

올해는 캠퍼스 밖에서 지낼 거야.

A **I'm living off campus this year.** I couldn't deal with all the noise at the dorms anymore.

B But how can you afford it on top of tuition?

A I can't I had to apply for a student loan.
I really hope I qualify

B I'm sure you'll get the money.

A 올해는 캠퍼스 밖에 집을 얻어서 지내려고. 기숙사의 소음을 더 이상 참아낼 수가 없어.

B 그런데 수업료에 집세까지 어떻게 감당하려고?

A 감당할 수 없어서 학자금 대출을 신청했어. 대출 자격이 되면 정말 좋을 텐데.

B 돈을 꼭 대출 받을 수 있을 거야.

학교

10 I'm bound to be late.

나 분명히 지각할거야.

A How often do the buses run?

B It depends on traffic but normally every 10 minutes or so.

A Well, **I'm bound to be late** if the bus doesn't come soon.

B Don't worry. In case the bus comes late, you can always get a cab as an alternative.

A 버스가 얼마나 자주 와?

B 교통상황에 따라 다르지만 보통 한 10분에 한 대 와.

A 음, 버스가 금방 오지 않으면 나 분명히 지각할 거야.

B 걱정하지 마, 버스가 만약 늦게 오면 대신 항상 택시를 탈 수 있잖아.

학교

11 I need to earn two foreign-language credits to meet my degree requirements.

학위 요건을 충족하려면 외국어 과정 2학점을 추가 이수해야 해.

A **I need to earn two foreign-language credits to meet my degree requirements.**

B Ouch! That doesn't sound like fun at all!

A 학위 요건을 충족하려면 외국어 과정 2학점을 추가 이수해야 해.

B 이런! 진짜 재미없겠다!

CHAPTER

10

비즈니스

비즈니스 **1**

It's not carved in stone.

확정된 것은 아니에요.

A Good to see you again, Ms. Kim. I have the price estimate for having your car repainted. Please take a look.

B Okay. Well, it's more than I expected. It's actually over my budget.

A Really? Well, **it's not carved in stone.** What's your budget?

A 다시 봐서 반가워요, 김씨. 차를 다시 칠한 작업에 대한 가격 견적서가 있어요. 보세요.

B 네. 음, 예상했던 것보다 더 많네요. 실제로 제 예산을 넘어요.

A 정말요? 음, 확정된 것은 아니에요. 예산이 얼마나 되죠?

비즈니스 **2**

I ruled it out.

저는 그것을 배제했어요.

A So, have you decided on the type of car you want to buy?

B I think so. At first, I considered an SUV, but the price range was a bite higher than I expected. So, **I ruled it out.** And I don't think a sedan is right for my age. So, I just made up my mind to buy a compact car.

A Sounds reasonable. So, re you meeting the dealer soon?

A 그래서 어떤 차종으로 사고 싶은지 정했어요?

B 그런 것 같네요. 처음에는 SUV를 고려했는데, 가격대가 제가 예상했던 것보다 좀 높았어요. 그래서 저는 그것을 배제했어요. 그리고 세단형 자동차는 제 나이와 안 맞는 것 같고요. 그래서 그냥 소형차를 사기로 결정했어요.

A 타당한 생각이네요. 그럼 중개인과 곧 만날 건가요?.

비즈니스 **3**

These are really hard to come by.

이건 정말 구하기 어려워요.

A Hey, look at that rack. Isn't that a Yann Becker jacket?

B Let me check the tag. Wow, it is! **These are really hard to come by.** I actually tried to buy one when they first came out, but they sold out before I got to the store.

A Really? You should buy this one, then. Is it the right size?

A 저 선반에 있는 것 좀 봐. 저거 얀 베커 재킷 아니야?

B 꼬리표 좀 볼게. 와아, 맞아! 이거 구하기 정말 어려운 건데. 실은 내가 처음 출시되었을 때 사려고 했었거든. 그런데 내가 매장에 가기도 전에 품절이었어.

A 그래? 그럼 이거 사면 되겠네. 맞는 사이즈 아니야?

비즈니스

4 You can say that again.

당신 말이 맞아요.

A I really don't like the new book cover design.

B Well, the color scheme is a little too loud for a novel.

A Yeah. **You can say that again.** We'd better have the designer change it.

A 새 책 표지 디자인이 정말 마음에 안 드네.

B 음, 소설책치고는 색 배합이 너무 강렬하긴 해요.

A 그래. 자네 말이 맞아. 디자이너한테 바꾸라고 해야겠어.

비즈니스

5 The rest is history.

나머지는 다들 아시는 대로입니다.

A Thank you for agreeing to meet with me. It's such an honor to get to interview you. So, what made you decide to form VCS?

B Well, I wanted to prove that K-pop could attract a wide variety of listeners all over the world. So, I auditioned a lo of youngsters, found these five talented boys, and **the rest is history.**

A Oh, tell me how you prepared them to succeed in the global market.

A 시간 내주셔서 감사해요. 인터뷰하게 돼 큰 영광입니다. 어떻게 VCS를 결성하게 됐어요?

B 음, K팝이 전 세계의 다양한 팬들을 끌어들일 수 있다는 걸 증명하고 싶었어요. 그래서 많은 젊은이들의 오디션을 통해 재능있는 친구 다섯 명을 찾아냈죠. 그 이후는 알려진 대로 교요.

A 아, 어떻게 전 세계 시장에서 성공하게끔 준비시켰는지 말씀해주세요.

비즈니스

6 Here's my two cents.

내 의견은 이렇습니다.

A The sales of our new dishwasher have been really disappointing.

B Well, **here's my two cents**: we need to lower the price. It's just too expensive for our customers.

A Maybe, but Marketing did choose that price based on consumer research.

A 우리의 새 식기세척기의 판매가 정말 실망스럽네요.

B 음, 내 의견은 이래요. 우리가 가격을 인하해야 한다는 거죠. 고객들에게 너무 비싸요.

A 아마도요, 하지만 마케팅팀이 소비자 조사를 바탕으로 가격을 책정했는걸요.

비즈니스

7 Easier said than done.

말이야 쉽조.

A The itinerary for my London trip is terrible. The flight leaves at six A.M., and I have to give a presentation on the same day!

B Well, you will have to get up early, but it's a long flight. Can't you just sleep on the plane?

A **Easier said than done!** I'm flying economy class, and those seats are tiny.

A 런던 출장 일정이 형편 없어요. 비행기가 오전 6시에 출발하는데 같은 날 발표를 해야 하거든요!

B 음, 일찍 일어나야겠지만, 긴 비행이잖아요. 비행기에서 자면 되지 않아요?

A 말이야 쉽죠! 이코노미 클래스를 타고 가는데 좌석이 작잖아요.

비즈니스

8 I was a little freaked out.

나는 약간 당황했습니다.

A Jane, you handled that client lunch really well.

B Thank you. **I was a little freaked out** when they asked me to try those foods I'd never seen before, but I reminded myself that we had to Impress them.

A Well, you certainly did that. I'm sure they'll want us to handle their account now.

A 제인, 고객 점심 접대를 아주 잘 했네요.

B 감사합니다. 본 적도 없는 음식을 먹어 보라고 했을 때는 약간 당황했지만, 그들에게 깊은 인상을 남겨야 한다는 걸 생각했어요.

A 음, 당신이 확실히 깊은 인상을 남겼어요. 이제 분명 우리한테 그들의 거래 건을 맡기고 싶어할 거예요.

비즈니스

9 Do you really think you can beat that price?

가격을 더 낮출 수 있다고 생각하세요?

A What are you asking for this model?

B I'll give you my best price:$3t a unit?

A Oh, come on. You must be kidding.

B why? **Do you really think you can beat that price?**

A 이 모델은 얼마입니까?

B 내가 해줄 수 있는 최상의 가격은 개당 35달러입니다.

A 자 농담 마시고요.

B 왜요? 가격을 이것보다 더 낮출 수 있다고 생각하시나요?

비즈니스

10 He is still a bit green.

그는 아직 초짜야.

A I don't know how I am going to finish this project this week.

B Why don't you ask John? He's a sharp guy.

A True, but **he's still a bit green** when it comes to business.

A 이번 주까지 과연 이 프로젝트를 끝낼 수 있을지 모르겠어.

B 존에게 물어보지 그래? 똑똑한 사람이잖아.

A 그렇기는 한데 비즈니스는 아직 초짜야.

비즈니스

11 We need to have a catchy jingle for our new commercial.

새 광고에 주목을 끌만한 CM송이 필요해.

A **We need to have a catchy jingle for our new commercial.**

B It should be something upbeat, but not too silly of childish.

A I agree. We want it too be catchy, but not annoying.

A 새 광고에 주목을 끌만한 CM송이 필요해.

B 좀 신나면서도 유치하거나 우습지는 않은 것으로 말이야.

A 맞아. 주목을 끌되 너무 자극적이지는 않아야 해.

비즈니스

12 The stock market has been very bullish lately.

요즘 주식 시장이 아주 강세야.

A **The stock market has been very bullish lately.**

B I know. My portfolio value has risen 23% in the last six weeks!

A I wish I had some extra money to invest right now.

A 요즘 주식 시장이 아주 강세야.

B 그러게 말이야. 내 포트폴리오 가치는 지난 6주간 23%나 올랐어!

A 지금 투자할 여윳돈이 있으면 좋을텐데.

비즈니스

13 The stock market is going south.

증권 시장이 내림세에 있습니다.

A How did the dow do today?

B It fell almost 40 points to 3645.27.

A Really? I'm in trouble, big trouble.

B I told you not to buy in this bear market.

A I only bought the blue chip stocks.

A 오늘 증권 시세는 어때요?

B 거의 40포인트 내려 3645.27이 됐어요.

A 정말요? 난 큰일났네요. 정말 큰일이에요.

B 주가가 내림세에 있는 지금은 사지 말라고 말했잖아요.

A 난 우량주만 샀을 뿐인데요.

비즈니스

14 The stock market has been rather bearish lately.

요즘 주식 시장이 좀 약세야.

A **The stock market has been rather bearish lately.**

B I know. I'm losing my shirt because of some bad investments!

A I'm glad I didn't follow your investment advice last month!

A 요즘 주식 시장이 좀 약세야.

B 그러게 말이야. 잘못된 투자 몇 번에 알거지가 돼가고 있어.

A 지난달에 네 말 따라서 투자하지 않은 게 정말 다행이다.

비즈니스

15 I'd better pass this time.

다음 기회로 하시죠.

A Do you feel like dropping in somewhere for a few drinks?

B Well, maybe **I'd better pass this time**, it's getting a little late.

A I know a place nearby that's very casual and relaxing.

B Okay, you've talked me into it.

A 잠깐 들러 술 한 잔 하는 게 어때요?

B 글쎄요. 다음 기회로 미루는 게 낫겠어요. 늦었잖아요.

A 가볍고 편안하게 한 잔 할 수 있는 장소를 아는데요.

B 좋아요. 당신 말대로 하죠.

비즈니스

16 I'd like to transfer $5,000.

5,000달러를 이체하고 싶습니다.

A **I'd like to transfer $5,000** from my savings account into my checking account.

B No problem. Can I have your account numbers?

A Sure, my savings account number is 374-56-90182, and my checking is 901-23-04959.

A 5,000달러를 제 저축계좌에서 당좌예금계좌로 이체하고 싶은데요.

B 알겠습니다. 계좌번호를 주시겠습니까?

A 네. 제 저축계좌는 374-56-90182번이고 당좌예금 계좌는 901-23-04959번이에요.

비즈니스

17 How much is the monthly rent?

한 달 임대료는 얼마죠?

A **How much is the monthly rent?**

B $1,500 per month.

A Oh, that's a lot of money. Maybe we need to look for a house with a cheaper rent.

A 한 달 임대료는 얼마죠?

B 한 달에 1,500달러입니다.

A 상당히 비싸네요. 임대료가 더 싼 집을 찾아봐야 할 것 같습니다.

비즈니스

18 Let's put it in writing and sign it.

그것을 문서화해서 서명합시다.

A Now I think we've been able to come to an agreement.

B Yes, all the problems have been ironed out, as far as we can see.

A Right. So **let's put it in writing and sign it.**

A 이젠 계약을 해도 될 것 같습니다.

B 그렇군요. 저희가 보기에도 모든 문제점들이 조정된 것 같습니다.

A 맞습니다. 그렇다면 문서화해서 서명을 합시다.

비즈니스

19 What day suits you best?

어느 날이 가장 적당해?

A Hello? This is Joshua Thomson, a friend of Michael. Can I speak to Jess Covey?

B This is she. You must be calling me for the blind date Michael was talking about.

A That's right.
I'm wondering **what day suits you best?**

B Well, my schedule is flexible.

A 여보세요? 전 마이클 친구인 조슈아 톰슨인데요. 제스 코베이 씨 있습니까?

B 제가 제스 코베이인데요. 마이클이 말하던 소개팅 때문에 전화하셨군요.

A 맞아요.
약속 날짜로 언제가 가장 적당하신지 물어보려고요.

B 글쎄요, 제 스케줄은 조정이 가능하니까 좋으실 대로 하세요.

비즈니스

20 Can we put off our plans until next week?

우리 약속 다음 주로 미루면 안 될까?

A Hello, This is Jess. Is Joshua there?

B Hi, Jess. How nice to hear your voice on the phone. What's up?

A I'm terribly sorry, but **can we put off our plans until next week?** Something came up unexpectedly at work.

B Not a problem. Let me know when you settle things.

A 여보세요. 전 제스인데요, 조슈아 있나요?

B 안녕하세요, 제스. 전화로 목소리 들으니 너무 반가워요. 무슨 일이에요?

A 정말 미안한데요, 우리 약속 다음 주로 미루면 안 될까요? 갑자기 회사에서 일이 생겨서요.

B 문제 없어요. 정리 되면 저한테 알려 주세요.

비즈니스

21 What is on your agenda tomorrow?

내일 스케줄이 어떻게 돼요?

A Hello. Joshua. This is Jess.
I'm calling to ask **what is on your agenda tomorrow?**

B Nothing special. Shall we meet up?

A Sure. I'm sorry about all the hassles I caused the other day.

B No worries.
Just don't go back on your word this time.

A 여보세요, 저 제스에요.
내일 스케줄이 어떤지 궁금해서 전화했어요.

B 특별한 일은 없는데요. 우리 내일 만날까요?

A 좋죠. 전에 약속 깨고 번거롭게 해 드려 죄송해요.

B 걱정마세요.
이번에 약속 깨지 않으시면 돼요.

비즈니스

22 I want my money working for me.

돈을 잘 굴리고 싶어요.

A I'd like to earn as much interest as possible. **I want my money working for me.**

B In that case, you need a term deposit.

A But once the money is in one of those, I can't touch it, right?

B Yes. But if you lock it up for six months or more, you earn a really good rate

A 가능한 한 많은 이자를 받고 싶어요. 돈을 잘 굴리고 싶네요.

B 그런 경우라면 정기예금이 필요하겠군요.

A 하지만 일단 돈을 거기에 넣으면 뺄 수 없는 거죠?

B 네. 그렇지만 6개월 이상 묶어두시면 이자가 아주 높아질 거에요.

비즈니스

23 You should use a big down payment.

계약금을 많이 내셔야 합니다.

A To lower your monthly payments, **you should use a big down payment.**

B I heard that I only need five percent of the value of the house.

A True.... but we don't recommend doing it that way.

B I don't want to put everything into the down payment. I still need money for taxes.

A 월부금을 줄이기 위해서는 계약금을 많이 내셔야 합니다.

B 듣기로는 집값의 5퍼센트만 내면 된다고 하던데요.

A 맞습니다…. 하지만 그 방법은 추천해드리지 않습니다.

B 돈을 전부 계약금에 쏟고 싶지는 않아요. 세금 낼 돈도 필요하거든요.

비즈니스

24 I'm sorry I have to decline your order.

죄송하지만 주문을 받을 수가 없습니다.

A I'd like to place an order for 30,000 units of model No. K-1 right away.

B **I'm sorry I have to decline your order** because our factory is already fully occupied with other orders at the moment.

A How long a wait will it be till you can process my order?

B I believe we could start on it later this week.

A K-1 모델 3만 개를 지금 즉시 주문하고 싶은데요.

B 주문을 받을 수 없어 죄송하군요. 현재 저희 공장이 이미 다른 주문들로 꽉 차서요.

A 얼마나 기다리면 주문을 받을 수 있겠어요?

B 이번 주말부터는 시작할 수 있을 것 같습니다.

비즈니스

25 What are you terms?

거래 조건이 어떻게 됩니까?

A I'll order this item. But first, **what are your terms?**

B When you established the letter of credit, make it so that the delivery date is a minimum of two months and a maximum of three months from the date of opening.

A That's kind of long but, okay.

A 이 제품들을 주문하겠어요. 그런데 우선 거래 조건이 어떻게 됩니까?

B 신용장을 개설할 때 납기는 개설 일자로부터 최소 2개월에서 3개월로 해 주십시오.

A 좀 길긴 하지만 그렇게 하죠.

비즈니스

26 I gave you my word.

약속 드렸잖아요.

A We've got to have that shipment no later than October 30.

B Don't worry. **I gave you my word.**

A If it arrives later than that, we'll be too late for the Christmas season.

B You can count on me 100%

A 그 선적은 늦어도 10월 30일까지는 도착해야 합니다.

B 걱정하지 마세요. 약속을 드렸잖아요.

A 만약 물건이 그보다 늦게 도착한다면 크리스마스 시즌을 놓치게 됩니다.

B 저를 100% 믿으셔도 좋습니다.

비즈니스

27 It's got a one-year warrantly.

이것은 1년 품질 보증이 되어 있어요.

A Excuse me, sir could you help me? I am looking for a fax machine for my office

B Yes of course, please follow me. May I show you the deluxe model? At $799 it's a bargain

A It's very nice, but it's pretty expensive.

B Well, in that case, let me suggest this machine at $249. It has a speakerphone, copier, and speed dialer.

A I like that model. **It's got a one-year warranty.** Wrap it up. I'll take it.

A 실례하지만, 도와주시겠습니까? 제 사무실용 팩스를 찾고 있어요.

B 네 물론이죠, 이쪽으로 오세요. 고급 사양은 어떠세요? 799불이면 헐값이죠.

A 아주 좋은데, 너무 비싸군요.

B 글쎄, 그렇다면 249불짜리 팩스를 권해 드릴게요. 스피커폰, 복사기, 단축 다이얼 기능이 있어요.

A 그 모델로 할게요. 이건 1년 품질 보증도 되어 있네요. 포장해 주세요. 그걸로 살게요.

비즈니스 28 That's pushing it.

무리한 요구입니다.

A I'd like to place an order for this model. But a lot depends on timing. I mean, when can you make shipment?

B Well, if you place an order now, the shipment can be made in January.

A Too late. How about December?

B **That's pushing it**, but we'll try our best.

A 이 모델을 주문하고 싶지만 때를 맞춰 줄 수 있느냐에 달렸습니다. 내 말은, 언제 선적해 줄 수 있느냐는 거죠.

B 지금 주문하시면, 글쎄요, 1월에 선적이 될 수 있겠는데요.

A 너무 늦네요. 12월엔 안 될까요?

B 무리한 요구입니다만, 최선을 다해보죠.

비즈니스 29 What would you suggest?

어느 정도 해드리면 되겠습니까?

A Due to the delay, my customers wouldn't accept the goods at the contracted amount, but demanded a discount.

B Okay, we can offer you some savings too, then. **What would you suggest?**

A Two dollars on every unit.

B We can accept that on our end.

A 지연되는 바람에 저희 고객들이 계약 단가로는 물건을 인수하지 못 하겠다며 할인을 요구했습니다.

B 좋습니다. 할인을 해 드리지요. 어느 정도면 되겠습니까?

A 개당 2달러씩 할인해 주세요.

B 좋습니다.

비즈니스 30 How long should we make the contract for?

계약 기간은 얼마로 할까요?

A Okay, I think you can go ahead and make up the contract.

B Good. **How long should we make the contract for?**

A Ordinarily, we make our contracts for a period of one year, with an option to extend for an additional year upon a verbal agreement of both parties.

A 자, 계약서를 우선 작성하는 것이 좋겠습니다.

B 좋습니다. 계약 기간은 얼마로 할까요?

A 일반적으로 1년 계약을 합니다. 쌍방의 구두 합의에 따라 추가로 1년 연장하는 걸 옵션으로 해서요.

CHAPTER

11

교통

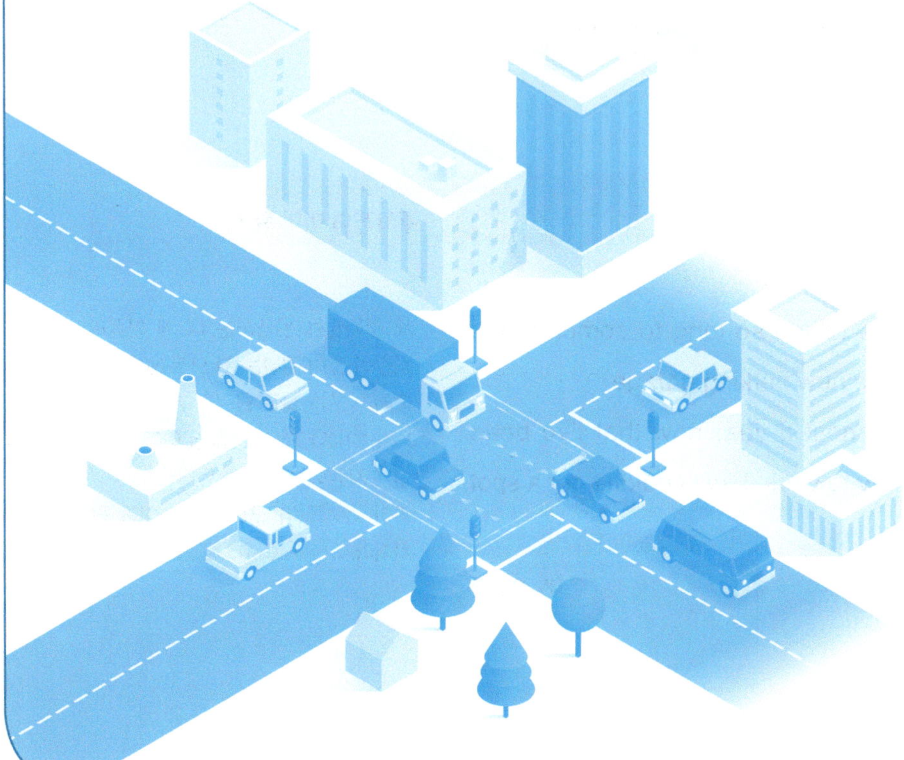

교통

1 speed bump.

과속방지턱

A How do you like the car's steering? It's very smooth, isn't it?

B Yeah, It's a pleasure to drive-much better than the other one. That's why it's good to take a test drive before making the final decision.

A Absolutely! Like I told you, this car is the better one for you. Oh! Watch out! **Speed bump** ahead!

A 자동차 핸들은 어떠세요? 아주 부드럽죠, 그렇죠?

B 네! 운전하는 게 참 즐겁네요, 다른 차보다 훨씬 나은 것 같아요. 그렇기 때문에 최종 결정하기 전에 시승해서 다행이에요.

A 물론이죠! 말씀드린 것처럼 고객님에게는 이 차가 더 좋을 겁니다. 오! 조심하세요! 앞에 과속방지턱요!

교통

2 pull into

주차하다.

A We're finally here at the hotel! Thanks for driving! Hey, what's wrong?

B I've got to use the restroom right now! Can you **pull into** the parking area for me?

A Sure, no problem. I'll meet you at the front desk, then.

A 드디어 호텔에 도착했네요! 운전하느라 수고했어요! 왜 그래요?

B 화장실에 바로 가야 해요! 나 대신에 주차장에 주차 좀 해줄래요?

A 물론이죠. 그러면 안내데스크에서 만나죠.

교통

3 The parking lot is already packed.

주차장이 이미 꽉 찼다.

A I wonder why it's taking so long to complete the construction of the new parking garage.

B Yes, it's been almost a year now that I've been taking the subway to work. I just couldn't get a spot in the office lot.

A Yeah, **the parking lot is already packed** by eight in the morning.

A 새 주차장을 완공하는 데 왜 이렇게 시간이 많이 걸리는 지 모르겠어.

B 그러게. 지하철로 출근한 지 지금 거의 1년이 다 돼 가는데 말이야. 사무실 주차장에는 자리가 없더라고.

A 맞아. 주차장이 오전 8시면 이미 꽉 차더라.

교통

4 You almost rear-ended it.

추돌할 뻔했어요.

A You're too close to the red car in front of you.

B But if I leave too much space, another car will try to get in front of me.

A Watch out! You almost hit that red car. **You almost rear-ended it.**

B It stopped so suddenly. I guess I should stay a bit back.

A 앞에 있는 빨간색 차와 너무 붙었어요.

B 그런데 차간 거리를 너무 많이 두면 다른 차가 앞에 끼어들려고 해요.

A 조심해요! 저 빨간색 차를 칠 뻔했어요. 추돌할 뻔했다고요.

B 저 차가 갑자기 멈췄어요. 좀 거리를 떼야겠군요.

교통

5 He pulled out in front of me without even signaling!

저 사람이 신호도 없이 내 앞으로 끼어들었어.

A Did you see what that guy just did? **He pulled out in front of me without even signaling!**

B That's really dangerous. I wish people would use their indicators when changing lanes.

A And they should shoulder-check, too.

A 저 사람 봤어? 신호도 없이 내 앞으로 끼어들었어!

B 정말 위험하네. 차선을 바꿀 때 사람들이 깜빡이를 켜야할 텐데.

A 그리고 고개를 돌려서 옆쪽도 잘 살펴야 해.

교통

6 Buying a car would cost me an arm and a leg.

차 사려면 너무 비싸.

A Talking three different busses to work is killing me.

B Why don't you buy a car then?

A **Buying a car would cost me an arm and a leg.**

B I'm sure if you shop around you can find a car that is within your means.

A 버스 두 번씩 갈아타고 출근하기 힘들어 죽겠어.

B 차를 한 대 사는 게 어때?

A 요즘에 차 사려면 기둥 뿌리 뽑히잖아.

B 돌아다녀 보면 네 예산에 맞는 차를 분명히 찾을 수 있을거야.

교통 7

It gets much steeper here.

여기 점점 가팔라지네.

A **It gets much steeper here.**
B This will tire us out.
A At least it will be downhill on the way home.

A 여기 점점 가팔라지네.
B 우린 완전히 기진맥진해질 거야.
A 그래도 집으로 가는 길은 내리막길이야.

교통 8

My car got rear-ended.

내 차가 뒤에서 받혔다고

A My car is in the shop again.
B When are you going to start driving more carefully?
A But this time it wasn't my fault! **My car got rear-ended.**

A 내 차가 또 정비소에 들어갔어.
B 넌 언제쯤 주의를 하며 운전할래?
A 이번엔 내 잘못이 아니야. 내 차가 뒤에서 받혔다고.

교통 9

They closed a lane of traffic up ahead.

앞에 길 하나를 막았어.

A We are moving at a snail's pace.
B **They closed a lane of traffic up ahead.**
A Everything always bottlenecks when drivers have to merge.

A 완전히 달팽이 속도로 움직이네.
B 앞에 길 하나를 막았어.
A 차가 합류되는 지점에는 늘 병목현상이 있게 마련이지.

교통 10

How long will the next bus be?

다음 버스가 올 때까지 얼마나 오래 기다려야 하나요?

A **How long will the next bus be?**
B About ten minutes.
A Really? How often do the buses run on this route?
B Every 20 minutes or so.
A That's not too bad.

A 다음 버스가 오려면 얼마나 걸릴 것 같습니까?
B 약 10분요.
A 그래요? 이 노선의 버스들은 얼마나 자주 다닙니까?
B 약 20분마다 다닙니다.
A 그렇게 나쁜 편은 아니군요.

교통

11 I locked myself out of the car.

나 차에다 열쇠 두고 잠갔어.

A I'm completely scatterbrained.
I locked myself out of the car again.

B Did you get your car key back?

A Fortunately, I know the number of a locksmith.

B If you are that absentminded, you should always carry a spare key in your wallet.

A 나 진짜 정신없다.
또 차에다 열쇠를 두고 잠갔어.

B 열쇠 다시 찾았어?

A 다행히 열쇠 수리공 전화번호를 알고 있어.

B 그렇게 정신이 없으면 열쇠 하나 더 만들어서 항상 지갑에 넣고 다녀야겠다.

교통

12 Pull over as soon as you can.

되도록 빨리 차를 한쪽으로 세워.

A I think that the officer in the police car wants you to pull over. He's flashing his lights.

B I guess he saw me make that illegal U-turn.

A Maybe it's about something else. But, **pull over as soon as you can.**

B Right. I don't want him to think I'm trying to start a high-speed car chase.

A 순찰차 안에 있는 경찰관이 차를 세우라는 것 같아.

B 내가 불법 유턴한 걸 본 거 같아.

A 다른 거 때문일지도 몰라. 그래도 되도록 빨리 차를 한쪽으로 세워.

B 그래. 우리가 과속 추월 경쟁을 하려 했다고 생각하지 않았음 좋겠다.

교통

13 Parking is going to be murder.

주차하기가 아주 힘들 거예요.

A **Parking is going to be murder.**

B I'm sure they have a giant lot; we'll be fine.

A Listen. We're going to get three early and take the best spot, right beside the exit.

B Right. It's a long walk to the gate, but then really easy to leave on the way home.

A 주차하기가 아주 힘들 거요.

B 주차장이 넓어서 괜찮을 거예요.

A 잠깐만요. 일찍 가서 출구 바로 옆 제일 좋은 자리에 차를 댑시다.

B 그래요. 입구까지는 한참 걸어야 하지만 귀가 길은 아주 쉽겠네요.

교통

14 We need short-term parking

단기주차로 해야겠다.

A We'll only be gone for a few days, so I guess **we need short-term parking.**

B Short-term is for less than a day. We need long-term.

A This is so complicated! Why didn't we just take a cab to the airport?

B Because taxis can be expensive. With the flat rate, parking is only about ten bucks a day.

A 며칠만 다녀올 거니까 단기주차로 해야 할 거 같아.

B 단기주차는 하루 미만을 말하는 거야. 우리는 장기주차를 해야 돼.

A 이거 너무 복잡하다! 공항까지 택시 탈 걸 그랬나?

B 택시는 비싸잖아. 균일요금이라서 주차비는 하루에 10달러 정도 밖에 안 해.

교통

15 The parts you can't see are called blind spots.

보이지 않는 곳을 사각지대라고 합니다.

A The rearview mirror is too small. I can't see everything behind me.

B **The parts you can't see are called blind spots.**

A Isn't it dangerous if I can't see all the cars behind me?

B Don't worry. You can see them in the side-view mirrors.

A 백미러가 너무 작아서 뒤에 안 보이는 게 많네요.

B 보이지 않는 곳을 사각지대라고 합니다. 모든 차에 다 있죠.

A 뒤에 오는 차를 다 볼 수 없으면 위험하지 않나요?

B 걱정 마세요. 사이드미러로도 뒤에 오는 차를 볼 수 있어요.

교통

16 That guy's facing some stiff fines.

저 남자 엄청난 벌금을 낼 거야.

A Did you see that guy? he jumped right over the turnstile without paying.

B A gate jumper. Don't sorry, though, the transit police will catch him.

A Well, it's not like it's a serious crime. The subway's not expensive.

B Sure, but nowadays the transit police are very strict. **That guy's facing some stiff fines.**

A 저 남자 봤어? 요금을 안 내고 개찰구 위로 뛰어넘어갔어.

B 불법 개찰자인데, 걱정 마. 교통경찰이 저 사람을 잡을 거야.

A 심각한 범죄는 아닌 거 같네. 지하철 요금이 비싼 것도 아니니까.

B 그렇긴 한데, 요즘 교통경찰은 아주 엄해. 저 남자는 엄청난 벌금을 낼 거야.

교통

17 It's got a lot of pickup.

이 차는 아주 빠릅니다.

A What makes this car so special?

B **It's got a lot of pickup.**

A I like fast cars.

A 이 차는 뭐가 특별한가요?

B 이 차는 가속이 아주 좋습니다.

A 저는 빠른 차를 좋아해요.

※ 차를 운전할 때 속도를 내는 것을 영어로 pickup이라고 합니다.

CHAPTER

12

미용실

미용실

1 I usually wear my hair up.

저는 보통 머리를 위로 묶고 다녀요.

A **I usually wear my hair up.**

B But you have beautiful hair. You should let it fall down your neck and back.

A 저는 보통 머리를 위로 묶고 다녀요.

B 하지만 손님 머리는 너무 아름다워요. 그냥 목이랑 등으로 흘러내리게 하세요.

미용실

2 Give me a buzz.

기계로 짧게 밀어주세요.

A Do you want me to keep your hair long?

B No, **give me a buzz.**

A 머리를 길게 놔둘까요?

B 아니요. 기계로 짧게 밀어주세요.

미용실

3 Do you think I'd look better with bangs?

앞머리를 가지런히 자르는 게 더 나은 것 같니?

A **Do you think I'd look better with bangs?**

B I generally don't like them. They look too square.

A Really? But I had bangs when we first met.... And you said you liked them.

B I lied. I was so happy when you grew them out.

A 앞머리를 가지런히 자르는 게 더 나은 것 같니?

B 난 대체적으로 앞머리 있는 걸 안 좋아해. 너무 고리타분해 보이잖아.

A 그래? 하지만 우리 처음 만났을 때 난 앞머리가 있었어…. 네가 좋다고 했고.

B 거짓말했어. 네 앞머리가 자라니까 정말 좋더라.

미용실

4 Please hold your head still.

머리를 움직이지 마세요.

A Wow! I have to turn around to look at this woman who just walked in.

B **Please hold your head still.**

A 와! 방금 들어온 여자를 보려면 고개를 돌려야 하는데.

B 머리를 움직이지 마세요.

미용실

5 You've got split ends.

머리카락 끝이 갈라졌네요.

A **You've got split ends.** I can fix that by trimming your hair all the way around your head.

B Thank you. You're a skilled and attentive hair stylist.

A 머리카락 끝이 갈라졌네요. 제가 전체적으로 다듬어 드릴게요.

B 감사합니다. 실력도 있고 정말 세심하시네요.

미용실

6 That haircut suits you.

그 헤어스타일 너한테 딱인데.

A I look very different with this haircut.

B But it seems to reflect your personality. **That haircut suits you.**

A 이 머리 스타일을 하니까 나같지 않은데.

B 근데 네 분위기에 잘 맞는 것 같아. 그 헤어스타일 너한테 딱인데.

미용실

7 I'd like a trim.

조금만 다듬어주세요.

A Do you want me to cut your hair in an entirely new style?

B No, **I'd like a trim.**

A 혹시 머리를 잘라서 헤어스타일을 확 바꾸고 싶으세요?

B 아니오, 그냥 다듬어 주세요.

미용실

8 I'd like a sensible haircut.

저는 보수적인 헤어스타일이 좋아요.

A I could shave one side of your head, if you want.

B No! **I'd like a sensible haircut.**

A 원하시면 제가 머리 한쪽을 밀어드릴 수 있는데요.

B 됐어요! 저는 보수적인 헤어스타일이 좋아요.

CHAPTER 13

전화

전화 1 I'm just calling to say hi. 그냥 안부 전화한 거야.

A Hi, Tommy.
B Hi, Steve. is anything the matter?
A No, not at all. **I'm just calling to say hi.**

A 안녕, 타미.
B 안녕, 스티브. 무슨 일 있니?
A 아니, 없어. 그냥 안부 전화한 거야.

전화 2 I'll have him get back to you. 바로 연락하라고 할게요.

A Hello, may I please speak to Bruce?
B Sorry, he's asleep, **I'll have him get back to you.**
A All right, thank you.

A 여보세요, 브루스 좀 바꿔주실래요?
B 미안하지만 자고 있거든요. 나중에 연락하라고 할게요.
A 알겠습니다, 고마워요.

전화 3 Can you hold, please? 잠시만 기다려주실래요?

A Hello, may I please speak to Mr. Williams?
B Yes. **Can you hold please?**
A Yes, I'll hold.

A 여보세요, 윌리엄스 씨 좀 바꿔주시겠어요?
B 예, 잠시만 기다려주실래요?
A 그러죠, 기다릴게요.

※ 전화를 끊지 말고 잠시만 기다려달라고 할 때 사용하는 표현으로, "Just a moment.", "Wait a minute!" 보다 더 많이 쓰인다.

전화 4 The reception is pretty poor. 수신이 잘 안 돼.

A I can't hear this station well.
There is a lot of static, which hurts my ears.
B Yes, **the reception is pretty poor.**
Let's listen to another station instead.

A 이 방송을 잘 들을 수가 없어.
잡음이 너무 많아서 귀가 아플 지경이야.
B 맞아, 수신이 잘 안돼.
차라리 다른 방송 듣자.

※ 요즘은 이런 경우가 거의 없지만 라디오의 수신 음질이 안 좋을 때 poor를 씁니다.

전화 5 The lines seem to be mixed up.

전화가 혼선이 된 것 같습니다.

A Is this Soongsil University?

B Yes, it is.

C No. You have the wrong number.

A **The lines seem to be mixed up.**

I'll hang up and call again.

B All right.

A 숭실대학교입니까?

B 네, 그렇습니다.

C 아니요. 잘못 거셨습니다.

A 혼선이 된 것 같군요.

끊었다 다시 걸죠.

B 그렇게 하세요.

전화 6 I'm sorry I'm calling at this late hour.

이렇게 늦게 전화를 걸어 죄송합니다.

A Hi, Kenny, how are you? This is Tom.

I'm sorry I'm calling at this late hour.

B It's Okay. What's the matter with you?

A Bad news.

I hope I'm not calling at a bad time.

B No, not at all.

A 안녕, 케니, 잘 지냈니? 나 탐이야.

늦은 시간에 전화 걸어 미안해.

B 괜찮아. 무슨 일이야?

A 나쁜 소식인데.

내가 좋지 않은 때에 전화를 하는 건지 모르겠다.

B 아니, 괜찮아.

전화 7 I'm calling from a pay phone.

공중전화로 전화하는 거야.

A Hi, Sandy. **I'm calling from a pay phone.** Could you give me the directions to your house again?

B Yes, turn left on Elm Street and then turn right on Oak Street.

A 안녕, 샌디. 공중전화로 전화하는 건데, 너희 집 가는 길 좀 다시 알려줄래?

B 그래, 엘름 가에서 좌회전한 다음에 오크 가에서 우회전하면 돼.

전화 8 Please hold.

끊지 말고 기다리세요.

A Thank you for calling e-bay. How may I help you?

B Yes. I just bought a scanner from your online shopping network, and I have a question about my bill.

A I'll connect you to the billing department, sir. **Please hold.** (Seconds later) I am sorry, sir. But all the lines are busy at the moment. Would you hold until the next representative becomes available?

A 이베이입니다. 전화 주셔서 감사합니다. 어떻게 도와드릴까요?

B 네. 얼마 전에 온라인 쇼핑 네트워크에서 스캐너를 구입했는데 청구서에 관해 질문이 있어서요.

A 대금 결제부로 연결해드리겠습니다. 끊지 말고 기다리십시오. (잠시 후) 죄송합니다만 지금 모든 선이 통화 중입니다. 다음 상담 직원을 기다리시겠습니까?

전화 9 Could you put me through?

전화 연결 부탁해요.

A Acme manufacturing, may I help you?

B Yes, please. this is Otto Kunstler from Swiss Trading Associates calling for Tom jones is in?

A Do you know which Department Mr. Jones is in?

B I think he's in Marketing. Could you look it up for me?

A No trouble. Hmm, it looks like he's in advertising

B Thank you. **Could you put me through, please?**

A 애크미 제조 회사입니다. 제가 도와드릴 일이 있을까요?

B 네, 저는 스위스 무역협회의 오토 쿤슬러인데 톰 존스씨와 통화하고 싶습니다.

A 톰 존스씨가 어느 부서에 계신지요?

B 마케팅 부서에 계신다고 알고 있어요. 확인해 주시겠습니까?

A 물론이죠. 음, 그 분은 홍보부에 계시네요.

B 감사합니다. 전화 연결 부탁드립니다.

전화 10 His extension is 1818.

그의 내선 번호는 1818입니다.

A How can I reach George Bush?

B **His extension is 1818.** In the future you can use that number to dial straight to his office.

A 조지 부시와 통화하려면 어떻게 해야 하나요?

B 그의 내선 번호는 1818입니다. 앞으로는 그 번호를 돌리면 바로 그분 사무실로 연결됩니다.

전화

11 No one by that name lives here.

여기 그런 사람 없는데요.

A Hi, is Michael there?

B **No one by that name lives here.**

What number were you calling?

A I was calling 351-5081.

I must have the wrong number.

A 안녕하세요. 마이클 있나요?

B 여기 그런 사람 없는데요. 몇 번으로 전화하셨죠?

A 351-5081로 했는데, 제가 전화를 잘못 걸었나 봐요.

CHAPTER

14

공항

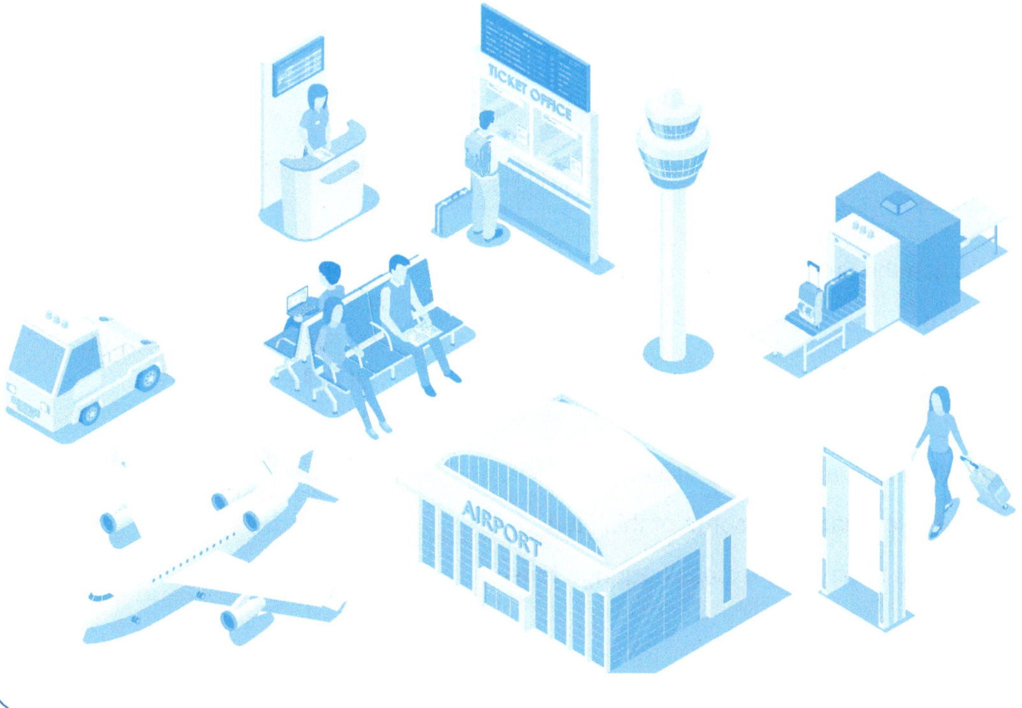

공항 1 Can you put me on the standby list?

대기자 명단에 올려줄 수 있나요?

A I'm sorry ma'am, there are no seats available on that flight.

B **Can you put me on the standby list?**

I need to get to Washington as soon as possible.

A Certainly, ma'am. Please check back at 6:30

A 죄송합니다만 그 비행기는 만석입니다.

B 대기자 명단에 올려줄 수 있나요? 워싱턴으로 가능한 한 빨리 가야 하거든요.

A 알겠습니다. 손님 6시 30분에 다시 확인해주세요.

공항 2 Is this a direct flight?

이 비행기는 직항인가요?

A **Is this a direct flight?**

B No, ma'am. There is a stopover in Honolulu.

A Do I need to catch a connecting flight?

B No, ma'am. You don't need to get off the plane.

A 이 비행기는 직항인가요?

B 아니요, 손님. 호놀룰루에서 한 번 경유합니다.

A 비행기를 갈아타야 하나요?

B 아니요. 갈아타실 필요는 없습니다.

공항 3 It's just under the limit.

중량 초과를 겨우 면했어요.

A Pleas place the first bag on the scale.

B Here we go!

It's the smallest one, so I'm sure it'll be fine.

A **It's just under the limit.**

I'll have to attack a "HEAVY" sticker to it.

B Uh oh. I better rearrange some of this stuff.

I dont's want to pay any excess baggage fees.

A 첫 번째 가방을 저울 위에 올리세요.

B 자 여기요!

가장 작은 거라서 분명 괜찮을 거예요.

A 중량 초과를 겨우 면했어요.

"과중" 스티커를 붙이겠습니다.

B 이런. 짐들을 다시 정리해야겠어요.

무게 초과비용을 내고 싶지는 않아요.

공항
4 The runways are a bit backed up.

활주로에 비행기들이 좀 밀려 있습니다.

A The captain has just informed us that there will be a slight delay.
B Excuse me, but why the delay? Is something wrong?
A Not at all. It's just that **the runways are a bit backed up**, because it's the busy season.
B Oh. Well, I hope it's our turn soon.

A 기장이 비행기 이륙이 약간 지연될 거라고 알려왔습니다.
B 실례지만, 왜 지연된 건가요? 뭐가 잘못됐나요?
A 아닙니다. 활주로에 이륙할 비행기들이 좀 밀려있을 뿐입니다. 성수기잖아요.
B 아, 그럼 우리 차례가 빨리 왔음 좋겠네요.

공항
5 How many bags will you be checking?

가방은 몇 개 부칠 건가요?

A **How many bags will you be checking**, sir?
B None. I only have this one carry-on suitcase.
A I'm sorry, sir.
That suitcase is too large for carry-on.
I'm afraid you'll have to check it.

A 가방을 몇 개 부칠 건가요?
B 없어요. 들고 탈 가방 하나만 있습니다.
A 손님, 죄송합니다만 그 가방은 가지고 타기엔 너무 큽니다. 부쳐야겠습니다.

공항
6 They are not allowed in.

그것들은 반입이 허용되지 않습니다.

A Oh, Mr. Kim, When I go to the US, is it possible to take some dried laver with me?
B Oh, sure. Any type of agricultural products that are dried are okay, but otherwise **they are not allowed in**, because they're afraid it may spread disease among farm crops in the US.

A 아, 김 선생님, 미국에 갈 때 마른 김을 좀 갖고 들어가도 될까요?
B 아, 물론이죠. 마른 농산물이면 무엇이든 괜찮지만 그렇지 않으면 반입이 허용되지 않습니다. 미국 내의 농작물에 질병을 전파시킬지도 모르기 때문이죠.

CHAPTER 15

우체국

우체국

1 I'm getting too many flyers in my mailbox.

우편함에 광고지가 너무 많이 와요.

A **I'm getting too many flyers in my mailbox.**

B There is nothing we can do about that here. We're not the ones delivering them.

A You're not? But then who is?

B Different companies. If you don't want flyers, put a "No Flyers" sticker on your mailbox.

A 우편함에 광고지가 너무 많이 와요.

B 저희는 어떻게 할 방법이 없습니다. 우체국에서 보내는 게 아니거든요.

A 여기서 보내는 게 아니라고요? 그럼 누가 보내나요?

B 다른 회사들이요. 광고지를 받지 않으려면 '광고지 사절' 스티커를 우편함에 붙이세요.

우체국

2 We have priority mail and overnight express mail.

특급 우편과 속달 우편이 있습니다.

A I would like to send this package to LA. What kind of service do you recommend?

B I recommend **priority mail or overnight express mail.**

A How long does each take?

B Overnight express arrives within 24 hours and priority takes about 2 to 4 days.

A 이 소포를 LA로 보내고 싶은데요. 어떤 서비스를 권해 주시겠어요?

B 특급 우편 또는 속달 우편을 권합니다.

A 각각 얼마나 시간이 걸려요?

B 속달 우편은 24시간 이내, 특급 우편은 2~4일 정도 걸립니다.

우체국

3 I'll have it rushed off to you.

서둘러 보내드리겠습니다.

A How soon will you send me the contract for the order of Cell-phones we talked about yesterday?

B I'll have our president sign it first, and sed it on to you by the 15th at the latest. So, after your boss signs off on it, please return one of the originals to me. We need it very urgently so we can order the raw materials.

A In that case, **I'll have it rushed off to you.**

A 오늘 상담했던 휴대전화 주문에 대한 계약서를 언제쯤 보내 주시겠습니까?

B 먼저 사장님의 서명을 받은 다음 늦어도 15일까지 보내 드리겠습니다. 그러니 귀사 사장님의 서명을 받은 뒤 원본 중 한 부를 제게 보내 주십시오. 원자재 주문용으로 매우 급하게 필요하니까요.

A 그러시다면, 서둘러 보내 드리겠습니다.

우체국

4 Can you have it sent by express mail?

속달 우편으로 보내주시겠어요?

A Did you bring a sample of model No. 65-K with you?

B Oh my god. It completely slipped my mind.
I'm sorry about that

A No problem. **Can you have it sent by express mail?**

B Sure thing. I'll get on the phone right away and have the company rush it off.

A 모델 65-K 의 견본을 갖고 오셨나요?
B 이럴 수가 있나. 깜빡 잊어버렸습니다. 죄송합니다.
A 그럴 수도 있죠. 속달로 보내주실 수 있죠?
B 물론입니다. 당장 회사에 전화를 걸어 빠리 보내도록 하겠습니다.

우체국

5 The mail is always slow around the holidays.

우편물 배송이 연휴 때는 항상 느려져.

A Have you made your list yet?

B List? Oh, you mean my Christmas list. Sure. I already gave it to Mom.

A Why would you give it to her?
I'm mailing mine directly to the Big Man at the North Pole.

B I hope it gets there in time.
The mail is always slow around the holidays.

A 목록 만들었니?
B 목록? 아, 크리스마스 선물 목록 말이지? 그럼, 벌써 엄마께 드렸지.
A 왜 엄마한테 드려?
난 북극에 있는 산타할아버지한테 직접 우편으로 보냈어.
B 늦지 않게 도착해야 할 텐데.
우편물 배송이 연휴 때는 항상 느려지잖아.

CHAPTER 16

축제·관람·체험

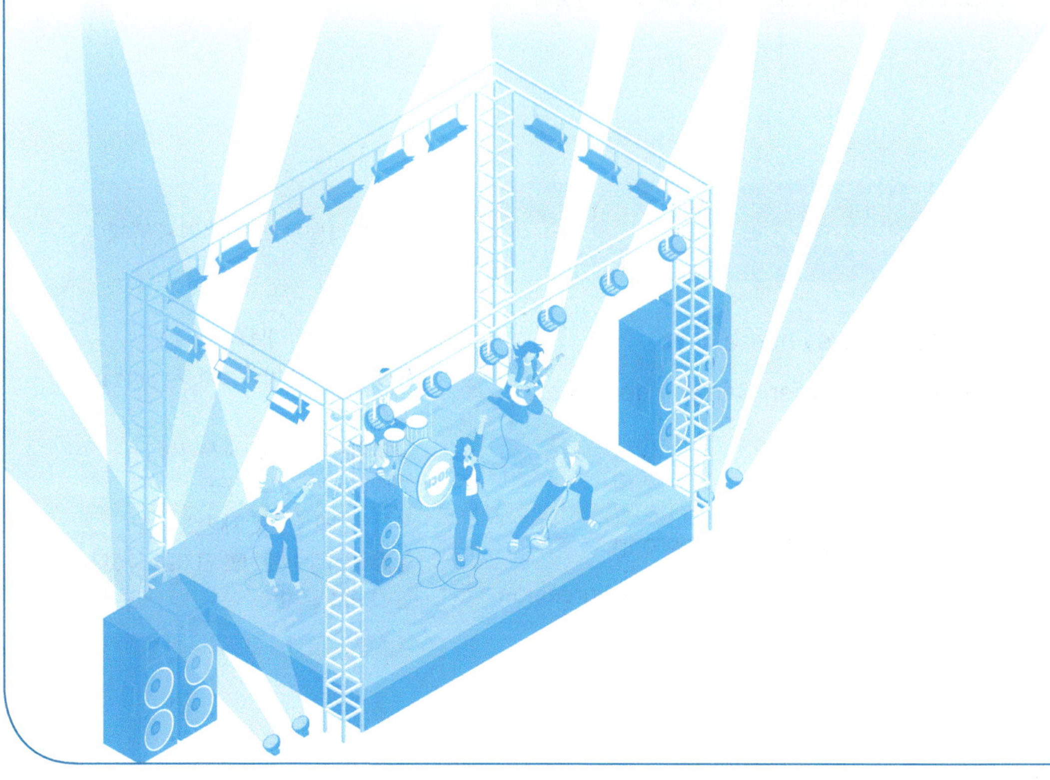

축제·관람·체험

1 Don't give up your day job.

본업에 충실하세요.

A So, what did you think of my performance?

B It was god for someone who's only been playing the piano for a few months, but **don't give up your day job.**

A I know I'm not Mozart. But I enjoy my piano class, so I think I'll stick with it anyway.

A 그래서 저의 공연은 어땠어요?

B 피아노를 친 지 몇 개월밖에 안 되는 사람치고 좋았어요. 하지만 본업에 충실하세요.

A 제가 모차르트가 아닌 건 알아요. 그래도 피아노 수업이 좋아서, 어쨌든 계속할 생각이에요.

축제·관람·체험

2 push past.

밀치다, 밀어젖히다.

A Hey, do you see that? I guess they started the fireworks!

B I can't see anything. Can you **push past** those people in front of you?

A You go ahead of me. You're way bigger than me!

A 저거 보여요? 불꽃놀이를 시작한 것 같아요!

B 아무것도 안 보이는데요. 앞에 있는 사람들 좀 밀어내 줄래요?

A 당신이 내 앞으로 가요. 당신이 나보다 훨씬 크잖아요!

축제·관람·체험

3 Those gorillas sure make a racket.

저 고릴라들은 화가 난 게 분명해.

A Let's go to the monkey house.

B It's just around the corner. Can you heart that? **Those gorillas sure make a racket.**

A I can hear one beating his chest.

B Maybe someone looked at them wrong. Making direct eye contact is a sigh of aggression.

A 원숭이 우리로 가보자.

B 모퉁이를 돌면 바로 있어. 저 소리 들려? 고릴라들이 화가 난 게 분명해.

A 가슴을 치는 소리가 들리네.

B 누가 고릴라를 잘못 쳐다봤나 봐. 눈을 똑바로 마주치면 공격을 하겠다는 뜻으로 알거든.

축제·관람·체험

4 I'm getting goosebumps.

소름, 닭살 돋다.

A This movie is so scary

B Hey, this isn't scary at all.

This movie is for little kids!

A No, it's not oh no! That monster is horrible!

I'm getting goosebumps!

B That "monster" is just a cute little elf!

What's the matter with you? You should try to relax.

It's not real. it's just a movie!

A but how can you be so sure?

Maybe this is a documentary and you don't even know it.

B No more of such nonsense!

How can this be a documentary?

A 이 영화 너무 무서워.

B 이봐 전혀 무섭지 않아.
이 영화는 어린이들이 보는 영화라고.

A 아니야. 그렇지 않아. 저 괴물 너무 무서워. 나 소름 돋은 거 봐.

B 저 "괴물"은 그저 귀여운 꼬마 요정일 뿐이야.
너 괜찮니? 진정해 저건 사실이 아니야 영화일 뿐이라고.

A 하지만 어떻게 확신해?
어쩌면 이건 다큐멘터리고 내가 그것을 모르고 있을지도.

B 이상한 소리 좀 그만 해!
이게 어떻게 다큐멘터리가 될 수 있니?

축제·관람·체험

5 I'm so pumped to see Death Purge live.

데스펄지의 라이브 공연을 보다니 정말 설렌다.

A It's the night of the big concert.

I'm so pumped to see Death Purge live.

B I heard they put on a really great show.

There're tons of dancers.

A I heard the bass player spits fire from his mouth.

B Awesome. Don't forget to bring your camera!

A 오늘 밤 멋진 공연이 펼쳐져.
데스펄지의 라이브 공연을 보다니 정말 설렌다.

B 굉장한 쇼가 펼쳐진대.
댄서들도 많이 나오고.

A 베이스 연주자가 입에서 불을 뿜는 쇼도 선보인다고 하더라.

B 멋지다. 카메라 가져오는 거 잊지마!

축제 · 관람 · 체험

6 Do you have a student discount?

학생할인 되나요?

A I would like a ticket for the Smithsonian, please.

B That will be $23, please.

A **Do you have a student discount rate?**

I'm an international student on vacation.

A 스미스소니언 입장권 하나 주세요.

B $23입니다.

A 학생할인 되나요? 여행 중인 국제학생인데요.

축제 · 관람 · 체험

7 I don't want to be in the nose bleed section.

제일 높이 있는 맨 뒷자리에 앉고 싶지 않아.

A So, which tickets should we get? Front row, center?

B Aren't those a bit expensive?

A We could get something a bit further back.

But I want to be close enough to really see the band.

B I know.

I don't want to be in the nose bleed section.

A 자, 어느 자리로 표를 살까? 앞쪽 줄, 가운데?

B 거기는 좀 비싸지 않을까?

A 좀 더 뒤쪽 자리를 사야 할 것 같아. 하지만 밴드가 보일 정도는 돼야 하는데.

B 그러게. 제일 뒤쪽 높이 있는 자리에 앉고 싶진 않아.

축제 · 관람 · 체험

8 It must be wall to wall people in there.

저기 안에 사람들로 발 디딜 틈이 없을 거야.

A Look at all the cars!

It must be wall to wall people in there.

B What did you expect?

There are a lot of big sales going on.

A Do you think we'll be able to find a place to park?

Do you see any empty spots?

B There's one over there. See it?

Grab it before someone else.

A 저 차들 좀 봐!
쇼핑몰에 사람들로 발 디딜 틈이 없을 거야.

B 당연한 거 아니야?
대대적인 세일들을 하고 있잖아.

A 주차할 곳을 찾을 수 있을까?
빈 공간 보이니?

B 저기 하나 있다. 보이지?
다른 사람 오기 전에 먼저 잡아.

축제·관람·체험

9 Did you get the right tickets?

티켓 제대로 끊었어요?

A **Did you get the right tickets?**

B I think so.... It's really complicated.

A Well, there are five of us, two adults and three kids. And we need ticktets that cover the entrance fees and unlimited redes.

B Let me double-check.

A 티켓 제대로 끊었어요?

B 그런 것 같아요…. 정말 복잡하더라고요.

A 성인 둘, 애들 셋, 모두 다섯 명이에요. 그리고 입장료와 자유이용권이 포함된 티켓이어야 해요.

B 다시 확인해볼게요.

축제·관람·체험

10 They might really like the merry-go-round.

아이들이 회전목마를 정말 좋아할 거 같아요.

A Let's take the kids on the Ferris wheel.

B Or, **they might really like the merry-go-round.**

A But they might not want to go on te kiddie rides.
Maybe they've outgrown them.

B We could try the bigger rides.
You'll have to take them on, though. I'm too afraid!

A 아이들을 페리스 관람차에 태웁시다.

B 아니면 회전목마도 정말 좋아할 거 같아요.

A 근데 애들이나 타는 건 안 타려고 할 거예요.
그런거 타기엔 이제 컸으니까요.

B 더 큰 놀이기구를 타도 되겠네요.
그럼 당신이 애들 데리고 타요. 난 너무 무서워요!

축제·관람·체험

11 There's a shuttle bus that runs all the time.

항시 운행하는 셔틀버스가 있어.

A How are we supposed to get all these bags all the way over there?

B Don't worry.
There's a shuttle bus that runs all the time.

A Great. Where does it pick us up?

B That's the best part. It just drives up and down the lot looking for people.

A 이 가방을 어떻게 다 저기까지 가져가지?

B 걱정 마.
셔틀버스가 수시로 다녀.

A 그거 좋은데. 어디서 타는 거야?

B 제일 좋은 게 그거야. 오고 가다가 사람을 보면 태워주지.

축제·관람·체험

12 Is this ride scary?

이 놀이기구 무서운가요?

A Are you all ready? Remember to keep your arms and legs inside the ride at all times.

B OK. Hey, **is this ride scary?**

A Well… there's a big drop and then the loop deloop.

B Sounds good. Can you just check the safety bar one more time?

A 준비 다 되셨나요?
팔다리는 항상 안쪽에 두셔야 합니다.

B 알겠어요. 이봐요. 이 놀이기구 무서운가요?

A 글쎄요… 크게 한 번 낙하한 다음 공중 회전을 하죠.

B 재미있겠네요. 안전바를 한 번 더 확인해주실래요?

축제·관람·체험

13 It'll make a great souvenir.

멋진 기념품이 될 거에요.

A Look over there by the drink stand.
Isn't that Charlie the Mouse?

B Sure. Look over there, kids.
It's your favorite character, Charlie.

A Look at all the kids kicking the poor guy.

B Let's go over and get our picture taken with him.
It'll make a great souvenir.

A 저쪽 음료수매점 옆에 좀 봐요.
저거 마우스 찰리 아니에요?

B 맞아요. 얘들아 저기 좀 봐라.
너희가 좋아하는 캐릭터 찰리야.

A 아이들 모두 불쌍한 찰리 아저씨를 발로 차고 있네요.

B 저기 가서 찰리와 사진 찍어요. 멋진 기념이 될 거에요.

축제·관람·체험

14 What are the hours of operation?

개관 시간이 어떻게 되죠?

A **What are the hours of operation?**

B The museum is open from 9AM to 6PM, Monday through Saturday.

A That's too bad.
I was hopping to see the exhibit on Sunday.

A 개관 시간이 어떻게 되죠?

B 박물관은 월요일부터 토요일까지 오전 9시에서 오후 6시 사이에 엽니다.

A 아쉽네요.
일요일에 전시회를 보려고 했는데.

15 Sound the alarm!

비상벨을 울려!

A Holy cow! That bird escaped from its cage.
Sound the alarm!

B The peacock? Don't worry.
It's allowed to roam free.

A Aren't the zookeepers worried that it'll run away?

B Why would it ever want to leave?
It's more than happy to hang out and steal food from the kids here.

A 저런! 저 새가 새장에서 나왔어.
비상벨을 울려!

B 공작새 말하는 거야? 걱정 마.
자유롭게 돌아다니도록 나둔 거야.

A 공작새가 도망갈까 봐 사육사들은 걱정이 안 되나?

B 왜 도망가고 싶겠어?
어슬렁거리며 여기 온 아이들 음식이나 뺏어먹는 게 더 좋을 텐데.

PART 3

기타

CHAPTER 17

회화에서 유용하게 쓰이는 단어

단어 1 turnover

이직률

A Can you believe the **turnover** at this company? Five co-workers have left just this month.

B It does seem strange. No one wants to hang around. Maybe they know something we don't.

A Could be. I'm going to start looking for another job next week, just to be safe.

A 우리 회사 이직률이 믿어져요? 이번 달에만 동료 직원이 다섯 명이나 그만뒀어요.

B 정말 이상한 것 같아요. 아무도 남아 있고 싶어 하지 않아요. 아마도 우리가 모르는 뭔가를 그들은 알고 있나 봐요.

A 그럴 수도 있어요. 혹시 모르니까 다음 주에 다른 회사를 알아보기 시작해야겠어요.

단어 2 hay fever

꽃가루 알레르기

A There's nothing I love more than a nice spring day. Just breathe in that air!

B My eyes are itchy, my nose has been running for days, and I can't stop sneezing.

A Oh, **hay fever**, right? guess allergies can really put a damper on spring.

A 난 이런 화창한 봄날이 무엇보다 좋아요. 공기 좀 마셔 봐요!

B 난 눈도 가렵고 콧물도 며칠째 줄줄 흐르고 재채기는 멈추질 않아요.

A 아, 꽃가루 알레르기군요. 꽃가루 알레르기는 정말 봄의 불청객이에요.

단어 3 pushover

만만한 사람

A Where are you headed? You said you were going to stay in today and get some rest.

B I was, but my girlfriend really wants to see me. She hates being alone and feeling bored.

A Oh, stop being a **pushover!** You have to say no to her sometimes.

A 어디에 가는 중이에요? 오늘은 집에서 쉴 거라고 했잖아요.

B 그랬는데 여자친구가 저를 매우 보고 싶어 해요. 그녀는 혼자 있는 것과 지루한 걸 싫어해요.

A 오, 만만한 사람이 되는 걸 그만둬요! 때때로 그녀에게 싫다고 해야 해요.

단어 4 road hog

난폭 운전자

A Look at that car in front of us. It's straddling two lanes. You should watch out.

B Yeah, I know. I hate **road hogs** who don't care about other drivers and people.

A Me too. They should learn how to drive. Hey, look at that! The police patrol car is pulling that car over.

A 우리 앞에 있는 차를 봐. 차선 2개를 걸치고 있어. 너는 조심해야 해.

B 알고 있어. 다른 운전자들과 사람들을 신경 안 쓰는 난폭 운전자들이 정말 싫어.

A 나도 그래. 저 사람들은 운전하는 방법을 배워야 해. 이봐, 저기를 봐! 순찰차가 저 차를 한쪽으로 대게하고 있어.

단어 5 backfire

역효과를 낳다

A Hey, how's the advertising campaign for the new product?

B Well, I'm thinking of making a TV commercial with a famous actress. If we find the right one, our product could be the product of the year.

A Hmm, using a celebrity spokesperson would get a lot of attention for the product, but it could **backfire** if she gets into a scandal. You'd better choose carefully.

A 저, 신제품을 위한 광고 활동은 어떻게 되고 있어요?

B 음, 유명한 여배우와 텔레비전 광고를 만들 생각인데요. 알맞은 사람을 찾으면 우리 상품이 올해의 상품이 될 거예요.

A 음, 유명인을 대표자로 쓰는 것은 상품에 많은 관심을 가져올 수 있지만 그 여배우가 스캔들이 나면 역효과가 날 거예요. 신중히 선택하는 게 좋아요.

단어 6 offhand

확인하지 않고 바로

A How many units of our new product did we sell last quarter?

B Oh, I don't know **offhand.** I'll check the data and let you know.

A Um, could you do it now? I think I'll need it in a moment.

A 지난 분기에 우리가 판매한 신제품이 몇 대인가요?

B 오, 확인하지 않고 바로 알 수 없어요. 자료를 확인하고 알려 줄게요.

A 음, 지금 할 수 있어요? 곧 필요할 것 같네요.

단어 7 blooper
우스꽝스러운 실수

A Did you see Mr. Scott's keynote speech yesterday? Everybody's talking about it. What's happened?

B Oh, that's right – you coulnd't attend the convention because of the meeting. Well, he was so nervous because of the big crowd that he kept making **bloopers**. He even mispronounced the name of our company!

A Oh my god! How can a perfectionist like him make that kind of mistake? He must be dying of embarrassment.

A 어제 스캇 씨의 기조 연설 봤어요? 다들 그 이야기만 하더라고요. 무슨 일 있었어요?

B 아, 맞아요, 어제 회의 때문에 컨벤션에 참석 못 했죠? 음, 관중들이 많아서 그런지 너무 긴장해서 어처구니없는 실수를 연발했지 뭐에요. 우리 회사 이름조차 잘못 말했다니까요!

A 맙소사! 그 사람같은 완벽주의자가 그런 실수를 저질렀다고요? 창피해서 죽을 심정이겠어요.

단어 8 epitome
전형

A You like to watch movies, don't you? Can you recommend something for me to watch this weekend?

B Classics are always the best choice! If you haven't already, why don't you see Francis Ford Coppola's *The Godfather?* It's the **epitome** of the gangster film. You won't regret it.

A I've never seen that one before. Sounds like it's worth checking out!

A 영화 보는 것 좋아하죠, 그렇죠? 제가 이번 주말에 볼 영화 한 편 추천해 줄 수 있어요?

B 명작들은 항상 옳은 선택이에요! 아직 못 봤다면, 프랜시스 포드 코폴라 감독의 〈대부〉를 보는 게 어때요? 갱스터 영화의 전형이죠. 후회하지 않을 겁니다.

A 그 영화는 본 적 없어요. 볼 가치가 있을 것 같네요!

단어 9 backseat driver

잔소리꾼

A You need to turn your blinker on now. How else will the other drivers know that you want to change lanes?

B Ugh, you're such a **backseat driver**. You know I like to wait until there's an actual opening in the other lane. Stop nagging me.

A Well, you don't exactly have a spotless driving record. I'm just trying to keep you from getting into another fender bender.

A 지금 방향 표시등을 켜야 해. 어떻게 다른 운전자들이 네가 차선을 변경하고 싶다는 것을 알겠니?

B 욱, 너 진짜 잔소리꾼이구나. 다른 차선 안에 실제 공간이 생길 때까지 내가 기다리고 싶어 하는 것을 알잖아. 잔소리 그만해.

A 음, 네가 티 없는 운전 기록을 가진 것은 아니잖아. 나는 그냥 네가 또 다른 접촉 사고를 내는 것을 막으려는 거야.

단어 10 knot

근육의 뻣뻣한 느낌

A Mr.Davis, I was told you're having leg pain. What seems to be the problem?

B I played soccer too much yesterday, so I have **knots** in my calves.

A I see. I'll prescribe you a pian reliever and a muscle relaxant. That should take care of it.

A 데이비스씨, 다리에 통증이 있으시다고 들었습니다. 어디가 불편하시죠?

B 어제 축구를 너무 심하게 했더니 종아리에 근육이 뭉친 것 같아요.

A 알겠습니다. 진통제와 근육이완제를 처방해 드리죠. 그럼 나아지실 겁니다.

단어 11 snug

딱 맞는

A Mom, can I get a new pair of jeans?

B What's the matter with you? I just bought you new jeans two weeks ago.

A Yes, but they've been a little **snug** since you washed them. I can't move my legs comfortably anymore.

A 엄마, 새 청바지 한 벌만 사 주실래요?

B 아니 왜? 보름 전에 새 걸 사줬잖니?

A 네, 그렇긴 한데 엄마가 한 번 세탁하신 후부터 좀 꽉 끼어서요. 이젠 다리를 편하게 움직일 수가 없어요.

단어 12 peachy — 훌륭한

A You look really happy these days.
B Oh, yeah. Everything in my life is totally **peachy**.
A Really? Well, I'm glad to hear that things are going well.
B Me, too. It's about time things in my life got better.

A 너 요즘 굉장히 기분 좋아 보인다.
B 아, 맞아. 요즘은 내 인생의 모든 일이 정말 잘 풀리는 것 같아.
A 그래? 음, 다 잘 되고 있다니 기쁘다.
B 나도 그래. 이젠 내 형편도 더 좋아질 때가 됐지 뭐.

단어 13 doormat — 당하고도 가만히 있는 사람

A What was up with those guys? It looked like they were yelling at you. I know you too well to believe that you did something to deserve that.
B You're right-I didn't. They just treat me like a **doormat** because they can, They're friends with the boss.
A That's terrible! You've got to talk to HR. Maybe they can step in.

A 저 사람들 왜 그런 거야? 너한테 막 소리치는 것 같던데. 넌 누구한테 면박당할 행동을 할 사람이 아니란 걸 내가 아는데 말이야.
B 맞아요. 그런 행동 안했어요. 제가 만만하니까 그냥 호구처럼 대하네요. 사장님이랑 친한가 봐요.
A 말도 안 돼! 인사과에 이야기해. 그쪽이 도와줄 수도 있잖아.

단어 14 wet blanket — 흥을 깨는 사람

A Ugh, the people at that table are so annoying, This bar sucks.
B Mike, you've done nothing but complain all evening. Stop being such a **wet blanket**. Remember that we're here to celebrate Alice's graduation, not hear about your problems.
A You're right. I guess I'm just not in the right mood for a party. Maybe I should just go home and let you guys have fun.

A 진짜, 저 테이블 사람들 짜증 나네. 여기 술집 별로네.
B 마이크, 너 저녁 내내 불평만 하고 있는 거 알고 있니? 제발 분위기 좀 망치지 마. 여기 온 건 앨리스 졸업 축하 때문이지, 너 불평 들어주려고 온 게 아니잖아.
A 그건 그래. 오늘 파티 할 기분이 아닌 것 같아. 그냥 나는 집에 가고, 너희들에게 폐 끼치지 않는 게 좋겠어.

단어

15 dawdle

꾸물거리다

A Could you drive a little slower? This road seems pretty narrow, and there's a steep drop-off on my side.

B Well, if we don't hurry, we're not going to make It to the hotel by check-in. I told you we shouldn't have **dawdled** at the beach for so long.

A Don't blame me! I wasn't the one who slept on the beach towel.

A 운전 좀 천천히 할래? 여기 도로도 좁은 듯한 데다가 내 쪽에 가파른 경사면도 있다고.

B 음, 서두르지 않으면, 호텔 체크인 시간에 못 맞춰 간단 말이야. 내가 해변에서 오랫동안 꾸물거리면 안된다고 했잖아.

A 나한테 뭐라 하지 말라고! 수건 깔아놓고 잔 사람이 누군데.

단어

16 tourist traps

관광객들에게 바가지를 씌우는 곳

A How was your trip to Bangkok, Latrice? I'm actually interested in going to Thailand.

B It was awesome! This was my fifth time, actually. I love the atmosphere of the city.

A Nice. Now can tell me where to go, avoiding **tourist traps.**

A 방콕 여행 어땠어요, 라트리스 씨? 나도 태국 여행에 관심이 있거든요.

B 너무 좋았어요! 사실 이번이 다섯 번째 여행이에요. 저는 도시의 분위기가 너무 좋아요.

A 좋네요. 그럼 바가지 씌우는 곳들 피하면서 갈 만한 곳들을 내게 말해줄 수 있겠네요.

단어

17 odd jobs

잡무, 임시적인 일

A Dave, was that you painting the Smiths' house last week? I thought I saw you as I drove by.

B Oh yeah, I do all sorts of **odd jobs** during the summer vacation. A lot of teachers do.

A That's a smart way to use your free time.

A 데이브, 지난주에 스미스씨 집을 도색한 게 당신이었어요? 운전하고 지나가다 본 것 같아서요.

B 아 맞아요, 전 여름방학 동안 모든 종류의 잡다한 일을 하거든요. 많은 교사가 그렇게 하죠.

A 여가를 보내는 영리한 방법이네요.

단어 18 hit-or-miss | 복불복

A Jared, have you read the latest Frederick Justice novel yet?

B No, I find that series to be **hit-or-miss**, so I was waiting to see whether other people liked it.

A Oh, you should definitely read this one. It's got a really great mystery.

A 재러드, 프레드릭 저스티스의 최신 소설 벌써 읽었나요?

B 아니요, 그 시리즈는 복불복이라서 다른 사람들이 좋아하는지 보기 위해 기다리고 있었죠.

A 아, 이번 것은 반드시 읽어 봐야 해요. 대단한 미스터리가 있어요.

단어 19 the ruling party / the opposition party | 여당 / 야당

A What are you reading?

B It's an article on the dispute between **the ruling party** and **the opposition party** over taxes.

A Oh, I hadn't heard about that. I hope they can come to an agreement soon.

A 뭘 읽고 있나요?

B 여당과 야당 사이의 세금 관련 논쟁에 대한 기사예요.

A 아, 저는 못 들어본 거네요. 빨리 합의에 도달했으면 좋겠네요.

단어 20 daily temperature range | 일교차

A Don't forget to take a jacket with you, Bill.

B But it's really sunny out. I don't need a jacket in this weather.

A The **daily temperature range** is still quite wide. It's cold in the evenings.

A 빌, 재킷 꼭 챙겨 가요.

B 하지만 밖이 정말 화창해요. 이런 날씨에는 재킷 안 입어도 돼요.

A 일교차가 여전히 심하잖아요. 저녁에는 아직 추워요.

단어 **21**

bank loan

은행 대출금

A The company is on the brink of bankruptcy.
We need cash, fast

B Have we tried to get extensions on our **bank loans**?
Can they give us an extra thirty days?

A We asked, and they turned us down flat.
We're going to need to find more investors.

A 회사가 파산 직전에 있어요.
지금 당장 현금이 필요해요.

B 은행에 대출금 연장 신청했어요?
30일 더 연장해줄 수 있대요?

A 요청해봤는데 한마디로 거절당했어요.
우린 더 많은 투자자들을 찾아야 할 거예요.

단어 **22**

blurry

흐릿한

A Any other symptoms? How's your vision?

B Sort of **blurry**, but usually only in the mornings.
Is it something serious, doc?

A Hard to tell. We'll have to run some more tests.
You'll need to stay in the hospital overnight.

A 다른 증상이 있나요? 시력은 어떠세요?

B 좀 흐릿한데 보통 오전에만 그래요.
심각한 건가요, 선생님?

A 아직 알 수 없어요. 몇 가지 검사를 더 해봐야 할 것 같아요. 병원에 하루 입원하셔야 돼요.

단어 **23**

freckle

주근깨

A The weather's been beautiful theses last few weeks.
I've been going to the beach a lot.

B Well, I can't stand all this sunny weather.
Look at my face! It's covered in **freckles**.

A Oh, my. It looks like you need a better hat and some stronger sunscreen. SPF 50 at least, I'd say.

A 요 몇 주 동안 날씨가 참 좋아요.
바닷가에 여러 번 갔다 왔어요.

B 음, 전 햇빛이 쨍쨍 나는 이런 날씨는 정말 싫어요.
제 얼굴 좀 보세요! 온통 주근깨투성이에요.

A 저런, 챙이 더 넓은 모자와 더 강력한 선크림이 필요할 것 같아요. SPF 지수가 적어도 50은 되어야 해요.

단어

24 second-choice school

2지망 학교

A Have you heard anything from the universities yet?

B I got into my safety school, but I'm still waiting for an answer from Harvard.

A Well, at least you know you got into your **second-choice school.**

A 대학에서 아직 연락 없었어요?

B 안전하게 하향 지원한 대학은 합격했는데, 아직 하버드대에서 연락 오기를 기다리고 있어요.

A 음, (하버드에서) 떨어지더라도 2지망한 학교에는 갈 수 있겠네요.

단어

25 hospitalized

병원에 입원한

A ... and then we realized he was having a heart attack! We called an ambulance right away.

B It sounds like your quick thinking saved his life. Good for you.

A Well, it was nothing, really. He's still **hospitalized**, but should be released next week.

A … 그러다 그가 심장마비를 일으켰다는 걸 알아차렸어요! 우린 바로 구급차를 불렀죠.

B 당신의 빠른 판단이 그의 목숨을 살린 것 같네요.
잘하셨어요.

A 사실 대단한 일은 아니었어요. 그는 아직 병원에 입원해 있지만 다음 주에 퇴원할 거예요.

단어

26 volley

받아치다

A How did Mr. Schnell do at the conference?

B He gave a great speech and then answered a lot of questions.

A Did he have any problems answering the questions?

B Not at all. he **volleyed** all the questions everyone asked.

A 회의에서 쉬넬 씨 어땠어요?

B 멋진 연설을 하고 여러 질문에 답변도 했죠.

A 질문에 답변할 때 문제는 없었나요?

B 전혀요. 모든 사람들의 질문을 다 잘 받아쳤어요.

단어 **27**

scratch

동등한

A I'm going to open a business with Allen.

B So who is going to be the majority partner?

A Neither of us. We are going to be **scratch** partners.

B It's good that you'll both have equal shares.

A 앨런과 사업을 시작하려고 해.

B 그럼 누가 주도권을 갖게 되는 거지?

A 둘 다 아니야. 동등한 조건으로 파트너가 되는 거거든.

B 둘이서 동등하게 출자하는 거라면 좋을 거 같은데.

단어 **28**

walk-in

예약하지 않고 가는 손님 [환자]

A Good evening, sir. Do you have a reservation?

B I'm sorry, I don't. I didn't realize you'd be so busy on a Tuesday.

A I'm sorry, but all the tables are booked; we can't accommodate **walk-ins**.

A 안녕하세요, 예약이 되어 있으신가요?

B 예약 안 했어요, 화요일에 사람이 많을 거라 생각 못했어요.

A 죄송하지만, 모든 테이블이 다 예약이 되어 있어요. 예약 없이 그냥 오시는 분은 받을 수 없어요.

단어 **29**

deadwood

쓸모없는 사람, 짐만 되는 사람

A No, thanks. We don't need any more line managers.

B We're talking about a capable manager.

A Look, we have enough **deadwood** as it is.

B I think she would be an invaluable asset to our company.

A 아니오, 괜찮습니다. 관리자는 더 이상 필요하지 않습니다.

B 제가 말씀드리는 사람은 유능한 관리자입니다.

A 보세요. 지금도 쓸모없는 사람들이 넘치고 있어요.

B 그녀라면 우리 회사에 매우 귀중한 인재가 될 텐데요.

단어 30 shoestring operation / budget

영세운영자금, 예산

A They're asking for payment in advance this time.

B Yeah, they're a typical **shoestring operation**. The company has been and continues to run on a shoestring budget.

A Well, what do you think?

A 그들이 이번에도 선불을 요하고 있어.

B 그래, 그들은 전형적인 영세업체야. 그 회사는 소자본으로 운영해 왔고 지금도 그래.

A 그럼, 어떻게 할까?

단어 31 interest

이자, 금리

A Rising **interest** rates are a result of rising inflation.

B Was it the other way around?

A It's really hard to determine which is the cause and which is the effect.

B Either way, I'm getting out of the stock market and putting my money into bonds.

A 금리가 상승하는 건 물가 상승률이 높아졌기 때문입니다.

B 그 반대 아닌가요?

A 사실 무엇이 원인이고 무엇이 결과인지를 결론짓기는 어렵습니다.

B 어느 쪽이든, 나는 주식투자를 그만두고 채권에 투자할 겁니다.

단어 32 corny

시시한

A I'd like to tell a few jokes now.

B That's okay. You don't have to do that.

A Why? Don't you like any of my jokes.

B Your jokes are too **corny**. And I've heard them all too many times.

A 재밌는 얘기 몇 개 해줄게.

B 됐어. 그러지 않아도 돼.

A 왜? 내 얘기가 싫으니?

B 네 얘긴 너무 시시해. 다 너무 많이 들어본 얘기들이야.

단어 33 dress code — 복장 규정

A I need to talk with Jim about the company **dress code**. He's not wearing appropriate clothes for the office.

B Just make sure you choose your words carefully. You don't want to offend him.

A I know. I'll make it clear I'm not attacking him personally.

A 회사 복장규정에 관해 짐과 이야기를 해야겠어요. 회사 옷차림이 적절하지 않아요.

B 단어 선택을 신중하게 하세요. 그가 기분 상하지 않게요.

A 네. 인신공격을 하기 위한 게 아니라는 걸 분명히 해둘게요.

단어 34 strong coffee — 진한 커피

A Are you OK? You look like a zombie.

B I wish I were dead. I am so hung over. I need to have some **strong coffee**.

A Here's my secret hangover cure: Drink lots of water and go back to sleep.

A 당신 괜찮아요? 꼭 산송장 같아요.

B 차라리 송장이 낫겠어요. 술이 아직도 안 깼어요. 진한 커피를 좀 마셔야겠어요.

A 제가 숙취 해소 비법을 알려드릴게요. 물을 잔뜩 마시고 다시 잠자리에 들어요.

단어 35 stocky — (체격이) 다부진, 다리가 굵은

A I hear short summer dresses are all the rage this season. Have you bought any yet?

B What? Just look at my legs! I'm too **stocky** for short dresses.

A Oh. I see what you mean. Oh well. There's always fall!

A 이번 여름에는 짧은 원피스가 유행이라고 들었어요. 당신은 아직 안 샀어요?

B 뭐라고요? 제 다리 좀 보세요! 짧은 원피스 입기에는 다리가 너무 굵잖아요.

A 아, 무슨 말인지 알겠어요. 어쩔 수 없죠. 가을은 항상 오는 법이니까요.

단어
36 step out
잠깐 자리를 비우다, 잠시 나가다

A I'm looking for Jim Fowler. Is he available now?

B Oh, I', sorry. He just **stepped out** for a few minutes.

A Where can I find him? It's urgent.

A 짐 파울러를 찾고 있는데요. 지금 계세요?

B 아, 죄송하지만 방금 잠시 자리를 비우셨어요.

A 어디 가면 짐을 만날 수 있을까요? 급하거든요.

단어
37 coop up
가두다

A Didn't you go snowboarding last year?

B I did. I also broke my leg on the first day and spent the rest of the vacation **cooped up** in the hospital.

A In that case, I guess you won't be doing that again this year.

A 작년에 스노보드 타러 가지 않으셨어요?

B 그랬죠. 첫 날 다리가 부러져서 남은 휴가 내내 병원에 틀어박혀 지냈어요.

A 그럼 올해는 스노보드 타러 안가겠네요.

단어
38 (one's) portfolio
자산 알람표

A My fund manager recommends that I diversify my investment **portfolio** because I have all my money in one stock.

B That makes sense. If one stock decreases in value, another is likely to increase, and you'll break even.

A Which stocks are profitable?

A 제 투자담당자가 투자 자산 구성을 다양화하라고 권고하네요. 제가 하나의 주식에만 투자하고 있거든요.

B 일리가 있는 말입니다. 만약 한 주식의 주가가 떨어져도 다른 건 오를 수 있으니까요. 그러면 손해는 안 볼 겁니다.

A 어떤 주식이 수익성이 있나요?

단어 39 temp — 임시직 직원

A Henry, do you have a number for the Globe H.R.?

B Sure. Are we short handed?

A One of the receptionists called in sick this morning. We'd better get a **temp** to help out for a day.

B Which of the receptionists is it?

A It's Clara. She sounded awful on the line.

B Okay. I'll work on it.

A 헨리, 글로브 인력 회사 전화 번호 알지?

B 그럼. 왜? 사람이 더 필요해?

A 안내 직원 한 명이 아파서 결근한대. 오늘 하루 일할 임시 직원을 구해야겠어.

B 안내 직원 누구?

A 클라라. 전화 목소리가 많이 아픈 것 같았어.

B 알았어. 바로 알아볼게.

단어 40 scuttlebutt — 소문

A There's something weird today. Everyone seems to have butterflies in their stomachs.

B There are good reasons for it.

A What's going on?

B Didn't you hear? The **scuttlebutt** is all around that an enormous scale of layoff is being planned.

A 오늘 뭔가 이상하네. 다들 매우 불안해 보여.

B 그럴 만도 하지.

A 무슨 일이야?

B 못 들었어? 대대적인 정리해고가 있을 예정이라는 소문이야.

단어 41 utility bill — 납부서

A Hello, I'm calling from the Public Utilities Commission. Is this Ms.Monroe's resident?

B That's right.
Is there something that I need to be informed of?

A Your record shows that you owe us $75.
Did you get your **utility bill** yet?

B Oh, yes. I completely forgot about the bill.
I'll wire the money as soon as possible.

A 여보세요, 공익설비 위원회인데요, 몬로양 댁인가요?

B 네, 맞는데요.
제가 알아야 할 사항이 있나요?

A 예, 몬로양 기록에 75달러 미납금이 있어서요. 고지서는 받으셨나요?

B 아, 네. 제가 받아 놓고 잊고 있었어요. 제가 되도록 빨리 송금하겠습니다.

단어
42 cram
벼락치기 공부를 하다

A I can't wait to get this mid-term over with. I've done nothing but study for the last 20 hours.

B I just reviewed some of the chapters last night. I never **cram** for tests.

A Well, whatever works for you. In my case, I usually do better when I study everything the night before.

A 이번 중간고사가 빨리 끝났으면 좋겠어. 지난 20시간 동안 공부 말고는 아무것도 못했어.

B 난 어젯밤에 몇 챕터를 훑어봤어. 난 벼락치기는 절대 안 하거든.

A 글쎄, 너한테 맞는 공부 방법이 있지. 나 보통 전날 밤에 모조리 공부하면 성적이 잘나와.

단어
43 wind chill factor
풍속냉각지수(체감 온도)

A How cold is it right now? It feels like it's minus ten, at least.

B Let me see.... According to my smartphone, it's only minus five.

A But that's without the wind. **Wind chill factor**, it's got to be much colder.

A 지금 날씨가 얼마나 추운 거예요? 적어도 영하 10도는 되는 것 같아요.

B 어디보자…. 스마트폰으로 검색해보니 영하 5도 밖에 안 되는데요.

A 하지만 그건 바람이 안 불었을 때 얘기고요. 체감온도는 훨씬 더 춥다고요.

단어
44 soap opera
(텔레비전, 라디오의) 연속극

A ... and then I told Brian he had better watch out, because....

B You know, you should really avoid all the office politics. It's going to get you into trouble.

A Sure, it might. But, it's like watching a **soap opera**. I can't help myself.

A 그리고 나서 브라이언에게 조심하는 게 좋겠다고 말했어요. 왜냐하면….

B 있죠, 사내 정치 문제들은 정말 관여하지 않는 게 좋겠어요. 곤란한 상황에 처하게 될 거에요.

A 네, 그럴지도 모르죠. 하지만 마치 연속극을 보는 것 같아요. 저도 어쩔 수가 없어요.

단어 **45** **tattletale** 고자질쟁이

A I wouldn't mention that to Gloria if I were you.
B Why not? She seems a very sympathetic person.
A No, not at all. I know from experience that she's a real **tattletale**.
B Really? Well, if that's the case, I'll take your advice.

A 내가 너라면 그걸 글로리아에게 말하지 않을 텐데.
B 왜? 그녀는 인정 있는 사람인 것 같던데?
A 아니, 전혀. 내 경험으로는 그녀는 고자질쟁이야.
B 정말? 그렇다면 너의 충고를 받아들일게.

단어 **46** **bylaw** (이사회의 구조와 해야 할 일을 정해 놓은) 내규·규칙·정관

A Did you see the minutes of the last board meetings? They **bylaws** were re-vised to reflect the company's new mission and vision.
B the board has developed an ambitious strategic plan. I agree with the new focus.
A The problem is that the board did not have a quorum when the vote was held.

A 지난번 이사회 회의록 봤어? 회사의 새로운 임무와 이상을 반영하도록 내규가 수정됐어.
B 이사회에서 야심차게 전략적인 계획을 만들어 냈지. 나는 새로 중점 둔 부분에 동의 해.
A 문제는 투표가 실시되었을 때 이사회는 정족수를 채우지 못했다는 거야.

단어 **47** **overstaffed** 과잉인원의

A Volume we're now **overstaffed** at sales levels.
B I know. We have a lot of people sitting around doing nothing.
A The problem is that we don't know how to do with them.
B Yeah, it's turning into a real morale problem.

A 판매량이 떨어지고 있는 지금 필요이상으로 판매 직원이 많네요.
B 알고 있습니다. 아무 일도 하지 않고 빈둥대는 사람이 너무 많아요.
A 문제는 그들을 어떻게 처리해야 할지 모른다는 점이죠.
B 네. 이제는 근로의욕에 관한 문제가 되고 있어요.

단어 48 brainstorm

여러 가지 착상을 모으다, 논의해 보다

A The chairman of the board convened an emergency meeting to discuss the president's sudden resignation from the company.

B I heard the board **brainstormed** for hours about how to handle the situation.

A One member even made a motion to dissolve the company. They tabled that motion indefinitely.

A 이사회 의장이 사장님의 갑작스런 사임을 논의하기 위해서 긴급회의를 소집했어.

B 이사회에서 그 사태를 어떻게 다룰지에 대해 몇 시간 동안 브레인스토밍을 했다던데.

A 한 이사는 심지어 회사를 해산시키자는 제안까지 했어. 이사들은 그 제안을 무기한으로 연기했지만.

단어 49 downsize

감원하다

A Hello, Mrs. Seymour. How are you?

B Never better. And you?

A I was **downsized** in April, and I've been looking for work ever since.

B That's a shame.
I'll try my best to find the right job for you!

A 여보세요, 세이모어양. 안녕하세요?

B 아주 좋아요. 안녕하셨어요?

A 저는 4월에 직장에서 해고돼 그때부터 계속 일자리를 찾고 있었어요.

B 유감이네요.
당신한테 맞는 일을 찾도록 최선을 다할게요.

단어 50 savvy

실용적인 지식

A Did you see how Tom got us free drinks at the bar? What a smooth talker!

B I know. He's got a lot of **savvy**. He knows how to make things happen.

A I could really use a friend like that.

A 술집에서 우리가 공짜 술을 얻어 마실 수 있게 톰이 어떻게 하는지 봤죠? 톰은 말주변이 참 좋아요!

B 맞아요. 그는 수완이 아주 뛰어나요. 그는 일이 되게 만드는 법을 알고 있어요.

A 톰 같은 친구가 있으면 정말 좋겠네요.

단어 51 cubicle

칸막이 방

A I heard they gave you a new desk.
You're moving up in the world.

B It's nothing. really. I don't have an office, yet.
It's just a new **cubicle**.

A I know that. But It's beside the window.
It's a cubicle with a view!

A 회사에서 새 책상을 사줬다면서요.
승진하신 거군요.

B 정말 별거 아니에요. 아직 사무실도 없어요.
그냥 칸막이 방 하나 새로 생긴 거에요.

A 알아요. 하지만 창문 옆이잖아요.
전망 좋은 칸막이 방이요!

단어 52 facelift

주름 제거 수술

A I think it's Botox. Look!
She can barely smile!

B No way. It was a **facelift**.
Just look at how tight the skin is over her cheeks.

A Nope. Definitely Botox.
I can tell. See how her forehead never moves?

A 보톡스 주사를 맞은 것 같아요. 봐요!
저 여자 잘 웃지도 못하잖아요!

B 아니에요. 주름 제거 수술을 받았어요.
양 볼의 피부가 팽팽한 것 좀 봐요.

A 아니라니까요. 분명 보톡스예요.
제가 알아요. 이마가 전혀 안 움직이는 거 보이죠?

단어 53 dicey

불확실한

A Do you have any information relating to the O'Brian Company?

B No. Why do you want to know about the company?

A A friend of mine says I can make a lot of money if I buy stock in O'Brian.

B I wouldn't if I were you.
The chances for success are **dicey**.

A 오브라이언 회사에 관한 정보가 좀 있나요?

B 아니오. 그 회사에 관해 왜 알고 싶어 하시죠?

A 제 친구가 오브라이언 주식을 사면 돈을 많이 벌거라고 해서요.

B 저라면 안 살 겁니다.
이윤을 낼 수 있을지 여부가 불확실하잖아요.

단어 54

informercial

홈쇼핑 광고

A Are you positive that the **informercial** will work?

B Sure. An informercial is most effective way of seeling products because it lead consumers to believe everything they see.

A Yeah. But the problem is its cost, It's incredivly expensive compared to a newspaper ad.

B We have no option though.
We have to make it happen within a few months.

A 홈쇼핑 광고가 정말 효과가 있을까?

B 그럼. 홈쇼핑 광고는 소비자가 보는 대로 믿게 만들기 때문에 가장 효과적인 판매 전략이야.

A 그래. 하지만 비용이 문제야.
신문 광고에 비해 너무 비싸.

B 하지만 다른 방법이 없잖아.
우린 몇 달 내로 승부를 봐야 해.

단어 55

get-together

모임

A I guess I'll be seeing you this Saturday.

B Saturday? Oh, no. Did we get called into work this weekend?

A Work? No, I'm talking about the **get-together** at the boss's house. It's this weekend. Sounds like you forgot all about it.

A 이번 주 토요일에 봐요.

B 토요일이요? 이런. 이번 주말에 회사에 출근하라는 통보를 받았던가요?

A 회사요? 아뇨, 사장님 댁에서 열리는 모임 얘기하는 거예요. 이번 주말이잖아요. 까맣게 잊고 있었나 보군요.

단어 56

cataract surgery

백내장 수술

A Tom goes in for his **cataract surgery** on the fifteenth.
He's really looking forward to it.

B Really? If I were him, I'd be totally scared.
An operation… on my eye!

A It's routine surgery.
We're not expecting any complications.

A 톰은 15일에 백내장 수술을 받아요.
그는 수술을 몹시 고대하고 있어요.

B 정말이에요? 나라면 완전히 겁먹었을 텐데.
수술을… 눈에 하는 거잖아요!

A 일상적인 수술이에요.
합병증 같은 건 없을 거예요.

단어
57

peachy

훌륭한

A You look really happy these days.

B Oh, yeah. Everything in my life is totally **peachy**.

A Really? Well, I'm glad to hear that things are going well.

B Me, too. It's about time things in my life got better.

A 너 요즘 굉장히 기분 좋아 보인다.

B 아, 맞아. 요즘은 내 인생의 모든 일이 정말 잘 풀리는 것 같아.

A 그래? 음, 다 잘 되고 있다니 기쁘다.

B 나도 그래. 이젠 내 형편도 더 좋아질 때가 됐지 뭐.

CHAPTER
18

회화에서 유용하게 쓰이는 숙어

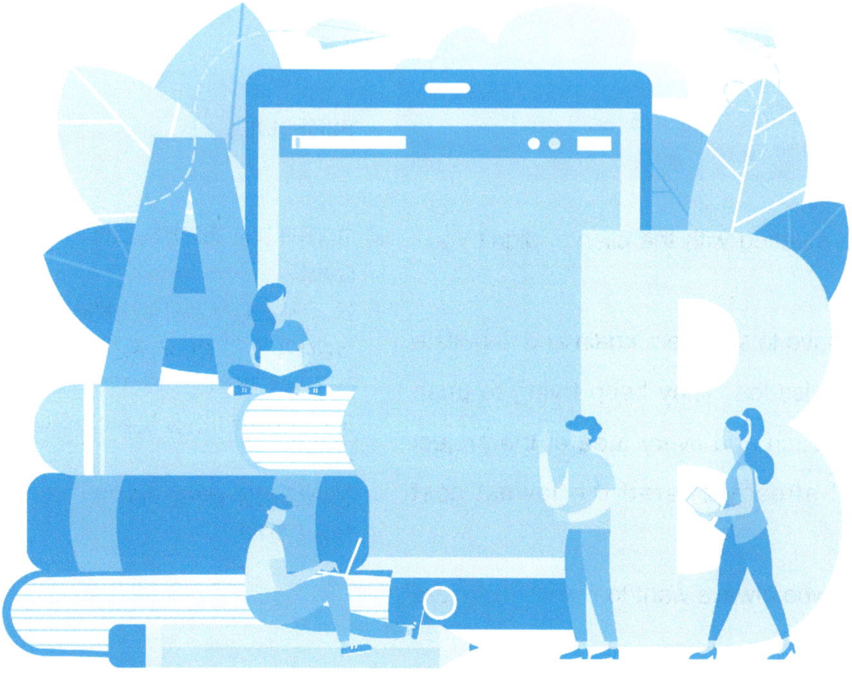

숙어

1 wear a cast

긴스를 하다

A It looks like all yor friends signed your cast. Someone even drew a nice heart!

B Actually, I hate this cast. I have to **wear it** for three more weeks, but it's always itchy.

A I know, a good trick: you can straighten a coat hanger and use that to scratch.

A 친구들이 다 와서 깁스에 사인을 했나 보네요. 예쁜 하트를 그린 사람도 있어요!

B 사실 깁스 싫어요. 앞으로 3주는 더 하고 있어야 하는데, 늘 가렵거든요.

A 내가 좋은 비결을 알아요. 옷걸이를 쫙 펴서 그걸로 긁으면 돼요.

숙어

2 grow apart

사이가 멀어지다

A You'll never guess who I ran into at the mall the other day. Dave Johnson.

B Seriously? I haven't seen him in ages. It's too bad, really. We used to be best friends.

A Sometimes, people just **grow apart**. Anyway, he said to tell you he says hi.

A 며칠 전에 쇼핑몰에서 내가 우연히 누구를 만났는지 넌 짐작도 못할 걸. 바로 데이브 존슨을 만났어.

B 정말? 그 친구 못 본 지 한참 됐는데. 안타까운 일이지. 우리 둘이 절친이었는데.

A 때로는 그냥 사이가 멀어지기도 하잖아. 어쨌든 그 친구가 너한테 안부 전해 달라고 했어.

숙어

3 cut corners

경비를 아끼다

A You just had a meeting with the clients, didn't you? How did it go?

B Well, I think I'll have to see them again and negotiate some additional issues. They keep trying to push coasts down in each and every area of the project even though I already offered the lowest cost estimates.

A Really? People who always want to **cut corners** are such a headache.

A 고객들과 방금 회의했죠, 그렇죠? 어땠어요?

B 음, 다시 만나서 추가적인 문제들을 협상해야 할 것 같네요. 제가 이미 최저 견적을 제안했는데도 프로젝트의 모든 부분에서 비용을 낮추려고 하더라고요.

A 정말요? 항상 경비를 아끼려는 사람들이 골칫거리죠.

숙어

4 hold a bake sale

빵 바자회를 열다

A Are you going to the school festival next week? I heard there was going to be a concert, or something.

B The freshman are doing that. But my class is **holding a bake sale** to raise money for orphans.

A Sounds good. It's nice to see students helping others.

A 다음 주에 하는 학교 축제에 갈 거니? 콘서트 같은 게 열릴 거라고 하던데.

B 그건 신입생들이 할 거예요. 하지만 우리 반에서는 고아 돕기 기금 마련을 위해 빵 바자회를 열어요.

A 그거 괜찮겠구나. 학생들이 다른 사람들을 돕는 걸 보는 건 기분 좋은 일이지.

숙어

5 ask for it

자초하다

A Why the long face? Oh! Is that the score sheet of the test you took a few weeks ago?

B Yes, and it's worse than I expected. This is a disaster.

A You **asked for it** by not studying. I told you not to go to that party the night before.

A 왜 시무룩한 얼굴이니? 아! 그건 몇 주 전에 본 시험 성적표지?

B 네, 그리고 예상보다 더 안 좋네요. 이것은 재앙이에요.

A 공부를 안 했으니 네가 자초한 일이지. 밤에 있던 그 파티에 가지 말라고 전에 말했잖아.

숙어

6 all the rage

대유행

A Hey, I asked Jenny out a few days ago, but I haven't found the perfect restaurant for our date yes. Can you recommend one? I'm going to see her tomorrow night.

B Haven't you heard about the restaurant that just opened on Elm and 7th? That place is **all the rage**.

A Really? Thanks for the heads-up. I'll book a table right now.

A 있잖아, 며칠 전에 제니에게 데이트를 신청했는데 아직 데이트할 만한 완벽한 식당을 못 찾았어. 추천해줄래? 내일 밤에 그녀와 만나기로 했어.

B 엘름가와 7번가에 막 개업한 식당에 대해 들어본 적 없어? 그 가게 대유행이야.

A 정말? 조언해줘서 고마워. 지금 당장 예약해야지.

숙어

7 a blessing in disguise

전화위복

A Your company's first software program has become a big hit-congratulations! It must be especially satisfying since you had a hard time for the last few years.

B Yeah. But as I look back, those years turned out to be **a blessing in disguise**. Without them, we never would have developed such a great program.

A That's right. So, what're your plans going forward?

A 당신 회사의 첫 소프트웨어 프로그램이 큰 성공을 했네요. 축하해요! 지난 몇 년 동안 고생했으니 특히 더 만족스럽겠어요.

B 네. 그런데 되돌아보면 그 몇 년들이 전화위복이 되었네요. 그 세월들이 없었으면 이런 훌륭한 프로그램을 개발하지 못했겠죠.

A 맞아요. 그래서 앞으로 계획은 어떻게 되나요?

숙어

8 mixed up

혼동한

A Do you have a minute to look at this guest list for the upcoming conference? I've just finished it.

B I have a meeting soon. But let me see.... Hmm, I remember that we'll have 315 people on the first day. But that's not what you wrote here.

A Oh, I got **mixed up**. I'll correct the number right away. Thanks a lot.

A 다가오는 회의를 위한 이 참석자 명단을 잠시 보겠어요? 방금 완성했어요.

B 곧 회의가 있어요. 그렇지만 어디 봅시다…. 음, 첫날에 315명이 오는 걸로 기억해요. 그런데 여기서 적은 것은 그렇지 않네요.

A 오, 제가 혼동했네요. 숫자를 바로 수정할게요. 정말 고마워요.

숙어

9 hit it off

서로 잘 맞다

A I'm so glad Steph joined our team! Look at her and Kevin. They get along so well.

B Yeah, they **hit if off** right from the start. It has changed the atmosphere of our sales team for the better.

A Definitely. I think we're going to be the most successful team this year.

A 스태프가 우리 팀에 합류해서 정말 기뻐요! 그녀와 케빈을 보세요. 사이가 정말 좋네요.

B 네, 바로 처음부터 서로 잘 맞았어요. 우리 영업부의 분위기를 더 좋게 바꿨네요.

A 분명히 그렇죠. 올해 우리가 가장 성공한 팀이 될 것 같아요.

숙어
10 lose track of time
시간 가는 줄 모르다

A Why didn't you answer the phone yesterday? I needed your opinion on how to promote our new product.
B Sorry. You know that I took the day off yesterday. I watched a baseball game on TV with my friends, and we **lost track of time.**
A Hmm, I'll let it slide this time. I just hope this kind of thing doesn't happen again.

A 어제 왜 전화를 안 받았어요? 신제품을 홍보하는 방법에 대해 당신의 의견이 필요했어요.
B 미안해요. 어제 저는 쉬는 날이었잖아요. 친구들과 텔레비전으로 야구 경기를 보다가 시간 가는 줄 몰랐어요.
A 음, 이번에는 넘어갈게요. 그저 이런 일이 다시는 없길 바라요.

숙어
11 face the music
비난을 받아들이다

A Oh, I'm screwed. I accidently split wine on my sister's brand new dress. She's really excited about wearing it this weekend. What should I do?
B Well, you can get it dry-cleaned, but you'll probably still have to **face the music** and tell her what you did.
A Do I have to? She's going to be so mad....

A 오, 망했어. 뜻하지 않게 언니의 새 드레스에 와인을 쏟았어. 이번 주말에 입을 거라고 정말 신나 했는데. 내가 뭘 해야 하지?
B 음, 드라이클리닝을 할 수 있겠지. 그렇지만 아마 여전히 비난을 받아들여야 할 거야. 그리고 네가 한 일을 그녀에게 말해야 해.
A 꼭 그래야 해? 몹시 화낼 텐데….

숙어
12 do the trick
효과가 있다

A Are you okay? What's wrong?
B I started getting a headache a few minutes ago and I really can't stand it.
A Wait a minute. Try one of these pills. They're what I take when I have a headache. That should **do the trick.** Trust me.

A 괜찮아요? 무슨 일이에요?
B 좀 전에 머리가 아프기 시작했는데 정말 견딜 수 없어요.
A 잠깐만요. 이 알약을 먹어 보세요. 제가 머리 아플 때 먹는 거예요 효과가 있을 거예요. 저를 믿으세요.

숙어

13 a deer in the headlights

너무 놀라서 얼어붙은

A How was the presentation to win the bid? I bet you gave it perfectly. Am I right?

B Unfortunately, no... I was so nervous that I forgot what to say in the middle of the pitch. I just stood there without saying anything for a while. I was such **a deer in the headlights**.

A Oh, no! So how did you get our of that situation?

A 유치를 따내기 위한 발표는 어땠어요? 완벽하게 잘 했을 것이라고 확신해요. 맞죠?

B 유감스럽게도, 아니요… 너무 긴장해서 설득하는 중간에 할 말을 잊어버렸어요. 한동안 아무 말도 못하고 그냥 거기 서 있었어요. 너무 놀라서 얼어붙었죠.

A 오, 이런! 그래서 그 상황을 어떻게 벗어났어요?

숙어

14 splash out

돈을 펑펑 쓰다

A Wow, what a beautiful painting! I had no idea you had such fancy things.

B Really? Well, how I live doesn't matter, right? Come on this way.

A Oh my goodness! Look at all of these bottles of vintage wine. You really like to **splash out** on luxuries, don't you?

A 와, 정말 아름다운 그림이네요! 이런 고급품들을 갖고 있는 줄 몰랐어요.

B 정말요? 음, 제가 어떻게 살든 문제가 되진 않죠, 그렇죠? 이쪽으로 오세요.

A 오, 세상에나! 이 고급 와인병들을 보세요. 당신은 사치품에 정말 돈을 펑펑 쓰는 것 같네요, 그렇지 않아요?

숙어

15 have a blast

즐거운 시간을 보내다

A So how was your trip to the States? I saw the pictures you posted on Facebook.

B It was awesome. Thanks to Panuly's hospitality, I **had a blast** every night. She took me everywhere from the tourist attractions to the bars and clubs. I really want to go there again.

A That's great! Let's visit her together next time!

A 그래서 미국 여행은 어땠니? 네가 페이스북에 올린 사진들을 봤어.

B 굉장했어. 파눌리의 환대 덕분에 매일 밤마다 즐거운 시간을 보냈지. 관광 명소부터 술집과 클럽가지 모든 곳에 데려다줬어. 거기에 꼭 다시 가고 싶어.

A 좋았겠구나! 다음에 같이 만나러 가자!

숙어

16 scrape through

간신히 합격하다

A How's your son Danny doing in college these days? Is he still not studying hard enough?

B He's doing better, actually. Almost getting kicked out last semester seems to have knocked some sense into him. I think he's going to be able to **scrape through**.

A That's great! Even if he doesn't end up with impressive grades, having a college degree will be helpful in the job market.

A 요즘 당신 아들 대니는 대학에서 잘 지내고 있어요? 아직도 공부를 열심히 안 하나요?

B 사실 좋아졌어요. 지난 학기에 거의 쫓겨날 뻔 한 일이 그를 정신 차리게 한 것 같아요. 간신히 상황을 잘 넘길 수 있을 것으로 보여요.

A 다행이네요! 인상 깊은 성적을 결국 못 받아도 대학 학위 취득은 취업 시장에서 도움이 될거예요.

숙어

17 under one's thumb

~의 수중에 있는

A Where's James? I saw him right here a couple of minutes ago.

B He just took off right after he got a phone call from his wife. He said she's waiting for him at home.

A Really? I didn't she had him **under her thumb** like that. By the way, are you still drink that beer? Let's get one more round!

A 제임스는 어디에 있어요? 몇 분 전에 바로 여기에서 봤는데요.

B 아내에게서 온 전화를 받고 나서 방금 나갔어요. 그녀가 집에서 기다리고 있다고 말하더라고요.

A 정말요? 그렇게 아내의 수중에 있는 줄 몰랐어요. 그런데 아직도 그 맥주를 마시고 있어요? 한 잔 더 합시다!

숙어

18 beat someone to it

~를 선수 치다

A You visited Sokcho las weekend, didn't you? How did you get there? Did you take the bus?

B No, I drove there. My mother wanted to use the family car for something else but I **beat her to it**.

A I see. Was there heavy traffic on the highway? I'm thinking of going there with my family next week.

A 지난 주에 속초 다녀왔죠, 그렇지 않아요? 거기에 어떻게 갔어요? 버스를 탔나요?

B 아니요, 거기에 운전해서 갔어요. 어머니가 다른 일로 가족이 쓰는 차를 사용하고 싶어 하셨는데, 제가 어머니를 선수 쳤죠.

A 알았어요. 고속 도로는 안 막혔나요? 다음 주에 가족들과 거기 갈 생각이에요.

숙어

19 brownie points

환심을 사서 얻은 점수(신임)

A What are you wrapping? Is it a present for your girlfriend or something?

B Yes. Actually, it's going to give her this diamond ring right after she wakes up.

A Wow! That's going to be awesome. You're going to earn some major **brownie points**.

A 뭘 포장하고 있어요? 여자 친구나 다른 사람에게 줄 선물이에요?

B 네. 사실 내일 제 여자 친구의 생일이에요. 그래서 그녀가 일어나면 바로 이 다이아몬드 반지를 줄 거예요.

A 와! 아주 멋지겠네요. 환심을 사서 큰 점수를 좀 얻을 수 있을 거예요.

숙어

20 with all due respect

외람되지만

A We need to start the production of the new smartphone model right now so that we can release it before our competitiors release their products.

B **With all due respect**, sir, I don't think that's a good idea. We haven't finished testing each and every function of the phone.

A Then why don't you guys step on it? We have to increase our market share in the next quarter. Don't you know that?

A 경쟁사들이 제품을 출시하기 전에 우리가 출시할 수 있게 새 스마트폰 모델 생산을 지금 당장 시작할 필요가 있어요.

B 외람되지만 그건 좋은 생각이 아닌 것 같습니다. 아직 휴대폰의 모든 기능에 테스트를 완료하지 못 했어요.

A 그럼 왜 서두르지 않는 거죠? 다음 분기에 우리는 시장 점유율을 높여야 해요. 이 일에 대해 몰라요?

숙어

21 bide one's time

때를 기다리다

A Dan, don't take this the wrong way, but-sometimes it seems like you don't even want to keep your job in this store.

B That's true, actually. I'm just **biding my time** here until my music career takes off. I'm in a rock band.

A Oh, I see. Well, good luck with that, I guess.

A 댄, 기분 나쁘게 받아들이지 마요. 그런데 때때로 당신은 이 상점에서 계속 일하고 싶어 하지 않는 것 같아요.

B 사실 맞아요. 저의 음악 활동이 급격히 인기를 얻을 때까지 그저 여기에서 때를 기다리고 있어요. 저는 록 밴드에 소속되어 있어요.

A 아, 알겠어요. 음, 그 일이 잘되길 바랄게요.

숙어

22 come a long way

많이 발전하다

A Hey, did you hear that Mr. Smith finally got promoted to marketing director? I just saw the news on the bulletin board in the lobby.

B Wow, he's **come a long way** since he started here as an intern. That's great.

A Yes, it is. I'm happy for him.

A 이봐요, 스미스 씨가 결국 마케팅 부장으로 승진됐다는 것을 들었어요? 로비에 있는 게시판에 쓰인 소식을 막 봤어요.

B 와, 그는 여기에서 인턴으로 시작한 이후로 많이 발전했네요. 대단해요.

A 맞아요. 그의 일로 정말 기분 좋네요.

숙어

23 sit on one's hands

수수방관하다

A The government kept **sitting on its hands** on the matter.

B He just sat on his ass at the critical juncture.

C She couldn't just look on with her arms folded when her friend was in trouble.

A 정부는 그 문제에 대해 계속 방관하기만 했다.

B 그는 그 중요한 시점에 아무 행동도 취하지 않고 방관하기만 했다.

C 그녀는 친구가 곤경에 처해 있는데 팔짱만 끼고 있을 수 없었다.

숙어

24 take (have) a breather

한숨 돌리다

A He was too busy all morning to **take a breather**.

B Let's **have a breather** and go get some coffee.

C I'd like to catch my breath for the weekend.

A 그는 오전 내내 숨 돌릴 사이도 없이 바빴다.

B 잠깐 숨 좀 돌리고 커피 마시러 가자.

C 나는 주말에 한숨 돌리며 잠시 쉬고 싶다.

숙어

25 light sleeper

잠을 깊게 못 자는 사람

A Hey, I saw you talking with James a few minutes ago. He looks so tired today. Do you happen to know why?

B Well, he said he's a **light sleeper** and last night his neighbor's dog was barking a lot. And he's allergic to dust. That's why his eyes are extra swollen.

A That's all? I thought he was sick and should take the day off.

A 저기요, 몇 분 전에 제임스와 이야기하는 것을 봤어요. 오늘 그가 매우 피곤해 보이던데요. 혹시 왜 그런지 알아요?

B 음, 그는 잠을 잘 못 잤고 어젯밤에 이웃집의 개가 많이 짖었다고 했어요. 그리고 그는 먼지 알레르기가 있어요. 그래서 그의 눈이 특히 더 부은 거예요.

A 그게 전부에요? 그가 아파서 하루 쉬어야 할 것 같았어요.

숙어

26 save face

창피를 면하다

A Did you hear that Mr.Salgado was the one who leaked the confidential information about our new project?

B What? I can't believe it! How could he do that? I've always trusted him. So, what's going to happen to him?

A Well, he'll definitely have to leave the company. If he's lucky, they'll let him **save face** by quitting before he's fired.

A 살가도씨가 우리의 새 프로젝트에 대한 비밀 정보를 누설한 사람이었다는 것을 들었어요?

B 뭐라고요? 믿을 수 없어요! 그가 어떻게 그럴 수 있죠? 항상 그를 믿었어요. 그래서 그는 어떻게 되는 건가요?

A 음, 분명 퇴사해야 할 거예요. 운이 좋다면 해고되기 전에 그만두는 걸로 창피를 면하게 해 주겠죠.

숙어

27 be caught red-handed

현행범으로 잡히다

A Hey, what's going on over there? I could hear the police siren from inside my office.

B A guy **was caught red-handed** trying to steal a bicycle parked in front of the coffeehouse. Do you see that guy wearing the blue hoodie?

A Yeah, I see him. He must have been really desperate.

A 이봐요, 저기에서 무슨 일이 있나요? 제 사무실에서 경찰 사이렌 소리가 들렸어요.

B 커피숍 앞에 세워 둔 자전거를 훔치려다가 현행범으로 잡혔어요. 파란색 후드 옷을 입은 저 남자가 보여요?

A 네, 보여요. 그는 정말 될 대로 되라는 식이었을 거예요.

숙어
28 run out of
~이 다 바닥나다

A Can you get me some copy paper? I need to make copies of today's meeting materials, but there's no paper in the tray.

B Okay. Well, this is the last pack in the supply cabinet. We're going to **run out of** paper soon.

A Oh, you'd better call the supplier and order more so that we have to no trouble making copies later.

A 복사 용지를 가져다주겠어요? 오늘 회의 자료를 복사해야 하는데 상자 안에 종이가 없네요.

B 알았어요. 음, 이게 물품함에 있는 마지막 묶음이네요. 곧 종이가 다 바닥나겠어요.

A 아, 나중에 복사하는 일에 문제가 생기지 않게 공급업체에 전화해서 더 주문하는 게 좋겠군요.

숙어
29 get a kick out of
~ 에서 쾌감을 느끼다

A He **gets a kick out of** driving fast cars.

B I **get a kick out of** riding a roller coaster.

C Viewers will be thrilled by its state-of-the-art visual effects.

A 그는 빠른 자동차를 운전하며 쾌감을 느낀다.

B 나는 롤러코스터를 타면서 희열을 느낀다.

C 관객들은 최첨단 시각 효과에 전율할 것이다.

숙어
30 drop someone off
~를 내려 주다

A Hey, are you leaving the office now?

B Yup. It's sic o'clock and I'm going to the movies with my friend later tonight. What's up?

A Well, my parents suddenly asked me to visit them, and I know you live near their place. So if it's possible, can you **drop me off** on your way home?

A 저기, 지금 퇴근하는 건가요?

B 네. 6시잖아요. 그러고 이따가 밤에 친구와 영화 보러 갈 거예요. 무슨 일이에요?

A 음, 부모님이 갑자기 집으로 오라고 했는데, 당신이 저희 부모님 댁과 가까운 곳에 산다는 것을 알아요. 그래서 가능하면 집에 가는 길에 저를 내려 주겠어요?

숙어

31 veg out

느긋하게 쉬다

A Hey, I'm going out to see my boyfriend. Do you even know that today is Saturday?

B Yeah, I do. That's why I'm going to **veg out** all day. By the way, can you grab me some chips and a couple of cans of beer when you come home?

A Don't you get tired of spending your weekends on the couch? Do something productive for once.

A 이봐, 나는 남자 친구를 만나러 나갈 거야. 오늘이 토요일인 것은 알고 있니?

B 응, 알아. 그게 내가 하루 종일 느긋하게 쉬려는 이유지. 그런데 집에 올 때 과자와 맥주 몇 캔을 좀 가져다주겠니?

A 소파에서 주말마다 시간을 보내는 것은 안 지겹니? 이번에는 생산적인 일을 해.

숙어

32 twist someone's arm

강요하다, 조르다

A You saw Jerry last night, right? He invited me to join you guys, but I couldn't make it because of the overtime. How's he doing?

B He hasn't changed at all. We were at the bar, and I was about to leave around midnight, but he **twisted my arm** to have another round. I went back home around 2 a.m.

A He's such a drinker, isn't he? You must be really tired.

A 어젯밤에 제리를 봤지? 그가 함께 놀자고 나를 초대했는데 초과 근무 때문에 참석할 수 없었어. 그는 어떻게 지내니?

B 전혀 변하지 않았어. 우리는 술집에 있었는데, 자정쯤에 내가 막 집에 가려고 하니깐 그가 한잔 더 하자고 졸랐어. 거의 오전 2시에 집에 들어갔지.

A 그는 정말 술꾼이야, 그렇지 않니? 너는 정말 피곤하겠구나..

숙어

33 let someone off the hook

~의 잘못을 봐주다

A Ji-soo, you came in on time today. Did you do the homework, too?

B I couldn't find the time to do it, actually. I was busy working at my part-time job last night.

A Hmm... I see. Well, I'll **let you off the hook** this time, but you know you should study hard to get the score you want, right?

A 지수야, 오늘 시간을 어기지 않고 왔구나. 숙제도 했지?

B 사실 숙제할 시간이 없었어요. 어젯밤에 아르바이트 하느라 바빴어요.

A 음… 알겠어. 이번에 네 잘못을 봐줄게. 하지만 원하는 점수를 받으려면 열심히 공부해야 한다는 것을 알 거야, 그렇지?

숙어

34 nine times out of ten

십중팔구

A How is it working with Andy? He's such a funny guy, right?

B I guess. I don't really like people who joke too much. **Nine times out of ten** they turn out not to be very reliable coworkers.

A Oh, don't worry. He's a good person. He just can't stand a serious atmosphere.

A 앤디와 일하는 것은 어때요? 그는 정말 재미있는 사람이에요, 맞죠?

B 그런 것 같아요. 사실 농담을 많이 하는 사람을 좋아하지 않아요. 십중팔구 진짜 신뢰할 만한 동료가 아닌 것으로 드러나죠.

A 아, 걱정하지 마세요. 그는 좋은 사람이에요. 그저 진지한 분위기를 참지 못해요.

숙어

35 drop the ball

실수하다

A Now, what you've got to do is distribute these surveys to the nine local retailers downtown. Here's the list of the stores' names and addresses.

B Okay. When does this have to be done by?

A You must be back by 3 p.m. And you should know that if you **drop the ball** again like you did the other day, you'll be in hot water.

A 이제 당신이 할 일은 시내에 있는 9개의 지역 소매점에 이 설문지를 분배하는 것이에요. 여기 상점 이름과 주소 목록을 받으세요.

B 알았어요. 언제까지 끝내야 하나요?

A 오후 3시까지 돌아와야 해요. 그리고 일전에 했던 것과 같은 실수를 다시 한다면 곤경에 처한다는 것을 알아두세요.

숙어

36 throw shade

헐뜯다, 깎아내리다

A Hey, you told me that Mike is very close to our director, Mr. Kim, right?

B Yeah. I see them talking together everdy day. But why are you asking about that?

A Well, I had a chance to have a meeting with Mr. Kim yesterday and he was totally **throwing shade** about Mike's job performance. I thought it was really weird.

A 저, 마이크랑 김 이사님이랑 무척 가까운 사이라고 했었죠, 맞죠?

B 네, 서로 이야기하는 모습을 매일 보는 걸요. 그런데 그건 왜 물어보는 거죠?

A 음, 어제 김 이사님이랑 회의를 할 기회가 있었는데, 마이크의 업무 능력에 대해서 깎아내리는 말을 하더라고요. 정말 이상하다고 생각했거든요.

숙어

37 jump the line

새치기하다

A Don't try to **jump the line.** Wait till your turn comes.

B They didn't allow her to cut in line.

C We all queued up. No one jumped the queue.

A 새치기하려 하지 말고 네 순서를 기다려라.

B 그들은 그녀의 새치기를 허용하지 않았다.

C 우리는 모두 줄을 섰다. 누구도 새치기하지 않았다.

숙어

38 long-winded

장황한

A I heard that you had dinner with Ted last night. I didn't know you two were friends. How do you know each other?

B We went to college together. I actually hadn't seen him for a few years, so we had a lot of catching up to do.

A Oh, that's nice. But I bet you were out until late. Ted's stories are always **long-winded**.

A 어젯밤에 테드와 저녁 식사했다고 들었어. 너희 둘이 친구인 줄 몰랐네. 서로 어떻게 알게 된 거야?

B 같이 대학을 다녔어. 사실 몇 년간 못 봐서 밀린 이야기가 많았지.

A 아, 그랬구나. 그런데 너희는 늦게까지 있었을 것이 분명해. 테드의 이야기는 항상 장황하잖아.

숙어

39 live up to

~의 기대에 부응하다

A You only have one semester left in college, right? What do you want to do after graduation?

B Well, my parents want me to get a decent office job. I think they're kind of right, but on the other hand, that's not the life that I want to lead.

A Hey, listen. You shouldn't worry about trying to **live up to** others' expectations. The most important thing is finding out what you really want to do.

A 이제 대학도 한 학기 남았네, 그렇지? 졸업 후에는 뭘 하고 싶니?

B 음, 부모님은 제가 제대로 된 회사에 취업하길 원하세요. 맞는 말이기도 하지만, 그건 제가 살고 싶은 인생은 아닌 것 같아요.

A 얘, 잘 들어. 다른 사람의 기대에 부응할 걱정은 할 필요가 없어. 가장 중요한 것은 네가 정말 하고 싶은 것을 찾는 거야.

숙어
40 vouch for
~을 보장하다

A Hey, you told me that you've been to Chiang Mai before, right? I'm looking for a hotel there. Can you recommend any?

B Sure. Are you looking at the price comparison website now? Let me see.... Oh! Do you see this one? I stayed there during my last visit. The price is reasonable and the service is fabulous! I can **vouch for** it.

A Really? Okay, I'll see if I can book a room there. Thanks a lot!

A 저기, 전에 치앙마이 가본 적 있다고 했었죠, 그죠? 제가 거기 호텔을 알아보고 있거든요. 어디 추천 좀 해줄래요?

B 물론이죠. 지금 가격 비교 웹사이트 보는 중이에요? 제가 좀 볼게요…. 아! 여기 보이죠? 지난번에 갔을 때 여기 머물렀어요. 가격도 적당하고 서비스도 아주 좋아요! 제가 보장할 수 있어요.

A 그래요? 알겠어요. 그럼 그곳의 방을 예약할 수 있나 알아볼게요. 너무 고마워요!

숙어
41 keep me in the loop
~에게 상황을 계속 알려주다

A Did you hear that the last presenter of tomorrow's convention will be late due to a flight issue? He missed the connection in Oslo. He's figuring out the way to get a ticket for another flight.

B Really? That's Mr.Patel, right? He's the most important speaker tomorrow. I've go to see the manager and tell him what's going on. And you've got to **keep me in the loop**. Did you hear me?

A Yes, sir. I'll let you know as soon as he calls me back.Thanks a lot!

A 내일 컨벤션의 마지막 발표자가 비행기 문제로 인해서 늦을 거라는 소식 들으셨어요? 오슬로에서 연결 항공편을 놓쳐서 다른 비행기 티켓을 구할 방법을 찾고 있대요.

B 뭐라고? 그 사람 파텔 씨 맞지? 내일 가장 중요한 발표자라고. 나는 부장님 만나서 현재 상황 보고할테니까, 내게 상황을 계속 알려줘요. 알겠죠?

A 알겠습니다. 연락 들어오는 대로 알려드리겠습니다.

숙어 42 on hold

통화 중인 사람을 기다리게 하는

A Hey, who are you talking to?

B Oh, I'm actually calling about getting a refund on the shirt that I bought a few days ago. But these guys have kept me **on hold** for almost five numbers.

A Really? Maybe you should hang up and call them again.

A 누구랑 통화중이에요?

B 아, 실은 며칠 전에 산 셔츠를 환불 받는 것 때문에 전화를 걸었거든요. 그런데 이 사람들이 거의 5분 넘게 절 기다리게 하고 있네요.

A 그래요? 혹시 모르니 전화를 끊고 다시 걸어 봐요.

숙어 43 tying up loose ends

마무리를 짓다

A Many readers are waiting for the next novel in your fantasy series. Can you give them a little hint about what they can expect?

B Well, the book will start by **tying up loose ends** from the previous story, but then it will send the characters on a new adventure.

A Sounds great! I'm looking forward to it. Thank you for the interview.

A 많은 독자들이 작가님의 판타지 시리즈의 다음 작품을 기다리고 있는데요. 독자들이 기대할 수 있도록 약간 힌트라도 줄 수 있으신가요?

B 음, 이번 책은 이전 이야기의 미진했던 부분을 잘 매듭짓는 것으로 시작할 거예요. 하지만 그러고 나서는 등장인물들이 새로운 모험을 하게 될 겁니다.

A 좋은 소식이네요! 저도 무척 기대가 됩니다. 인터뷰 해주셔서 고맙습니다.

숙어 44 just this once

이번 한 번만

A Did you finish editing the article I sent you a couple of days ago? It was supposed to be done today.

B Oh, Mr.Klein. I've been busy working on the exclusive interview. Is it okay if I get the article back to you tomorrow?

A You know I don't like it when work is turned in late. But okay. I'll wait **just this once**.

A 이틀 전에 제가 보낸 기사를 다 편집했어요? 오늘 마무리하기로 했는데요.

B 오, 클라인 씨. 독점 인터뷰 일로 계속 바빴어요. 내일 기사를 보내 드려도 될까요?

A 알다시피 저는 업무 결과물이 늦게 제출되는 것을 좋아하지 않아요. 하지만 알았어요. 이번 한 번만 기다릴게요.

숙어
45 in my book
이번 한 번만

A Unless our team starts working harder, we're not going to reach our sales quota for this quarter. What do you think we should do?

B Well, **in my book**, the best way to get results is by rewarding success, not punishing failure. Why don't we offer some kind of prize for the person with the most sales?

A Hmm... that could work. I'll think of some ideas for prizes.

A 좀 더 열심히 일하지 않으면 우리 팀은 이번 분기의 판매 할당량을 도달하지 못할 거예요. 우리가 어떻게 해야 할까요?

B 음, 제 생각에, 좋은 결과를 얻을 수 있는 가장 좋은 방법은 잘한 부분에 대해선 보상하고 못한 부분에 대해서는 나무라지 않는 것 같습니다. 영업 실적이 가장 좋은 사람에게 상을 주는 것이 어떨까요?

A 음… 괜찮을 것 같네요. 상으로 뭘 줄지 생각해보도록 할게요.

숙어
46 get past
~의 곁을 지나가다

A Mike, how's it going? You look like you're having a long day.

B Yeah, you're right. I'm exhausted due to the new research project. Can I **get past** you to the coffee machine?

A Go ahead. So, is it the one that the CEO talked about at the meeting?

A 마이크, 어떻게 지냈어요? 긴 하루를 보내는 것 같네요.

B 네, 맞아요. 새 연구 프로젝트 때문에 진이 다 빠졌어요. 커피 자판기로 가려는데 지나가도 될까요?

A 그러세요. 그래서 그 프로젝트가 회의에서 사장님이 말씀하셨던 건가요?

숙어
47 curl up
웅크리다

A Ta-da! Here we are! You've never been to a get cafe before, right?

B Right! Wow, pets are literally everywhere! Look at this cat! She's **curled up** into a little ball. She's so cute!

A Oh my God! So cute! I have to pet her!

A 짜잔! 우리 도착했어! 전에 애완동물 카페에 와본 적 없지, 그렇지?

B 네! 와, 애완동물들이 말 그대로 사방에 있네요! 이 고양이 좀 봐요! 작은 공처럼 웅크리고 있어요. 너무 귀여워요!

A 어머나! 너무 귀엽다! 만져봐야겠어!

숙어

48 pay peanuts

박봉을 주다

A So, you're looking for a place in the city center, right? How may rooms do you want it to have?

B Well, I have a wife and three daughters, so I need at least three bedrooms. But I'm **paid peanuts**, so I'm not sure if I'll be able to find a place within my budget.

A Well, why don't you tell me your price range, and I'll let you know if it's reasonable for a place like that in this area?

A 그래서 도심에 있는 집을 찾고 있어요? 방이 몇 개 있는 집을 원하나요?

B 음, 아내와 세 딸이 있어요. 그래서 적어도 침실 3개가 필요해요. 그런데 제가 박봉을 받아서 제 예산 내에 집을 찾을 수 있을지 모르겠네요.

A 음, 가격 범위를 저에게 말해 주고 제가 이 지역에서 그런 집을 구하기 위한 적당한 금액인지 알려 주는 건 어떨까요?

숙어

49 second nature

몸에 배이는 것

A I heard that you've been working as a receptionist. How's it going?

B Not bad. I like my coworkers, and my hours are pretty good. But I have found it hard to be cheerful and polite all of the time.

A Yes, I can see how that would be tiring. But I bet that it'll become **second nature** after a while.

A 접수원으로 일해왔다면서요, 어떠세요?

B 그럭저럭 나쁘지 않아요. 동료들이 좋고 근무 시간도 꽤 만족해요. 하지만 항상 밝고 공손한 모습을 유지하는 게 어렵게 느껴져요.

A 그렇죠, 얼마나 힘들지 알 것 같아요. 하지만 좀 지나면 몸에 배일 것이라 확신해요.

숙어

50 on thin ice

위험한 상태로

A Oh my God! I'm so glad I made it here on time.

B Seems like you were in quite a hurry. What's wrong with being a few minutes late?

A Well, I've been **on thin ice** with my supervisor ever since I made some calculation mistakes on my last project. I don't want to give her even the smallest reason to chew me out.

A 맙소사! 제시간에 여기 도착해서 정말 기뻐.

B 너 엄청 급하게 온 것 같구나. 몇 분 정도 늦는 게 어때서 그래?

A 그게, 지난번에 진행한 프로젝트에서 내가 계산을 좀 잘못한 이후로 줄곧 부장님과 관계가 위태위태해. 부장님한테 혼날 여지가 있는 사소한 꼬투리라도 잡히고 싶지 않다고.

숙어

51 shell out for

거금을 쓰다

A Hi, I'm thinking of moving this year. Since you helped me to find my current house two years ago, you know what it looks like. This time. I want to move to a nicer place.

B I got it. You know, I can show you many nice places that you'd be satisfied with. The question is, are you ready to **shell out for** a new place?

A Yes, I am. I've been saving up. When can we look at those properties?

A 안녕하세요, 저는 올해 이사할 생각이에요. 당신은 2년 전에 현재의 우리 집을 찾는 걸 도와줘서 이 집이 어떤지 알잖아요. 이번에는 더 좋은 집으로 이사 가고 싶어요.

B 알았어요. 알다시피 당신이 만족할 만한 좋은 집들을 많이 보여 줄 수 있어요. 문제는, 새 집에 거금을 쓸 준비가 되었나요?

A 네, 그럼요. 돈을 모았어요. 그 집들을 언제 볼 수 있을까요?

숙어

52 blow the whistle on

~을 밀고하다

A I saw a notice on the bulletin board saying that Mr.Miller will be relocated to the west branch. That seems totally out of the blue to me. Do you have any clue what's going on?

B Well, it became clear that he was the one involved in the bribery case last year. Somebody **blew the whistle on** him.

A Wow! What shocking news! I never would've thought he would do something shady like that.

A 게시판에서 봤는데 밀러 씨가 서부지점으로 이동될 거라고 하던데. 나한테는 너무 갑작스러운데 말이지. 무슨 일인지 알아?

B 음, 작년에 뇌물수수 사건에 연루된 것이 판명이 났나 봐요. 누군가 그를 밀고했대요.

A 아! 충격적인 소식이네! 그 사람이 그런수상한 일을 할 거라고는 생각해본 적 없는데.

숙어

53 bail out

손을 떼다

A Hey, wasn't Mike involved in the software development project? I just bumped into that project team in a meeting room, but there was no Mike. What happened?

B Oh, he decided to **bail out**. I think he couldn't take the pressure.

A Really? But it was his best chance to prove himself and get promoted. I think he should've stuck with it.

A 이봐, 마이크가 소프트웨어 개발 프로젝트에 관여하지 않았었나? 방금 회의실에서 그 팀이랑 마주쳤는데 마이크가 없던걸. 무슨 일 있었니?

B 아, 그 프로젝트에서 빠지기로 했어. 압박감을 견딜 수가 없었던 것 같아.

A 그래? 그래도 능력을 증명해서 승진할 수 있는 최고의 기회였잖아. 계속 버텼어야 했다고 생각해.

숙어

54 boil down to

~로 귀결되다

A So, did you read the new sales strategy proposal I e'mailed you a couple of days ago?

B Oh, I did. But I found it a little unclear. I think you should clarify what it is that you really wan to emphasize.

A Well, it all **boils down to** one point: we need to expand our sales area. I guess I'd better edit it to make that ore obvious.

A 이봐, 마이크가 소프트웨어 개발 프로젝트에 관여하지 않았었나? 방금 회의실에서 그 팀이랑 마주쳤는데 마이크가 없던걸. 무슨 일 있었니?

B 아, 그 프로젝트에서 빠지기로 했어. 압박감을 견딜 수가 없었던 것 같아.

A 그래? 그래도 능력을 증명해서 승진할 수 있는 최고의 기회였잖아. 계속 버텼어야 했다고 생각해.

숙어

55 on the double

빨리

A Did you finish packing all of your bags? We need to leave for the airport in 20 minutes.

B Not yet, mom. I'm still choosing which clothes to bring.

A Okay. But pease finish up **on the double**. Otherwise, we might be late for the flight.

A 짐 모두 다 쌌니? 20분 뒤에 공항으로 출발할 거야.

B 아직요, 엄마. 무슨 옷을 가져가야 할지 아직 고르고 있어요.

A 알겠다. 하지만 빨리 끝내렴. 안 그러면 비행기 놓칠 수도 있으니까.

숙어

56 Kodak moment

진귀한 풍경

A Hey, did you see the basketball game last night? It was neck and neck until the very end.

B Really? I missed it because I was out with some friends. Tell me more about it.

A Man, it was full of amazing 3-pointers and slam dunks. And when the game finished, the players all hugged the coach. It was a real **Kodak moment**. You should've watched it!

A 이봐, 어젯밤에 농구 경기 봤나? 마지막까지 접전에 접전이었어.

B 그래? 나는 친구들이랑 밖에 있느라고 경기를 놓쳤거든. 자세히 좀 말해 봐.

A 이런, 멋진 3점 슛이랑 덩크 슛이 많이 터진 경기였어. 경기 끝나자마자 선수들 전부가 감독이랑 포옹을 했지. 정말 멋진 광경이었어. 너도 봤어야 했는데!

숙어

57 give someone the cold shoulder

쌀쌀맞게 대하다

A Wow, this party looks like it's going to be really fun! Let's have a blast, okay?

B Definitely! Oh! There's Mike over there. What are you going to do? Please don't **give him the cold shoulder** again. It's really awkward for the rest of us.

A I know. But when I see him face to face, I feel so angry about the way he treated me when we were dating. I can't promise anything.

A 와, 이 파티 정말 재미있겠는걸. 신나게 즐겨봅시다, 좋지?

B 물론이지! 어! 저기 마이크다. 어떻게 할 거니? 제발 다시는 마이크한테 쌀쌀맞게 대하지 마. 네가 그러면 우리 나머지 다 어색해지잖아.

A 나도 알아. 그런데 마이크 얼굴을 직접 보면 말이지. 우리가 사귈 때 날 대했던 태도 때문에 너무 화가 치밀거든. 아무것도 약속할 수는 없어.

숙어

58 cry buckets

펑펑 울다

A Hey, you told me that you saw the new Janet Carmen movie, right? How was it?

B Oh! You should watch it! I went with my mom and both of us **cried buckets**.

A Really? It sounds like it's worth checking out.

A 저, 자넷 카르멘이 나오는 신작 영화 봤다고 얘기했었잖아요? 어땠어요?

B 네! 꼭 봐야 해요! 전 엄마랑 가서 봤는데 둘 다 펑펑 울고 나왔어요.

A 그래요? 볼 만한 영화인 것 같네요.

숙어

59 in the dark about

~에 대해 아무것도 모르는

A Do you know when they're going to hire a new employee to replace Stan?

B I don't even know if they're going to do that. I'm totally **in the dark about** management's plans.

A Yes, they do tend to keep things behind closed doors. I hope they make some kind of announcement soon.

A 스탠을 대체할 새 직원을 언제 채용할지 알아요?

B 채용할지조차 모르겠어요. 경영진의 계획에 대해 완전히 아무것도 몰라요.

A 네, 그들은 계획을 비공개로 유지하는 경향이 있죠. 곧 발표 같은 거라도 하면 좋겠네요.

숙어

60 put something else on the back burner

뒤로 제쳐 두다

A Hey, what are you doing this weekend? My friends and I are going camping on Saturday. Do you want to join us?

B Oh, I've got to get ready for a big English test in two weeks. I have to **put everything else on the back burner** for now. Sorry. But count me in next time!

A Okay. Next time! And good luck with the test.

A 이번 주말에 뭐해요? 친구들이랑 토요일에 캠핑 가기로 했는데 같이 갈래요?

B 아, 2주 뒤에 있는 중요한 영어 시험 준비를 해야 해요. 지금은 다른 건 다 뒤로 제쳐 두어야 해요. 미안해요. 다음 번엔 끼워주세요!

A 그래요. 다음엔 꼭 같이 가요! 그리고 시험 잘 봐요.

숙어

61 take the edge off

완화시키다

A Hey, you're still here in the office? It's 9 p.m. Did you eat dinner yet?

B Not yet. I'm going to eat after I finish editing this design.

A You're so hardworking. Here, you can have my banana. It'll help you **take the edge off** your hunger.

A 이봐, 아직도 사무실에 있는 거야? 밤 9시야. 자네 저녁은 먹은 거야?

B 아직이요. 이 디자인 편집을 끝낸 다음에 먹을 거예요.

A 정말 열심히 일하는군. 자, 여기 내 바나나 먹어. 허기가 좀 달래질 거야.

숙어

62 the apple of my eye.

가장 사랑하는 사람(것), 눈에 넣어도 안 아픈 존재

A Lately, I've been tasking care of my grandson. He is so lovely.

B That sounds so sweet. But isn't he bothering you a little?

A Yes, he is. But I love the way he is. He is **the apple of my eye**.

A 나 요즘 우리 손자 돌보고 있어. 그 녀석 너무 사랑스럽다니까.

B 정말 사랑스럽다. 그런데 걔가 널 좀 괴롭히지 않니?

A 그렇지. 그래도 나는 그 모습 그대로 사랑해. 그 아이는 나에게 무엇보다도 소중한 존재야.

숙어

63 move up in the world

승진하다, 출세하다

A Do you remember Mike, the one who left our company about two years ago?

B Yeah, he worked in Business Development, right?

A That's right. I have a friend who's been in touch with him. She told me that he started his own business after he quit here. Now he has more than 500 employees under him. He's **moved up in the world**, don't you think?

A 2년 전쯤에 퇴사한 마이크라고 기억하세요?

B 아, 사업 개발팀에서 일했었죠?

A 네. 그 사람이랑 연락하고 지내는 친구가 한 명 있는데, 여기 그만둔 다음에 사업을 시작했대요. 지금은 부하 직원이 오백 명 이상 된다고 하네요. 출세했네요, 그렇지 않아요?

숙어

64 come to the same thing

결국엔 마찬가지가 되다

A I'll be busy all weekend downloading my favorite songs.

B Really? When you get down to it, downloading pirated music for frese online and stealing CD from a store really **come to the same thing**.

A Come on, it's not THAT bad.

A 이번 주말 내내 좋아하는 노래들 전부 다운로드 받느라 바쁠 거야.

B 그래? 불법 음악을 공짜로 다운로드 받는 거나 매장에서 CD를 훔치는 거나 결국 같은 거라고.

A 이봐, 그게 그렇게 나쁜 건 아니라고.

숙어

65 brace yourself

마음의 준비를 하다

A I don't know why I feel so lazy these days. For some reason, I don't want to do anything but just veg out at home.

B Maybe it's because of the weather. But anyway, you should **brace yourself**. Midterms are coming.

A I know I'll get myself together before then.

A 요즘 왜 이렇게 게으름 피우는지 모르겠어. 왠지 아무 것도 하기 싫고 집에서 뒹굴 거리기만 하고 싶네.

B 아마도 날씨 탓 아닐까? 하지만 어찌 됐든 마음의 준비는 해야지. 중간고사가 다가오고 있잖아.

A 알아. 그전까진 정신 차려야지.

숙어

66 out of line

무례한, 도를 넘는

A You've worked at that school for about 3 months, right? How's work?

B Well, there's a co-teacher that's always **out of line**, but we had a little talk and now things are better.

A That's good to hear.

A 그 학교에서 세 달 정도 일했죠? 일하는 건 좀 어때요?

B 음, 협력수업을 함께 진행하는 선생님이 항상 무례한 말을 하곤 하는데, 이야기를 좀 나누고 나서 지금은 괜찮아졌어요.

A 잘됐네요.

숙어

67 drop someone a line

연락하다

A Hey, Mike told me that you're moving to Prague for a new job. Is that true?

B Yes, I'll be relocating soon. I'll probably be there for about 3 years.

A Really? **Drop me a line** once you get settled in. So, when are you living?

A 마이크한테 들었는데 새 일자리 때문에 프라하로 이사 간다는 게 사실이에요?

B 네, 곧 이사할 거예요. 3년 정도 있을 것 같아요.

A 정말요? 자리 잡으면 연락해 주세요. 그러면 언제 떠나세요?

숙어

68 a slap in the face

모욕, 황당한 일

A I'm really looking forward to Mike's birthday party this Saturday. Did you respond to his text message invitation yet?

B What? I didn't get one! And when I bumped into him on the street this morning, he didn't say anything about a party. Not a word. What **a slap in the face**!

A Don't freak out just yet. I'm sure there's been a misunderstanding. Maybe he thinks he already told you about it.

A 이번 주 토요일 마이크 생일 파티가 너무 기대된다. 초대 문자 메시지에 답장했어?

B 뭐라고? 나는 못 받았는데. 게다가 오늘 아침에 마주쳤을 때도 파티 한다는 말을 하지도 않던데. 진짜 한마디도 안 했어. 너무 황당하다!

A 흥분을 가라앉혀. 오해가 있었던 걸 거야. 네게 이미 말했다고 생각하고 있을 수도 있지.

숙어

69 hold water

이치에 맞다

A You're finally here! Everybody's in the meeting room waiting for you to show up. What happened?

B Uh... I left home on time, but there was traffic. Sorry.

A What? I know you only live 2 blocks from here. That excuse doesn't **hold water**. Whatever. Just go in there and start the presentation. But you and I are going to have a talk afterwards, you hear?

A 이제 오네요! 회의실에서 모두들 기다리고 계세요. 왜 늦은 거예요?

B 어… 제때 나왔는데, 차가 좀 막혀서요. 죄송합니다.

A 뭐라고요? 여기에서 두 블록 거리에 사는 거 알고 있다고요. 그런 변명은 어불성설이잖아요. 뭐 됐고요. 빨리 들어가서 발표 시작하세요. 이따가 끝나고 얘기해요, 알겠죠?

숙어

70 ball and chain

속박하는 것, 걸림돌

A I wish I hadn't decided to settle down and have a family in my early twenties.

B Oh, really? What makes you say that?

A I feel like my decision became a **ball and chain**, that's preventing me from pursuing my dream to travel the world.

A 20대 초반에 결혼하고 정착해서 가족을 이루기로 결정하지 않았으면 좋았을 텐데.

B 뭐라고? 무슨 소리야?

A 그 결정이 이제 보니까 세계를 여행하고 싶은 내 꿈을 가로막는 걸림돌인 것 같아.

숙어

71 throw me off balance

헷갈리게 하다

A Jenny sent me a message last night that really **threw me off balance**. Could you look at it?

B Hmm... weird. She's the one who dumped you, right? And now she's saying she misses you? I think she's playing games.

A I don't know. She doesn't seem like that kind of person. Maybe she really did change her mind.

A 어젯밤에 제니가 헷갈리게 하는 메시지를 보냈는데, 좀 볼래?

B 음… 이상하군. 그녀가 널 찬 거잖아. 그런데 이제 와서 네가 그립다고? 내 생각엔 장난치는 것 같은데.

A 모르겠어. 그럴 사람은 아닌데 말이지. 정말 마음이 바뀐 걸 수도 있지 않을까?

숙어

72 have one's nose in the air

오만하게 굴다

A Who's that guy you were talking to? Seems like I've never seen him before.

B Hi, honey. He works in the accounting department at my office. I don't like him much-he always **has his nose in the air**. I'm surprised he acknowledged me just now, actually.

A Well, I hope we don't bump into him around here again, then. So, what do you want to eat for dinner?

A 대화 나눈 사람 누구야? 전에 본 적 없는 사람 같은데.

B 왔구나. 회계 부서에 일하는 사람인데, 사실 맘에 안드는 사람이야. 항상 거만하게 굴거든. 사실, 방금 나를 아는 척해서 깜짝 놀랐지 뭐야.

A 음, 이 근처에서 다시는 안 마주쳤으면 좋겠다. 그럼, 저녁 뭐 먹을래?

숙어
73 by the numbers

원칙에 따라서

A Mr. Green, can you give me some tips to prevent bid rigging for this project? I don't want to have any problems with the law.

B Well, if just do our work **by the numbers**, I don't think there'll be anything to worry about.

A The situation isn't that simple. Look at this e-mail. There's something going on between somebody in management and a couple of companies.

A 그린 씨, 입찰 담합을 방지할 수 있는 조언 좀 해 주실 수 있나요? 법적으로 골치 아프기 싫거든요.

B 음, 그건 원칙에 따라 하기만 하면, 아무 걱정할 필요가 없을 것 같은데.

A 상황이 그렇게 단순하지 않아서 말이죠. 이 이메일 좀 보세요. 경영진 중의 누군가와 두 회사 사이에 뭔가 있는 것 같아요.

숙어
74 off the charts

대단한, 엄청난

A Hey, what are you looking at? Oh, my... Is that your cell phone bill? Why is it so high?

B I have no idea. You know I'm not the type of person who's always on the phone or anything.

A Of course. You've got to call your service provider and find out what's going on. $600 is just **off the charts.**

A 이봐, 뭐 보고 있는 거야? 세상에… 그거 휴대폰 요금 명세서야? 왜 이리 많이 나왔어?

B 모르겠어. 내가 항상 휴대폰 붙들고 사는 사람도 아니라는 거 잘 알잖아.

A 그렇지. 통신사에 전화해서 어떻게 된 건지 알아봐. 600 달러라니 말도 안 돼.

숙어
75 on a side note

여담이지만

A Thanks for the presentation, Mike. It sounds like the project is on the right track.

B Thank you, ma'am. I'll keep you posted as we proceed.

A Great. And **on a side note**, the graphics in your presentation were very impressive. Maybe you could give the rest of the team some tips on that.

A 발표하느라 수고했어요, 마이크. 프로젝트가 수월하게 진행되고 있는 것 같군요.

B 감사합니다. 진행 상황은 수시로 보고 드리겠습니다.

A 좋아요. 이건 여담인데, 발표에 사용된 그래픽 아주 좋았어요. 나머지 팀 사람들에게도 조언을 좀 주면 좋을 것 같아요.

숙어
76 go blank
머리가 하얘지다

A Hey, how was the job interview? Did you do what I told you?

B Yes, I did everything you said. But it was no use. As soon as the interviewer asked a question, I **went blank**. I'm sure I won't get a callback.

A Dang! Well, I'm out of ideas. Is there such a thing as a professional interview consultant? If so, I think you should see one.

A 면접 어땠어? 내가 말해준 대로 했니?

B 응, 얘기해준 대로 다 했어. 그런데 하나도 소용없던데. 면접관이 질문을 던지자마자, 머리가 하얘지더라. 회신은 못 받을 것 같아.

A 이런! 그러면 방법이 없는데. 전문 면접 자문가라는 것도 있나? 있다면 네가 만나봐야겠네.

숙어
77 stuffed to the gills
잔뜩 먹어 배가 부른

A All right, time for dessert! Let's see, do you want cake of pie?

B Are you kidding me? I'm **stuffed to the gills** after that meal! How can you possibly eat anything else?

A I always have room for dessert! I think I'll get the apple pie with ice cream.

A 자, 디저트 먹자! 어디 보자, 케이크와 파이 중 뭐 먹을래?

B 무슨 소리야? 나는 식사하고 나니까 배가 너무 부른걸! 그렇게 먹고 들어갈 자리가 있어?

A 항상 디저트 공간은 남아 있지! 그럼 나는 아이스크림 얹은 사과파이를 먹을까 해.

숙어
78 make one's jaw drop
입이 쩍 벌어지게 하다

A So, you went to Jim's cocktail party las Saturday, didn't you? How was it?

B It was like I was in another world. All of the guests showed up in designer clothes and shoes. And their cars **made my jaw drop.**

A That's because most of them are from rich families. Jim met them at his private high school.

A 지난 토요일 짐네 칵테일파티에 갔지? 어땠어?

B 완전 다른 세상 같더라고. 손님들이 전부 명품 옷이랑 구두로 치장하고 말이지. 몰고 온 차들을 보니까 입이 쩍 벌어지더라.

A 그건 그들 대부분이 부잣집 사람들이라 그럴 거야. 짐이 사립 고등학교 시절에 만난 사람들이야.

숙어

79 feel left out

소외감을 느끼다

A About the night out we're planning.... Shouldn't we invite Jim? He's also a member of our team.

B He is, but we hardly know him. It's only been a week since he was hired.

A Then going out drinking is the perfect way to get to know him! Besides, do you want him to **feel left out?**

A 우리가 계획 중인 회식 말인데요…. 짐을 초대해야 하지 않을까요? 그 사람도 우리 팀 일원이잖아요.

B 그렇기는 한데, 그 사람에 대해 잘 모르잖아요. 입사한 지 일주일밖에 안 됐으니까요.

A 그러니까 같이 한잔하면서 알아갈 수 있는 좋은 기회가 아닐까요? 그리고 짐이 소외감 느끼게 하고 싶어요?

숙어

80 sour grapes

오기

A Wow, what a nice suit! It must have cost you a couple thousand dollars.

B It did, actually. Does it really look all right, though? I just saw Tony, and he said it makes me look fat.

A Oh, I'm sure that was just **sour grapes**. He always pouts when other people have nice things.

A 와아, 정장 멋지다! 한 2,000달러는 들었겠는데?

B 사실 맞아. 근데 정말 괜찮아 보여? 방금 토니를 만났는데 뚱뚱해 보인다고 하더라고.

A 아, 그건 그냥 오기를 부리는 거야. 그는 남들이 비싼 물건 사면 꼭 뿌루퉁해져.

숙어

81 get out of hand

감당할 수 없게 되다

A Are you going to bring Jim to the party tonight?

B Of course. He's so fun to have around. He knows how to make people laugh.

A I guess. Just don't let him drink too much. Things always **get out of hand** when he gets drunk.

A 오늘 밤 파티에 짐 데리고 갈 거야?

B 물론이죠. 같이 있으면 얼마나 재미있는데요. 사람들을 웃겨주거든요.

A 뭐, 그렇긴 하지. 하지만 술은 너무 많이 마시지 않게 챙겨. 취하면 감당이 안 될 테니.

숙어
82 young at heart
마음은 청춘인

A Look! Mr.Cruise is in line for a roller coaster with the sales representatives!

B Oh, he loves roller coasters. He may be in his sixties, but he's **young at heart**.

A I had no idea! He always seems so serious around the office.

A 저기 봐요! 크루즈 씨가 영업 담당자들과 롤러코스터 타는 줄에 서 있네요.

B 아, 크루즈 씨는 롤러코스터 좋아해요. 60대지만 마음은 청춘이죠.

A 전혀 몰랐어요! 사무실에서는 항상 진지한 모습이니까요.

숙어
83 rain or shine
무슨 일이 있더라도

A Did you see that there's been an earthquake in the area we're flying to tomorrow?

B I did. But it wasn't a very serious one. Anyway, we're going there **rain or shine**.

A Are you sure? An earthquake isn't just a little bit of bad weather!

A 우리가 내일 비행기 타고 가는 지역에 지진이 났다는 것을 봤나요?

B 네. 그런데 그렇게 심각한 것은 아니던데요. 어쨌든, 무슨 일이 있어도 우리는 가는 겁니다.

A 정말이에요? 지진은 날씨가 좀 안 좋은 정도의 하찮은 문제가 아니에요.

숙어
84 give or take
~의 차이는 있어도 대략

A I heard you're going to be relocated to the Shanghai branch. When are you leaving?

B I'll probably fly out on the last day of October, **give or take** a couple of days.

A Really? Why didn't you let me know earlier? We should go out for dinner sometime soon.

A 상해 지사로 부서 이동한다고 들었어요. 언제 떠나나요?

B 며칠 차이는 있을지 몰라도 아마 10월 말일쯤에 떠날 것 같아요.

A 그래요? 왜 일찍 알려주지 않았어요? 조만간 저녁식사나 하러 가죠.

숙어

85 pick up after

~의 뒤치다꺼리를 하다

A I can't keep sharing an apartment with you if you're going to be so messy.

B Hey, you know I'm used to my mom **picking up after** me. I just need time to adjust.

A You've had 3 months! That's enough time to learn not to leave your clothes on the floor.

A 이렇게 엉망으로 지내면 이 아파트에서 같이 살 수가 없어.

B 이봐, 알다시피 난 어머니가 청소해주시는 것에 익숙한 사람이라서 적응할 시간이 필요해.

A 벌써 세 달이나 살았다고. 옷을 바닥에 두지 말아야 하는 것 정도는 충분히 알 때 아니야?

숙어

86 have a heart of gold

상냥한 마음을 가지다

A Excuse me. Weren't you on the corner of 5th and Elm a couple of days ago?

B Let me think.... Yeah! I was on the way to the mall to get some clothes. Why?

A I saw you helping an old lady on the street and was really touched. You **have a heart of gold.**

A 실례합니다. 이틀 전에 5번가랑 엘름가 모퉁이에 있지 않았나요?

B 글쎄요…. 아! 네, 옷 사려고 몰에 가는 길이었어요. 왜 그러시죠?

A 당신이 길에서 할머니를 도와 드리는 모습을 보고 정말 감동했어요. 따뜻한 마음의 소유자세요.

숙어

87 someone's true colors

~의 본심, 진짜 모습

A Why didn't you break up with Lloyd? I thought things were going well.

B I saw **his true colors** when we took a trip together last weekend. He has a bad temper.

A Oh, I'm sorry to hear that. Well, better to find that out sooner rather than later.

A 로이드랑 왜 헤어진 거야? 잘되고 있는 줄 알았는데.

B 지난 주말에 같이 여행 갔을 때 그 사람의 진짜 모습을 보고 말았지. 성격이 별로더라고.

A 아, 안됐네. 그래도 빨리 알게 됐으니 다행이네.

숙어

88 go down the wrong pipe

사레들리다

A You're eating so fast. Why don't you slow down?

B I haven't eaten anything today. I'm starving.

A Okay. But beg careful. If any food **goes down the wrong pipe**, you'll be in big trouble.

A 너무 빨리 먹는 것 같은데 좀 천천히 먹는 게 어때요?

B 오늘 아무것도 안 먹어서 배가 너무 고프거든요.

A 그래요. 하지만 조심해요. 음식 먹다가도 사레라도 들리면 곤란해질 테니까요.

숙어

89 be up to something

뭔가 꿍꿍이가 있다

A Have you seen Tim and Chris lately? I think they'**re up to something**.

B What makes you say that?

A They're always standing by themselves and whispering. I wonder what they're planning.

A 최근 팀이랑 크리스 본 적 있어요? 그 둘 요즘 뭔가 꾸미고 있는 것 같아요.

B 왜 그렇게 이야기하는 거죠?

A 그 사람들 항상 같이 꼭 붙어서 소곤거리든요. 무슨 일을 꾸미는 건지 궁금해요

숙어

90 sitting pretty

여유롭게 살다

A I just dropped by Jenny's bakery and she said it's not going well.

B Oh, really? Well, since she's from a rich family, she's **sitting pretty** anyway.

A Then she's running a business just for fun?! Wow, I'm jealous of her.

A 방금 제니의 제과점에 들렀다 왔는데 가게가 잘 안된다고 하네요.

B 아, 그래요? 음, 부잣집 딸이니 그래도 여유롭게 살겠죠.

A 그럼 제니는 사업을 그냥 재미로 한다는 건가요? 와, 정말 부럽네요.

숙어

91 pull some strings

연줄을 대다

A Oh no, the tickets for the Julia Arnold concert are all sold out! How disappointing.

B Well, I know a guy who could **pull some strings** and get you a ticket. I could give him a call.

A You'd do that for me? That would be amazing!

A 이런, 줄리아 아놀드의 콘서트 티켓이 매진됐네요! 실망스럽네요.

B 음, 내가 힘을 좀 써서 표를 구해줄 수 있는 사람을 한 명 알아요. 통화 한번 해볼 수 있어요.

A 그래 줄 수 있어요? 그러면 너무 좋겠네요.

숙어

92 bundle up

옷을 따뜻하게 입다

A Leo, haven't you looked outside yet today? It's snowing!

B Oh, really? Then just one sweater won't be enough. I'd better **bundle up**!

A Definitely! I'll go look for your winter hat and gloves.

A 리오야, 오늘 바깥을 아직 안 봤니? 지금 눈이 오네.

B 어, 그래요? 그럼 스웨터 하나만 입으면 안 되겠네요. 따뜻하게 입는 것이 좋겠네요.

A 당연하지! 내가 겨울 모자와 장갑을 찾아볼게.

숙어

93 go bananas

흥분하다

A How was the concert? I heard that Mike Sheldon made a surprise appearance.

B Yeah, and it was great! The whole crowd **went bananas** when he came onstage.

A I'll bet! He's one of the most popular musicians around these days.

A 콘서트 어땠나요? 마이크 셸던이 깜짝 등장했다던데요.

B 네, 너무 좋았어요! 마이클이 무대에 나타났을 때 관객 모두가 흥분했어요.

A 당연히 그랬겠죠! 요즘 가장 인기 있는 음악가 중 한명이니까요.

숙어
94 make any difference
영향을 주다, 상황을 변화시키다

A I've been having trouble with dandruff in my hair recently, What should I do?

B You should use a special shampoo for your scalp. That should take care of the problem.

A Really? Some articles say that won't **make any difference**. I don't know what to believe.

A 최근 비듬 때문에 고생하고 있어요. 어떻게 해야 할까요?

B 두피에 맞는 특별한 샴푸를 사용해야 해요. 그러면 해결될 겁니다.

A 그래요? 몇몇 기사에는 특수 샴푸를 써도 별 차이가 없을 거라고 하던데요. 뭘 믿어야 할지 모르겠네요.

숙어
95 hot air
거짓말, 허풍

A Mark told me you're thinking about changing jobs.

B Yes. Pam offered me a position in the business she's planning to set up soon. The salary would be incredibly good.

A Oh, haven't you heard about her? You can't believe what she says. She's full of **hot air**.

A 마크는 당신이 이직을 생각 중이라고 말해주던데요.

B 네. 팸이 곧 시작할 업체에 자리를 하나 제안했는데요. 연봉이 너무 좋아요.

A 아, 그녀에 대해 못 들었어요? 그녀가 말하는 걸 믿으면 안 돼요. 하는 이야기들이 다 허풍이래요.

숙어
96 hat in hand
저자세로

A This is too much work to finish by the end of this week. I need more time.

B Okay. Why don't you ask Mr.Givens to extend the deadline?

A I told him I could handle this project. I'd hate to go back now **hat in hand**, and admit I was wrong.

A 이 일은 이번 주말까지 끝내기엔 양이 너무 많아요. 시간이 더 필요해요.

B 알겠습니다. 그럼 기븐스 씨에게 마감일을 연장해달라고 하는 게 어때요?

A 이 프로젝트 잘 처리할 거라고 이미 말씀 드렸어요. 그런데 이제야 다시 가서 내 판단이 틀렸다고 굽실거리긴 싫어요.

숙어
97 on the mend
회복 중인

A How was your weekend, Min-Jung? You said you caught the flu on Thursday, didn't you?

B Yes, so I took some medicine and stayed home to rest. I feel like I'm **on the mend** now.

A Good. You'll need to be in good shape with the exam coming up.

A 주말 어떻게 보냈어요, 민정 씨? 목요일에 독감에 걸렸다고 했지요?

B 네, 그래서 약 먹고 집에서 쉬었어요. 이제 좀 회복되는 것 같아요.

A 잘됐군요. 다가오는 시험에 대비해 컨디션을 잘 유지해야 해요.

숙어
98 without batting an eye
눈 하나 깜짝 안 하고

A You know what? James is much braver than people say.

B Really? What makes you say that?

A At lunch yesterday, a huge bug landed on the table, and he smashed it **without batting an eye.**

A 있잖아, 제임스가 사람들이 말하는 것보다 더 용감하다더라.

B 그래? 어쨌길래 그렇게 말하는 거야?

A 어제 점심 식사 중에 큰 벌레가 테이블에 앉았는데, 눈 하나 깜짝 안 하고 때려잡던데.

※ eye 대신 eyelid(눈꺼풀) 또는 eyelash(속눈썹)를 쓰기도 하며, 'without blinking an eye.' 'without turning(moving) a hair'로 표현하기도 합니다.

숙어
99 out of left field
뜬금없는

A Do you think that space aliens exist?

B What? That question was totally **out of left field.** I mean, we've been talking about our careers.

A Oh, sorry! I can expalin-the TV behind you is playing and ad for a movie with aliens.

A 외계인이 존재한다고 믿어?

B 뭐라고? 그 질문은 완전히 뜬금없잖아. 아니, 지금까지 직장생활 이야기하고 있었잖아.

A 아, 미안! 그게 말이지, 너 뒤에 있는 TV에서 외계인 나오는 영화를 광고하고 있거든.

숙어

100 in the family way

임신 중인

A Ms.Jennings isn't in today. Do you know what happened to her?

B Didn't you hear? She's **in the family way.** She's gone on maternity leave.

A Oh, how nice for her. But... who should I talk to about the Erikson account?

A 제닝스씨가 오늘 자리에 없네요. 어쩐 일인지 혹시 아세요?

B 아직 못 들었어요? 제닝스씨 임신했잖아요. 출산 휴가 갔어요.

A 아, 잘된 일이긴 합니다만…. 그럼 에릭슨사 건은 누구와 상의해야 하죠?

숙어

101 stretch the truth

진실을 왜곡하다

A Hey, Jim! Why did you tell Nina that you nursed me trough cancer?

B Ah, sorry about that. I wanted to impress her by showing her that I'm a very considerate man.

A OK, but you **stretched the truth** too far this time. I mean, I just had a bad flu!

A 저기, 짐! 왜 니나한테 내 암투병 기간 동안 네가 돌봤다고 말한 거야?

B 아, 미안해. 내가 사려 깊은 사람이라는 걸 보여줘서 그녀에게 좋은 인상을 주고 싶었어.

A 알겠는데, 이번엔 사실을 너무 왜곡한 것 같다. 난 좀 심한 독감에 걸린 것뿐이었잖아.

숙어

102 pressed for time

시간에 쫓기는

A John, could you proofread this manuscript by 1 p.m. and send it to the publishing team?

B Hmm... It's 11:30 now. I don't' think I can finish it in an hour and a half.

A I know you'll be **pressed for time**, but it really ahs to be done by then. Just do your best.

A 존, 1시까지 이 원고 교정 보고 출판부로 보내주겠어요?

B 음… 지금이 11시 30분인데요. 한 시간 반 안에 못 끝낼 것 같아요.

A 시간 압박을 느낄 것은 알겠지만 그때까지 반드시 마쳐야 해요. 최선을 다해주세요.

숙어

103 tall order

무리한 요구

A This break room is really gross. We need to get employees to start cleaning up after themselves.

B That's going to be a **tall order**. People don't like to change their habits.

A That's true, but we still have to try. Just look at this sink!

A 이 휴게실 정말 지저분하네요. 직원들에게 이용 후 뒷정리를 하라고 해야겠네요.

B 그건 무리한 요구일 겁니다. 사람은 대개 자기 습관을 바꾸는 걸 좋아하지 않잖아요.

A 그렇긴 해도 얘기는 해봐야죠. 이 싱크대를 좀 봐요!

숙어

104 all wound up

초조한

A Do you know why Ciara is pacing up and down the corridor?

B I think she's **all wound up** because she's next to get a performance review.

A Oh, dear. Boy, am I glad I'm a freelancer.

A 시아라 씨가 왜 복도를 왔다 갔다 하는지 알아요?

B 아마 직원 업무 평가를 받을 다음 차례라서 초조할 겁니다.

A 오, 저런. 정말 나는 프리랜서라 다행이네요.

숙어

105 get under one's skin

거슬리게 하다

A Hey, you look irritated, Arianna.

B Yeah. I just can't stand Mario's voice, so everything he says **gets under my skin.**

A Oh, I guess you haven't heard his brother's voice.

A 아리아나. 짜증이 나 보이네.

B 응, 마리오의 목소리를 듣는 게 견딜 수가 없어서 그가 말하는 모든 것이 거슬려.

A 아, 그의 형 목소리는 아직 못 들어본 것 같구나.

숙어

106 mess around

빈둥거리다

A Mom, could you give me ten bucks?

B Stop **messing around** and finish your chores!

A I already finished doing the dishes and mowing the lawn!

A 엄마, 10달러만 주실래요?

B 그만 빈둥거리고 빨리 집안일 끝내!

A 이미 설거지랑 잔디 깎는 일을 다 끝냈다구요!

숙어

107 keep tabs on

~을 예의주시하다

A You bought another new suit? It seems like you're spending a lot of money these days.

B Well, why not? I have a good job, and I want to enjoy life.

A OK, I understand. I just hope you're **keeping tabs on** your balance.

A 새 정장 또 산 거니? 요즘 돈 많이 쓰는 것 같다.

B 좀 그래도 되지 않을까요? 좋은 직장도 다니고 있고 인생을 즐겨야죠.

A 알겠다. 나는 단지 네가 은행 잔액도 잘 봤으면 한다.

숙어

108 bring the house down

청중을 열광하게 하다

A You went to the Russell Beevers show, right? How was it? He's my favorite stand-up comedian.

B It was great. He's so funny. He told a joke about dating that **brought the house down.**

A Ah, I wish I'd gone! You're really lucky.

A 러셀 비버스 공연에 다녀왔죠? 어땠어요? 제가 제일 좋아하는 스탠드업 코미디언이거든요.

B 최고였어요. 그는 너무 웃겨요. 연애에 관한 농담을 했는데 사람들이 모두 열광했어요.

A 아, 저도 갈걸 그랬어요. 정말 부럽네요.

숙어

109 flat out

딱 잘라 말해서, 한마디로

A Hey, did you talk to Mike about the presentation he gave yesterday?

B Yeah, I did. He asked me about it this morning and I told him **flat out** that it was terrible.

A Oh, good. Someone needed to let him know.

A 어제 발표에 대해서 마이크에게 이야기했나요?

B 네, 했어요. 오늘 아침에 물어보길래 한마디로 형편없었다고 말했어요.

A 아, 잘하셨어요. 누군가는 알려줘야 할 필요가 있었어요.

숙어

110 Just let sleeping dogs lie

긁어 부스럼 만들지 말고 잠자코 있다

A You're late again, Mike. That's the third time this week!

B Well, this time I got stuck in traffic. Should I go and explain the situation to Mr. Givens?

A I don't think he noticed that you weren't here. You should probably **just let sleeping dogs lie**.

A 마이크, 자네 또 늦었어. 이번 주만 세 번째야!

B 아, 이번에는 차가 막혀서 늦었어. 기븐스 씨에게 직접 가서 말씀 드려야 하나?

A 자네가 없는 걸 눈치채지는 못하신 것 같던데. 괜히 긁어 부스럼 만들지 말고.

숙어

111 out of place

어울리지 않는, 어색한

A You went to Jim's birthday party, didn't you? How was it? Did you have fun?

B Um... actually I felt a little **out of place**. Most of the guests were big sports fans.

A Oh, did they talk about sports the whole time? That must have been boring for you.

A 짐 생일파티에 다녀왔죠? 어땠어요? 재미있었나요?

B 음… 사실 좀 어색했어요. 온 사람들 대부분이 스포츠 열성 팬들이라서요.

A 아, 그럼 파티 내내 스포츠 이야기만 했다는 거예요? 정말 지루했겠네요.

숙어

112 stick out

눈에 띄다

A The staff photos from last month's shoot are ready. Want to see? Here's the group photo.

B Sure! Let's take a look.... Oh my, I really **stick out** because of that red shirt, don't I?

A Yes, but you look nice! Don't worry about it.

A 지난달에 찍었던 직원 사진들이 나왔어요. 볼래요? 여기 단체 사진이 있어요.

B 그러죠! 봅시다…. 이런, 빨간 셔츠 때문에 내가 너무 튀어 보이지 않아요?

A 그렇긴 한데 멋져요! 걱정하지 마세요.

숙어

113 have a way with

~에 솜씨가 있다

A Wow, look at my puppy! She's not barking at all, even though she's never met Mike before.

B I think he **has a way with** pets. I've seen him with cats before, and they love him, too.

A Unbelievable! I've got to go ask him what the secret is.

A 어머, 우리 강아지 좀 봐요! 마이크를 처음 보는데도 전혀 짖지 않네요.

B 마이크는 애완동물을 다루는 솜씨가 있는 것 같아요. 전에 고양이들이랑 같이 있는 걸 봤는데 녀석들이 그를 좋아하더라고요.

A 대단하네요! 비밀이 뭔지 물어봐야겠어요.

숙어

114 drag your feet

꾸물거리다

A Jaden, turn off the TV now. It's time to study for tomorrow's quiz.

B Mom, can't I watch a little longer? This show will be over in 10 minutes.

A Don't **drag your feet!** Go into your room and open your books right now!

A 제이든, 이제 TV 꺼야지. 내일 시험 공부할 시간이네.

B 엄마, 조금만 더 보면 안 돼요? 이 프로그램 10분 안에 끝나요.

A 꾸물거리지 마! 당장 방에 들어가서 책 펴!

숙어
115 waste one's breath

입만 아프다

A I've been telling Ashanti to buy a warmer coat.

B You're **wasting your breath.** She doesn't take advice from anybody.

A I'm just worried she'll end up catching a cold.

A 아샨티에게 더 따뜻한 코트를 사라고 줄곧 얘기했거든요.

B 그런 말 해 봤자 소용없어요. 그녀는 누구의 조언도 듣지 않아요.

A 나중에 결국 감기 걸리게 될까 걱정돼서요.

숙어
116 get some shut-eye

한숨 자다

A Jane, you're going home already? It's only 8 p.m.!

B I was up until 3 a.m. last night because my cat got sick, I have got to **get some shut-eye.**

A Oh, really? Well, that's understandable. Have a good rest!

A 제인, 벌써 집에 가는거예요? 8시밖에 안 됐는데요.

B 어제 고양이가 아파서 새벽 3시까지 깨어 있었는데요. 그래서 눈 좀 붙이려고요.

A 아, 그래요? 그럴 수 있겠네요. 잘 쉬어요!

숙어
117 crow's feet

눈가의 잔주름

A Can I help you, sir?

B Well, I'm looking for something for my mother. She's worried about her **crow's feet** these days.

A OK. We have several products for wrinkles. Please follow me.

A 무엇을 도와드릴까요?

B 음, 어머니를 위한 제품을 찾고 있는데요. 요즘 눈가의 잔주름 때문에 걱정이시라서요.

A 알겠습니다. 주름을 위한 제품들이 몇 개 있어요. 저를 따라오세요.

숙어

118 without a hitch

별 탈 없이, 순탄하게

A The event wrapped up **without a hitch.**

B The task was done on oiled wheels.

C The wedding ceremony went off without a hiccup.

A 그 행사는 별 탈 없이 순조롭게 마무리됐다.

B 일은 순탄하게 마무리됐다.

C 그 결혼식은 별 탈 없이 진행됐다.

숙어

119 know one's way around

~에 대해 훤히 알다

A I'm thinking of going on a day trip to Jeonju. Have you ever been there?

B No, but talk to Min-Ho. He **knows his way around** the city because he's from there.

A Really? I'll go ask him about it right now.

A 전주에 당일치기로 여행이나 가려 하는데 가본 적 있어요?

B 아니요, 민호한테 물어보세요. 전주 출신이라 그 도시에 대해 잘 알아요.

A 그래요? 바로 가서 물어봐야겠네요.

숙어

120 rub it in

아픈 곳을 들추다

A I still can't believe that I beat you by 100 points. I thought you said you were good at darts!

B Don't **rub it in**! I was just playing for fun.

A All right, I'll let it go. So, want to get some nachos?

A 100점 차이로 내가 이기다니 아직도 믿을 수가 없네. 난 네가 다트 잘하는 줄 알았는데.

B 그만 좀 들먹여라! 난 그냥 재미로 했던 거야.

A 알겠어, 넘어갈게. 나초 좀 먹을래?

숙어
121 worth a shot
해볼 만한 가치가 있다

A Anna, have you thought about getting acupuncture for your back pain?

B Um, I don't really believe in alternative medicine.

A Don't you think it's **worth a shot**, though? It's not like anything else has worked.

A 애나, 허리 통증에 침을 맞아볼 생각은 안 해봤나요?

B 글쎄요. 대체 의학은 믿지 않아서 말이죠.

A 그래도 시도는 해볼 만하지 않아요? 다른 방법들이 효과가 있진 않았잖아요.

숙어
122 the gravy train
돈방석

A I heard Charlie's getting married.

B Yes, he's going to marry Denise, whose family owns one of the largest entertainment companies in Asia.

A Wow! He ended up on **the gravy train** after being single for a decade!

A 찰리가 결혼한다는 소식을 들었어요.

B 네. 드니스랑 결혼하는데 그녀의 가족이 아시아에서 가장 큰 연애기획사 중 하나를 소유하고 있죠.

A 와! 10년간 싱글로 지내다가 결국 돈방석에 앉게 됐군요.

숙어
123 play dumb
알면서 모르는 척하다 (시치미 떼다)

A Hey, the twenty-dollar bill I left on the table is gone. Did you take it?

B No-I didn't even see it. I've just been playing games on my phone.

A Don't **play dumb!** You were alone in the room! Give me my money!

A 이봐, 내가 테이블에 올려놓은 20달러짜리 지폐가 없어졌는데 네가 가져갔어?

B 아니, 있었는지도 몰랐어. 휴대전화기로 게임만 하고 있었어.

A 모르는 척하지 마! 이 방에 너만 있었잖아. 내 돈 내놔!

숙어

124 strike a chord

심금을 울리다

A I can't believe that Calvin Fleming might win the election. I think his ideas are terrible.

B So do I, but it seems like they really **strike a chord** with some voters.

A Why can't people see that he'd be an awful mayor? It's so frustrating!

A 켈빈 클레밍이 선거에서 이길지 모른다니 믿을 수가 없네요. 그의 공약은 형편없는 것 같거든요.

B 나도 그렇게 생각합니다만, 바로 그 공약이 특정 유권자들의 마음을 움직이는 것 같군요.

A 그가 시장이 되면 형편없을 거라는 걸 사람들을 왜 모르는 걸까요? 정말 좌절되네요!

숙어

125 over the counter

처방전 없이 살 수 있는

A Excuse me. I'm looking for a certain medication. I wrote its name on this piece of paper.

B Let me see.... Oh, I'm sorry, but that's not available **over the counter**.

A That means I need a prescription, right? OK. I see.

A 실례합니다. 어떤 약을 사려고 하는데요. 종이에 이름을 써 왔습니다.

B 어디 봅시다…. 아, 죄송하지만 이건 일반 의약품이 아니네요.

A 그럼 처방전이 필요하다는 말씀이죠? 알겠습니다.

숙어

126 come to one's senses

정신을 차리다

A Hey, did you hear that Mike failed to get promoted again? I'm sorry for him.

B I'm not! He should **come to his senses** and realize that he'll never succeed with that poor attitude.

A I suppose. It still seems unfair given how long he's worked here, though.

A 저기, 마이크가 이번 승진에서 또 제외됐다고 하네요 참 안됐어요.

B 안됐기는요. 그 사람 이제 정신 차리고 그런 불량한 태도로는 성공할 수 없다는 걸 깨달아야 해요.

A 그렇긴 하죠. 그래도 그가 일한 연차를 따져보면 불공평한 것 같긴 해요.

숙어

127 dead on one's feet

녹초가 되다

A Oh, you're back from the conference. How was your first visit to South Africa?

B It wasn't bad, but because of the tight schedule and jet lag. I'm **dead on my feet** now.

A I know how you feel. I felt the same way when I went to that conference a couple of years ago.

A 아, 회의에서 돌아왔군요. 남아공은 첫 방문이었는데 어땠어요?

B 나쁘진 않았는데, 빡빡한 스케줄이랑 시차증 때문에 아주 힘드네요.

A 어떤 상태일지 알아요. 저도 2년 전에 그 회의 다녀 왔을 때 그랬었거든요.

숙어

128 call someone on the carpet

~를 불러 야단치다

A You look so frustrated. What's up?

B Well, my boss **called me on the carpet** this morning because I forgot to attach an important document to an e-mail I sent to him.

A Wasn't that the big project you told me about?

A 매우 언짢으신 것 같아요. 무슨 일이에요?

B 음, 이메일에 첨부해야 할 중요한 문서를 빼먹어서 아침에 상관에게 혼났어요.

A 전에 내게 말했던 대규모 프로젝트 아니었어요?

숙어

129 have pins and needles

(몸이) 저리다

A I **have pins and needles** in my legs when I'm on my knees.

B He has been on pins and needles all day, waiting for her call.

C She felt like she was on pins and needles.

A 나는 무릎을 꿇고 있으면 다리가 저리다.

B 그는 그녀의 전화를 기다리며 안절부절못했다.

C 그녀는 바늘방석에 앉아있는 기분이었다.

숙어

130 flake out

약속을 깨다

A Hey, seems like you need help with that project you're working on. Why don't you ask Fabio for some help?

B Honestly, I don't want to. I've worked with him a few times, and he always ended up **flaking out.**

A Oh? So that's why you stopped asking me for help.

A 진행하고 있는 프로젝트에 도움이 필요한 것 같은데 파비오에게 요청해보는 것 어때요?

B 솔직히, 그러고 싶지 않네요. 몇 번 같이 일해 봤는데 그는 항상 결국 약속을 깨더라고요.

A 그래요? 그래서 더 이상은 저한테 도움을 청하지 않는 거였군요.

숙어

131 horse of a different color

전혀 별개의 이야기

A Hey, do you want to play basketball this weekend? My team needs someone to fill in for Valerio.

B Well, I love ball games. but basketball is a **horse of a different color.**

A Oh, then can you recommend someone who can possibly join us?

A 이번 주말에 농구 경기 할래? 우리 팀에 발레리오를 대신할 사람이 필요해서 말이야.

B 구기 종목을 정말 좋아하지만, 농구를 별개의 이야기더라고.

A 아, 그럼 가능하면 같이할 수 있는 사람 좀 추천해줄래?.

숙어

132 extend the deadline

마감일을 연장하다

A You're at the office late. Do you have a lot to do?

B I have to finish writing this article. It's due tomorrow, but I'm not even close to done. I may be up all night.

A Maybe the editor in chief can **extend the deadline.** Is it a big story?

A 늦게까지 사무실에 있네요. 할 일이 많아요?

B 이 기사 작성을 끝내야 해서요. 내일까지 마감인데 끝내려면 아직 멀었어요. 아마 밤을 새워야 할 것 같아요.

A 편집장님이 어쩌면 마감일을 연장해 줄 수도 있어요. 비중이 큰 기사예요?

숙어
133 brick in his hat
술에 취한

A What's up with Jimmy over there? He's so loud.
B Don't mind him. He's just got a **brick in his hat**.
A Really? But it's only 2 P.M.

A 저기 지미가 왜 저러죠? 너무 시끄럽네요.
B 신경 쓰지 말아요. 그냥 술 취한 거니까요.
A 정말요? 지금 오후 2시밖에 안 됐는데요.

숙어
134 bring me to book
~를 문책하다

A Hey, you look stressed out.
B I'm sure the boss is going to **bring me to book** for raising my voice at him,
A Just hope you don't get fired.

A 스트레스를 받고 있는 것 같네요.
B 언성을 높인 것 때문에 상사가 날 문책할 것이 틀림 없으니까요.
A 해고만 안 당하길 바랄 수밖에요.

숙어
135 nerves of steel
강심장, 담력

A I was scared to death, but Jagger faced the thugs bravely.
B Wow, he really has **nerves of steel**.
A Yeah, I was quite impressed. He didn't back down at all.

A 나는 정말이지 무서웠는데, 재거가 용감하게 깡패들을 상대하더군요.
B 와, 대단한 강심장이네요.
A 네, 꽤 인상적이었어요. 전혀 물러서지 않더라고요.

숙어
136 be wet behind the ears
애송이의, 풋내기의

A He **is still wet behind the ears**, and he has a lot to learn about life.
B He attempted to dupe the young man who was still green behind the ears.
A She is still not dry behind the ears.

A 그는 아직 머리의 피도 안 마른 친구여서 인생이 뭔지를 많이 배워야 한다.
B 그는 아직 경험이 많지 않아 미숙 한 그 젊은이를 속이려 들었다.
A 그녀는 아직 머리의 피도 안 마른 애송이일 뿐이다.

숙어

137 down in the mouth

풀이 죽은

A Did you hear the news that Sean Paul's dog died in a car accident?

B Oh! That's why he's so **down in the mouth**. I'm sorry to hear that.

A Let's take him to his favorite Jamaican restaurant.

A 션 폴 씨의 강아지가 교통사고로 죽었다는 소식 들었어요?

B 아! 그래서 그렇게 풀이 죽어 있군요. 유감이네요.

A 그분이 좋아하는 자메이카 식당에 데려가죠.

숙어

138 give it a rest

그쯤 해 둬요.

A Everything in China is much cheaper. You can drink as much beer as you want for 10 dollars. And th food is....

B **Give it a rest** about China already! You've been talking about it nonstop for an hour!

A Oh, have I? I'm sorry. But you know what? There really is a lot to like about it.

A 중국은 모든 게 훨씬 싸요. 10달러면 맥주도 맘껏 마실 수 있어요. 그리고 음식도….

B 이제 중국 이야기 좀 그만해요! 한 시간 내내 쉬지 않고 계속 그 이야기만 하고 있잖아요!

A 아, 그랬나요? 미안해요. 그런데 말이죠, 중국은 맘에 드는 것이 너무 많아요.

숙어

139 a dry run

예행연습

A Your band is performing at Webster Hall tomorrow, right?

B Yes. We actually just did **a dry run** of the performance to make sure there won't be any technical problems.

A That's good. I'm really looking forward to tomorrow. really is a lot to like about it.

A 당신의 밴드가 내일 웹스터 홀에서 공연하죠?

B 네. 사실 기술적인 문제가 있는지 확인하기 위해 방금 공연 예행연습을 했어요.

A 좋네요. 내일이 정말 기대됩니다.

숙어

140 fit to drop

기진맥진한

A You participated in the city marathon, didn't you? How was it? Did you finish the race?

B Yeah, but I was **fit to drop** after only the first mile of the race.

A That's why you should always try to keep fit.

A 당시 마라톤대회에 참가했죠? 어땠어요? 완주했나요?

B 네, 하지만 경기 첫 한 마일만 뛰고 나서 완전히 지쳐버렸어요.

A 그러니까 항상 건강을 유지해야 하는 거라고요.

숙어

141 settle old scores

오래된 원한을 갚다

A Hey, did you hear that Cassius Carter's going to enter the competition this year?

B No. That'll be awesome!

A Yeah, it's time to **settle old scores** with George Farmer, the current champion.

A 케시어스 카터가 올해 대회에 출전할 거라는 소식 들었어요?

B 아니요. 그러면 대단하겠는데요!

A 그렇죠. 현 챔피언인 조지 파머에게 복수할 때가 오는군요.

숙어

142 get the upper hand

우위를 점하다

A How was the soccer match last night?

B It was neck and neck in the first half, but our team **got the upper hand** when the top scorer of the opposing team was shown a red card.

A That's good! When is the next match?

A 어젯밤 축구 경기 어땠어요?

B 전반전에는 막상막하였는데 상대팀의 득점왕이 퇴장을 당하고 나서는 우리 팀이 주도권을 쥐었어요.

A 잘됐군요! 다음 경기는 언제죠?

숙어

143 back to earth

현실로 돌아오다

A Look at Sonny and Thelma! They look so happy.

B Yeah, they jus got married a couple of months ago, right?

A That's right. Now they think marriage is utterly blissful as newlyweds, but they'll come **back to earth** soon enough.

A 소니와 델마 좀 봐요. 아주 행복해 보이네요.

B 네, 두 달 전에 결혼했죠?

A 맞아요. 지금은 신혼이라 너무 행복하겠지만 머지않아 현실로 돌아올 겁니다.

숙어

144 lost for words

할 말을 잃은

A How are you doing?

B I just found out my coworkers helped pay for my medical bills. I'm **lost for words.**

A Wow, I'm glad it all worked out.

A 어떻게 지내세요?

B 동료들이 내 병원비 내는 걸 도와주었다는 걸 방금 알게 되었어요. 말로 형용할 수 없네요.

A 와, 잘되었다니 기쁘네요.

숙어

145 chase one's tail

헛수고하다

A How's the project you're working on going so far?

B Well, I'm trying not th **chase my tail** this time.

A You should take a break from it. Who knows? You might have a breakthrough.

A 지금 하고 있는 프로젝트는 어떻게 되어가고 있어요?

B 음, 이번에는 헛수고하지 않으려고요.

A 좀 쉬었다 해요. 혹시 알아요? 돌파구를 찾을지.

숙어

146 on the fritz

제대로 작동하지 않는

A Hey, where are you headed?

B The washing machine at my place is **on the fritz**, so I'm on my way to the laundromat.

A Okay, I'll see you around.

A 어디 가는 길이야?

B 집 세탁기가 고장 나서 빨래방에 가는 길이야.

A 그래, 또 보자.

숙어

147 have itchy fingers

몸이 근질근질하다

A Summer vacation is only a week away. Do you have any plans?

B Well, I'm thinking of going to Mongolia with my family. What about you?

A Um... I might take it easy, but I'm sure as soon as I begin to relax, I'll **have itchy fingers** to do something-anything-productive.

A 여름휴가가 이제 1주일밖에 안 남았네요. 계획 있어요?

B 음, 가족들이랑 몽골에 가려고 해요. 당신은요?

A 음… 아마 쉴 것 같긴 한데, 쉬려고 하면 분명 뭐라도 생산적인 걸 하려고 몸이 근질근질할 거예요.

숙어

148 in the heat of the moment

홧김에

A How was the party last weekend? I heard that Max and Todd got into a fight.

B Yeah, they were playing a drinking game and got too excited **in the heat of the moment.**

A Well, I hope they've made up. They've been friends for such a long time.

A 지난 주말에 파티 어땠어요? 맥스랑 토드가 싸웠다던데요.

B 네, 술 게임을 하다가 홧김에 너무 흥분했죠.

A 음, 둘이 화해했길 바라요. 오랫동안 친구였잖아요.

숙어

149 at the buzzer

종료 직전에

A Hey, did you see the game? I missed it because I fell asleep early.

B Oh! You missed a good one. Leonard scored a goal right **at the buzzer!**

A He did it again? He deserves an award.

A 그 경기 봤어? 일찍 잠들어서 못 봤거든.

B 아, 재미있는 경기를 놓쳤구나. 레너드가 종료 직전에 골을 넣었어.

A 또 넣었다고? 상 받을 만하다.

숙어

150 read the room

분위기를 파악하다

A I can't believe nobody laughed at that joke I made in the meeting.

B You've got to **read the room.** Nobody was in the mood for a joke right then.

A Well, I was hoping th joke would lighten the mood. I guess I was wrong.

A 회의에서 내가 한 농담에 아무도 웃어주지 않았다니 믿을 수가 없어요.

B 분위기를 파악했어야죠. 바로 그때는 아무도 농담을 받아줄 기분이 아니었으니까요.

A 음, 농담이 분위기를 밝게 만들어 주길 바랐는데요. 내 생각이 틀렸던 것 같네요.

숙어

151 a trial run

예행연습

A Did you see the notice that there will be **a trial run** of the product launch tomorrow?

B Yeah, I did. I think it's a good idea. The plan for the event is quite complicated.

A I agree. Hopefully we'll be able to catch all of the potential problems tomorrow.

A 내일 제품 출시 행사의 예행연습이 있을 거라는 공지 봤어요?

B 네, 봤어요. 좋은 생각 인 것 같아요. 행사 계획이 꽤 복잡하더라고요.

A 맞아요. 내일 발생할 수도 있을 문제들을 모두 포착할 수 있으면 좋겠네요.

숙어

152 sick at heart

상심한

A What's wrong with Michelle? She seems sad.

B Yes, she's been **sick at heart** since her dog died in a car accident.

A Ah... I'm sorry to hear that. We should do something nice for her.

A 미셸 무슨 일 있어요? 슬퍼 보이네요.

B 네, 애완견이 차 사고로 죽은 이후로 계속 상심해 있어요.

A 아… 정말 안됐네요. 그녀를 위해 뭔가 좋은 일을 해야겠어요.

숙어 153 jump the gun 섣불리 행동하다

A I heard from Damon that P&J agreed to the merger. Should I write a press release?

B No-let's not **jump the gun**. We should wait until the contract is signed.

A Oh, is there a chance that the deal will fall through? I thought it was pretty certain.

A 데이먼한테 들었는데 P&J 사가 합병에 동의했다고 합니다. 보도자료를 쓸까요?

B 아니요, 섣불리 행동하지 맙시다. 계약서에 서명할 때까지 기다려야 해요.

A 아, 설마 거래가 실현되지 못할 가능성이 있을까요? 나는 꽤 확실하다고 생각했는데요.

숙어 154 talk around the problem 말을 빙빙 돌리다

A I can't believe Dave is still leaving the office lights on. I asked him not to do that.

B Well, did you ask him clearly? Sometimes you **talk around the problem.**

A Hmm... I mean, I said that it wastes a lot of electricity. Couldn't he understand my point?

A 데이브가 여전히 사무실 조명을 켜두다니 믿을 수가 없어요. 그렇게 하지 말라고 했거든요.

B 음, 분명하게 이야기했어요? 가끔씩 당신은 문제점을 에둘러 말하잖아요.

A 음… 그게, 전력 낭비라고 말하긴 했어요. 내 요점을 알아듣지 않았을까요?

숙어 155 put your heart into 열과 성을 다하다

A So, what are you going to do after you graduate from college?

B Well, I got a job offer from a tech company, but I dont's know if I should take it.

A Why not? I think you should accept it and **put your heart into** whatever work they assign to you.

A 대학을 졸업하면 뭘 할 거죠?

B 음, 기술 회사에서 취업 제의를 받긴 했는데, 받아들일지는 잘 모르겠어요.

A 왜 안 해요? 나는 당신이 그 제의를 수락하고, 주어지는 어떤 일이든지 열과 성을 다해야 한다고 생각해요.

숙어

156 getting gray hair from

~ 때문에 골치가 아프다

A I hear you moved into a new apartment. How is it?

B Terrible! I'm **getting gray hair from** my upstairs neighbor stomping around at night. I barely slept las night.

A How awful! Have you tried asking them to be quieter?

A 새 아파트에 입주했다면서요. 어때요?

B 끔찍해요! 밤에 쿵쿵거리는 위층의 이웃 때문에 골치가 아파요. 어젯밤에도 간신히 잠들었어요.

A 정말 끔찍하네요! 좀 더 조용히 해달라고 요청해 봤어요?

숙어

157 in the blink of an eye

순식간에, 금방

A Mike, I just sent you an e-mail. Can you pease proofread the report in the attached file?

B Sure. I'll have it back to you **in the blink of an eye.**

A Well, don't look over it too fast! I don't want you to miss any mistakes.

A 마이크, 방금 이메일 보냈어요. 첨부 파일 안에 있는 보고서를 교정해 주시겠어요?

B 물론이죠. 바로 해서 보내드리죠.

A 음, 그래도 너무 급히 검토하진 말아요! 어떤 실수도 놓치지 않았으면 해요.?

숙어

158 hit hard

큰 타격을 입은

A Did you hear that the government has decided to offer financial support to small businesses?

B Yeah. It's a good thing. They've been **hit hard** by the social distancing measures.

A True. Some small businesses in my neighborhood have gone out of business already.

A 정부가 소규모 사업체에 재정 지원을 하기로 결정했다는 소식 들었어?

B 응. 다행이야. 그들이 사회적 거리두기 조치로 큰 타격을 입었잖아.

A 맞아. 우리 동네에 있는 몇몇 소규모 사업체들은 이미 폐업했어.

숙어

159 sound someone out

누구를 슬쩍 떠보다

A Did Ms. Stone talk to you about the proposal I gave her?

B No-why? Do you want me to **sound her out** about it?

A Yes, if possible. I'm really excited about the idea, and I want to know what she thinks of it.

A 혹시 스톤씨가 내가 그녀에게 준 제안서에 관해 이야기하던가요?

B 아니요. 왜요? 내가 그것에 관해 그녀를 슬쩍 떠볼까요?

A 가능하면요. 나는 이 방안이 참 좋은 것 같아서 그녀가 어떻게 생각하는지 알고 싶거든요.

숙어

160 have seen one's day

전성기가 지났다

A Did you go to the party that Gloria hosted the other night?

B Yeah, but it was just... not bad. She doesn't have the status that she used to.

A That's why I didn't go. I know she's still one of the richest women in the city, but I think she'**s seen her day.**

A 저번 밤에 글로리아가 열었던 파티에 갔나요?

B 네, 그런데 뭐… 그냥 그랬어요. 그녀는 예전 같지 않더라고요.

A 그래서 안 간 겁니다. 여전히 우리 시에서 가장 부자이긴 해도, 그녀의 전성기는 이미 끝났죠.

숙어

161 hit a sour note

찬물을 끼얹다

A What did you do to Lily last night? She looked really upset when she left.

B I was just trying to make her smile, but I guess I **hit a sour note** when I told a joke about a family trip.

A Oh yeah, her father passed away just a few weeks ago. Did you forget?

A 어젯밤에 릴리한테 무슨 짓을 한 거죠? 나갈 때 매우 언짢아 보이던데요.

B 웃겨 주려고 그랬는데요, 가족 여행에 대해 농담을 했을 때 분위기를 망친 것 같아요.

A 이런, 그녀의 아버지가 몇 주 전에 돌아가셨잖아요. 잊었어요?

숙어

162 blow off some steam

기분을 풀다

A Well, it's time to call it a day. What are you doing after work?

B Nothing, just going home to relax. How about you?

A Mr. Sanders gave me a lot of stress today, so I've got to **blow off some steam.** Want to get a drink at the bar before you go home?

A 음, 이제 마칠 시간이네요. 퇴근하면 뭐 할 거예요?

B 딱히 없어요. 집에 가서 쉬려고요. 당신은요?

A 샌더스 씨가 오늘 스트레스를 많이 줘서 기분을 좀 풀려고요. 집에 들어가기 전에 술집에서 한잔할래요?

숙어

163 play hard to get

밀당하다, 비싸게 굴다

A You told me that you asked Janice out, didn't you? What did she say?

B She said she'd think about it, but that was three days ago. I think she might not be interested in me.

A Or maybe she's **playing hard to get.** Why don't you ask her one more time?

A 재니스에게 데이트 신청했다고 했죠? 그녀가 뭐라고 하던가요?

B 생각해 보겠다고 했는데, 그게 3일 전이었어요. 아마 나에게 관심이 없는 것 같아요.

A 아니면 밀당하는 걸 수도 있고요. 한 번 더 신청해보는 게 어때요?

숙어

164 across from the restaurant

식당 맞은편에서

A All right, everyone. Here we are. We're going to have lunch at this Italian restaurant before continuing on our tour.

B Where will the bus driver pick us up after lunch?

A He'll pick you up in about an hour **across from the restaurant.** Not in front of it! Make sure you cross the street.

A 좋아요, 여러분, 다 왔어요. 관광을 이어 가기 전에 우리는 여기 이탈리아 식당에서 점심을 먹을 겁니다.

B 점심 식사 후에 버스 기사가 어디에서 우리를 픽업하죠?

A 기사가 대략 한 시간 후에 식당 맞은편에서 픽업할 겁니다. 식당 앞이 아니고요. 길을 꼭 건너주세요.

숙어

165 clear one's name

결백을 증명하다

A The real culprit confessed his crime and she could **clear her name.**

B She pledged to do everything to vindicate her honor.

C He was glad that the truth made his name white again.

A 진범이 범죄를 자백해 그녀는 오명을 벗을 수 있었다.

B 그녀는 오명을 씻고자 무슨 일이든 하겠노라 다짐했다.

C 그는 진실이 자기의 오명을 씻어 줘서 기뻤다.

숙어

166 be good with

~을 잘하다, ~에 밝다

A Everyone acknowledges that he **is good with** words.

B She **is good with** her hands.

C He **is** not **good with** numbers.

A 모두들 그가 말주변이 좋다는 점을 인정한다.

B 그녀는 손재주가 뛰어나다.

C 그는 숫자에 약하다.

숙어

167 nip in the bud

~의 싹을 없애다, 미연에 방지하다

A You have to **nip** a bad habit **in the bud.**

B The police are trying to **nip** the violence **in the bud.**

C We have to crush their plot in the egg.

A 나쁜 버릇은 초기에 싹을 잘라 버려야 한다.

B 경찰은 폭력을 미연에 방지하려고 애쓰고 있다.

C 우리는 그들의 음모를 미연에 방지해야 한다.

숙어

168 pay a heavy fine

많은 벌금을 내다

A Why do you think some people drink and drive? It's very dangerous, and they have to **pay a heavy fine** if they are caught.

B Well, maybe they think they'll get away with it.You're probably right.

A A lot of people are overly confident when they're drunk.

A 왜 일부 사람은 음주 운전을 할까? 엄청 위험하고 또 걸리면 많은 벌금을 내야 하잖아.

B 글쎄, 아마도 안 걸리고 넘어갈 수 있다고 생각하나 봐.

A 아마도 그런 것 같아. 많은 사람이 취했을 때 너무 자신만만하잖아.

숙어
169 in a flash

순식간에, 전광석화같이

A Ten years flew by **in a flash.**

B He solved the math problem in a twinkle.

C It passed by like a bolt of lightning.

A 10년이 눈 깜짝할 사이에 흘러갔다.

B 그는 그 수학 문제를 순식간에 풀었다.

C 그것은 전광석화처럼 지나갔다.

숙어
170 hit the nail on the head

정곡을 찌르다

A His criticism **hit the nail on the head.**

B Her answer hit the mark.

C He hit it right on the nose.

A 10년이 눈 깜짝할 사이에 흘러갔다.

B 그녀의 대답은 핵심에 적중했다.

C 그가 정확히 맞혔다.

숙어
171 that being said

말 나온 김에

A **That being said**, let's decide when to hold our next meeting.

B Speaking of which, when will he go back to his country?

C While we re at it, let's talk about the issue.

A 말 나온 김에 다음 모임 일정을 잡읍시다.

B 얘기가 나온 김에 말인데, 그는 언제 자기 나라로 돌아가나요?

C 말 나온 김에 그 문제에 대해 얘기를 해보자.

숙어
172 be taken aback

놀라서 기겁하다

A He **was taken aback** by her unexpected answer.

B They **were taken aback** by his abrupt proposal.

C He was struck dumb at her audacity.

A 그는 그녀의 예기치 못한 대답에 깜짝 놀라 어안이 벙벙했다.

B 그들은 그의 갑작스러운 제안에 놀라 기가 막혔다.

C 그는 그녀의 뻔뻔함에 놀라 말문이 막혔다.

숙어

173 egg on

부추기다

A She is trying to **egg on** me and him to fight each other.

B He goaded her on to lie.

C That will only incite others to follow suit.

A 그녀는 나와 그가 서로 싸우도록 부추기려 하고 있다.

B 그는 거짓말을 하도록 그녀를 부추겼다.

C 그것은 다른 사람들을 따라 하도록 자극만 하게 될 것이다.

숙어

174 eat one's words

식언하다, 말을 번복하다

A You're going to **eat your words** when you lose all of your money.

B I'm sure she will swallow her words in a few days.

C He made a commitment to support our project, but he went back on his words later.

A 가진 돈을 다 잃고 나면 당신이 한 말을 지키지 않게 될 것이다.

B 나는 그녀가 며칠 안에 자기 말을 번복하리라 확신한다.

C 그는 우리 프로젝트를 지원하겠다고 해놓고 나중엔 그 말을 지키지 않았다.

숙어

175 go through the roof

천정부지로 폭등하다

A Oil prices will **go through the roof** in a near future.

B Today my stocks hit the ceiling.

C I bet she is going to hit the roof.

A 유가는 가까운 장래에 천정부지로 치솟을 것이다.

B 내가 보유하고 있는 주식이 오늘 폭등해 상한가를 기록했다.

C 그녀가 화가 나서 길길이 날뛸 것이 분명하다.

숙어

176 have a silver tongue

말솜씨가 뛰어나다

A He **has a silver tongue.** You will never beat him in debate.

B He often turns his mistakes to his advantage with his smooth tongue.

C She married a man who has a ready tongue.

A 그는 언변이 뛰어나다. 당신은 토론에서 결코 그를 이기지 못할 것이다

B 그는 뛰어난 화술로 자신의 실수를 유리하게 뒤바꿔놓곤 한다.

C 그녀는 말주변이 좋은 남자와 결혼했다.

숙어

177 be(get) on one's high horse

거들먹거리다

A She **got on her high horse** after having become famous.

B I really hate to see him put on airs.

C She's very rich, but she never gives herself airs.

A 그녀는 유명해지고 난 뒤 거만해졌다.

B 나는 그가 으스대는 꼴을 보는 것이 너무 싫다.

C 그녀는 엄청난 부자이면서도 결코 젠체하는 적이 없다.

숙어

178 shoot one's mouth off

말을 함부로 하다

A Don't **shoot your mouth off** without thinking.

B You should not shoot off at the mouth without proof.

C She hates him running off his mouth.

A 아무 생각 없이 입을 함부로 놀리지 마라.

B 아무런 증거 없이 함부로 말해서는 안 된다.

C 그녀는 그가 경솔하게 떠벌리는 것을 싫어한다.

숙어

179 play (work) both sides (of the street)

양다리를 걸치다

A He always **plays both sides of the street** at meetings.

B You can't sit on the fence any longer.

C China is **playing both sides** against the middle, making ill use of the current situation.

A 그는 회의 때 늘 애매한 중립적 태도를 보인다.

B 당신은 이제 더 양다리를 걸칠 수 없게 됐다.

C 중국은 현 상황을 악용해 이간질하고 있다.

숙어

180 mooch off

~에게 빈대 붙다

A He always **mooches off** his friends.

B She has been **mooching off** of her brother for years.

C I don't want to sponge off my parents any more.

A 그는 늘 친구들에게 빈대 붙는다.

B 그녀는 수년 동안 오빠에게 빌붙어 살아왔다.

C 나는 더 이상 부모님께 얹혀살고 싶지 않다.

숙어

181 hang in

견디다, 버티다

A **Hang in** there. It's almost finished.

B He decided to stick it out for a year.

C You don't have to tough it out on your own.

A 조금만 참아. 거의 다 끝났어.

B 그는 1년간 참으며 견뎌보기로 했다.

C 너 혼자서 어려움을 참고 견딜 필요가 없다.

숙어

182 throw (have) a tantrum

짜증을 내다, 성질을 내다

A He **threw a tantrum** and walked out of the office.

B The child **throws a tantrum** when his parents doesn't buy him a toy he wants.

C She'll throw a fit if she finds out.

A 그는 성질을 부리고는 사무실을 나가 버렸다.

B 그 아이는 원하는 장난감을 부모가 사주지 않으면 떼를 쓴다.

C 그녀가 사실을 알고 나면 난리를 피울 것이다.

숙어

183 go down the drain

헛수고가 되다

A All his efforts **went down the drain.**

B I don't want his efforts to go to waste.

C His mother is very apprehensive that he may go wrong by any chance.

A 그의 모든 노력이 수포로 돌아갔다.

B 나는 그의 노력이 물거품 이 되길 원하지 않는다.

C 그의 어머니는 그가 혹시라도 잘못될까 봐 노심초사하고 계신다.

숙어

184 have a genius for

재주가 있다

A He seems to **have a genius for** making friends.

B This student seems to have a knack for technology.

C I think she is gifted with cooking skills.

A 그는 친구 사귀는 재주가 뛰어난 것 같다.

B 이 학생은 기술 분야에 재능이 있는 것 같다.

C 내 생각에 그녀는 요리 기술에 재주가 있다.

숙어

185 make a scene

소란을 피우다, 야단법석을 떨다

A They **made a scene** in a public place.

B He said he didn't want to cause a scene.

C Don't make a fuss about a minor thing like that.

A 그들은 공공장소에서 소란을 피웠다.

B 그는 소란을 일으키고 싶지 않다고 말했다.

C 그런 작은 일로 소란 피우지 말기 바란다.

숙어

186 have an upset stomach

배탈이 나다, 체하다

A You should avoid cold food when you **have an upset stomach**.

B She had a severe stomachache after eating some raw oysters.

C Some kids have a stomach upset when they drink milk.

A 배탈이 났을 때는 차가운 음식을 피해야 한다.

B 그녀는 생굴을 먹고 심한 배탈이 났다.

C 어떤 아이들은 우유를 마시면 배탈이 난다.

숙어

187 cut to the chase

바로 본론을 말하다

A Let's **cut to the chase**, since we don't have all day.

B Stop beating around the bush, just get to the point.

C I'm busy now, so just hit the high spots.

A 시간이 많지 않으니 곧바로 본론으로 들어갑시다.

B 말을 빙빙 돌리지 말고 단도직입 적으로 본론을 말해라.

C 내가 지금 바쁘니까 바로 요점만 말하라.

숙어

188 get cold feet

주눅이 들다, 겁을 먹다

A He always **gets cold feet** before a blind date.

B She **got cold feet** and could not say anything.

C He feels small in her presence.

A 그는 소개팅하기 전에 늘 긴장 하고 떤다.

B 그녀는 기가 죽어 아무 말도 하지 못했다.

C 그는 그녀가 있으면 주눅이 든다.

CHAPTER 19

속담

속담 1 The walls have ears.

낮말은 새가 듣고 밤말은 쥐가 듣는다.

A Hey, you know some people from HR, don't you? There've been rumors circulating here and there about personnel changes. Have you heard anything?

B Yes, but **the walls have ears**. Why don't we talk about this at lunch?

A Really?! The rumors aren't groundless? This is going to be a big issue!

A 자네 인사과 사람들 좀 알지, 그렇지? 요즘 인사이동에 대한 소문이 여기저기서 돌고 있잖아. 혹시 들은 것 있나?

B 응, 그런데 누가 들을 수도 있으니 이따 점심시간에 이야기하는 것이 어떨까?

A 정말?! 그럼 그 소문들이 근거 없는 게 아니라는 거야? 이거 엄청난 이슈가 되겠군!

속담 2 I'll eat my hat.

손에 장을 지지다.

A The day has come. Let's see if Mike asks Delta out. You said if he does, you'd give me five grand. Remember?

B Of course, I do. **I'll eat my hat** if he asks her out.

A Uh-oh, look who's coming over there!

A 드디어 그날이야. 마이크가 델타한테 데이트 신청하는지 어디 보자. 그렇게 하면 네가 나한테 오천 불 준다고 했어. 기억하지?

B 물론이지. 마이크가 데이트 신청하면 내가 손에 장을 지진다.

A 저기 봐! 저기 온다!

속담 3 What goes around comes around.

뿌린 대로 거두는 법이죠.

A Hey, did you hear that Jenny cheated on Mike? I'm shocked.

B I'm not. Mike cheated on his last girlfriend. **What goes around comes around.**

A Really? That's even more surprising! I guess I don't know Mike that well.

A 이봐, 제니가 마이크 몰래 바람피웠다는 소식 들었어? 충격이야.

B 아니, 난 별로. 마이크는 전 여자친구 몰래 바람피웠어. 뿌린 대로 거두는 법이지.

A 정말이야? 그건 더 충격이다! 내가 마이크를 잘 몰랐던 것 같다.

속담 4 if you can't stand the heat, get out of the kitchen.

절이 싫으면 중이 떠나야죠.

A I'm really sick of this job. I never have any free time. What should I do?

B Well, they say **if you can't stand the heat, get out of the kitchen.**

A I guess you're right. I really wanted to succeed here, but it's just too much work.

A 이 일 정말 지겹다. 쉴 틈이 전혀 없어. 어떻게 해야 하지?

B 음, 절이 싫으면 중이 떠나는 것 아니겠어?

A 네 말이 맞긴 해. 정말로 여기서 성공하고 싶었는데 일이 너무 많다.

속담 5 Look who's talking!

사돈 남 말 하네요!

A Mike looks so sleepy all the time. It's really unprofessional.

B **Look who's talking!** I saw you doze off at your desk a while ago.

A Hey, you know I worked overtime last night!

A 마이크는 항상 졸려 보여요 정말 프로답지 못해요.

B 당신이나 잘 좀 해요! 좀 전에 당신이 책상에서 조는 거 봤다고요.

A 이봐요, 나 어제 야근한 것 알잖아요!

속담 6 It wouldn't hurt to try.

밑져야 본전이다.

A Wow, this job sounds perfect for me. But I'm missing a few of the required qualifications...

B Well, why not apply anyway? **It wouldn't hurt to try**. The worst that can happen is that you won't get an interview.

A Hmm... OK, I will apply. Thanks for the encouragement, Mike.

A 와, 이 일은 나에게 딱 맞을 것 같아요. 근데 제가 몇 가지 필수 자격 요건을 충족시키지 못하네요.

B 음, 그냥 지원해 보는 게 어때요? 밑져야 본전이잖아요. 최악의 경우라고 해 봤자 면접을 못 보는 게 다 인걸요.

A 으음… 좋아요, 지원해 볼게요. 격려해 줘서 고마워요, 마이크.

속담 **7**

There's light at the end of the tunnel.

고생 끝에 낙이 있다.

A Keeping this resolution to do better in school is nearly killing me.

B Really? What is the hardest part?

A No matter how much I study, there's always another test just around he corner.

B **There's light at the end of the tunnel.** keep your eye on the prize: graduation.

A 학교 성적을 올리겠다는 결심을 지키느라 거의 죽을뻔했어.

B 그래? 어떤 게 가장 어려웠어?

A 아무리 공부를 많이 해도 시험이 끊일 새가 없더라고.

B 고생 끝에 낙이 오는 법이야. 네가 받을 상을 생각해. 졸업 말이야.

속담 **8**

The icing on the cake.

금상첨화

A It sounds like you got a really good deal on your car.

B But that's not it. There's more.

A What more could there possibly be?

B Well, **the** real **icing on the cake** is that my dad is going to pay for the whole thing.

A 너 차 정말 싸게 잘 산 것 같아.

B 그게 전부가 아니야. 또 있다니깐.

A 또 뭐가 있는데?

B 음, 진짜 금상첨화인 것은 바로 우리 아빠가 돈을 전부 내주실 거라는 거지.

속담 **9**

Curiosity killed the cat.

너무 많이 알려고 하면 다친다.

A Come on. Tell me what's in the bag.

B No way. It's a secret.

A I just have to know what's in there.

B You know what they say. **Curiosity killed the cat.**

A 야, 가방 안에 뭐가 있는지 말 좀 해봐.

B 절대 안 돼. 비밀이야.

A 난 거기 뭐가 들었는지 알아야만 하겠어.

B 너 사람들이 하는 말 알지? 너무 많이 알려고 하면 다친다니까.

속담

10 Everyone has a skeleton in his closet.

털어서 먼지 안 나는 사람 없다.

A Michael Bang has said that he is running for Congress.

B Really?

I don't think he is qualified to be a lawmaker.

A Why not?

B He is dirt, didn't you know that?

A Well, **everyone has a skeleton in his closet.**

A 마이클 뱅이 국회의원으로 출마한대.

B 정말? 그 친구는 국회의원이 될 자격이 없는데.

A 왜?

B 그 친구는 쓰레기 같은 인간이야. 몰랐어?

A 글쎄, 털어서 먼지 안 나는 사람은 없어.

속담

11 The opera's never over till the fat lady sings.

사람 팔자 시간문제다.

A I hear that Kenny made a fortune in the garbage hauling business. Is that true?

B Yes, that's true.

A As I know, he was down and out after filing for bankruptcy.

B Right. But he didn't throw his hands. He began to haul garbage, and made over a million dollars.

A Really? Well, **the opera's never over till fat lady sings.**

A 케니가 쓰레기 수거사업에서 큰돈을 벌었다는데 사실이니?

B 응. 맞아.

A 나는 케니가 파산신고를 하고는 완전히 망한 것으로 알고 있거든.

B 맞아. 그러나 포기하지 않고 쓰레기 수거를 시작해서 1백만 달러 이상을 벌었데.

A 정말? 음. 사람 팔자 시간문제로군.

속담

12 Nobody likes a back-seat driver!

뒤에서 감 놔라 배 놔라 하는 거 좋아하는 사람 없어.

A You should have filled up with gas at the last gas station.

B And, are you sure that this is the fastest way to get to the restaurant?

A Hey, **nobody likes a back-seat driver!**

A 이전 주유소에서 기름을 넣었어야지.

B 그리고 이게 식당가는 가장 빠른 길 맞아?

A 야, 뒤에서 감 놔라 배 놔라 하는 거 좋아하는 사람 없어!

속담

13 Time is on your side.

시간이 해결해 줄 거야.

A I don't know if I should sell my apartment now, or wait for the prices to rise.

B Prices are sure to go up over the next year, so you should wait. **Time is on your side.**

A You're probably right.

A 아파트를 지금 매도해야 할지 가격이 오를 때까지 기다려야 할지 모르겠네.

B 매매가는 내년에도 고공행진일 테니 기다려봐. 시간이 해결해 줄 거야.

A 네 말이 맞는 거 같아.

속담

14 It runs in the family.

피는 못 속인다.

A I heard your daughter won a prize at the science fair.

B Yes. I'm very proud of her. She worked so hard on her project.

A Well, I guess **it runs in the family.**

B Yeah, she gets it from her mother!

A 네 딸이 과학전람회에서 상 탔다며.

B 응, 너무 자랑스러워. 연구 과제를 진짜 열심히 준비했거든.

A 피는 못 속이나 보네.

B 맞아. 엄마를 닮아서 그래.

속담

15 Clean up your act.

행동 조심해라 점잖게 행동해라.

A **Clean up your act**, Steven. I'm afraid you're giving your family a bad name.

B If I'm giving my folks a bad reputation, that's none of your business.

A No wonder they say you are the black sheep of your family.

B Look, Kenny! Mind your own business, will you?

A 스티븐, 행동 좀 조심해라. 네 집안 망신을 시키고 있잖아.

B 내가 집안 망신을 시킨다고 해서 네가 상관할 바는 아니잖아.

A 사람들이 너를 집안의 말썽꾸러기라 부르는 것도 무리가 아니군.

B 이봐 케니! 넌 네 일이나 신경 쓰지 그래?

속담
16 Time and tide will wait for no man.

시간은 사람을 기다려주지 않는다.

Hey, Jess. It's me, Michael. I was wondering if you are still interested in the blind date I mentioned the other day. I have talked to my friend, Joshua about you and he is really dying to see you. I was thinking you guys will meet each other this Friday evening. Drop me a line if you are okay with it. I have a hunch that you guys will make a good couple. **Time and tide will wait for no man.**

제스, 나 마이클이야. 네가 아직도 전에 내가 말한 소개팅에 관심이 있는지 궁금해. 내 친구 조슈아한테 네 얘길 했더니 보고 싶어 난리야. 내 생각엔 너희들 이번 주 금요일에 서로 만났으면 좋겠는데 만약에 괜찮으면 연락해 줘. 너희 둘 잘 될 것 같은 예감이 들어. 시간은 사람을 기다려주지 않아.

속담
17 A man is known by the company he keeps.

친구를 보면 그 사람을 알 수 있다.

Hey, Michael. It's me, Jess. Thanks for setting me up with Joshua. Actually I'm not fond of meeting strangers, but I'm going to give it a shot. I'm sure he will be good natured like you just like in the saying "**A man is known by the company he keeps.**" I'll be in touch after the date.

마이클, 나 제스야. 조슈아랑 소개팅 주선해 준 것 고마워. 사실 나 낯선 사람들 만나는 것 좋아하지 않지만 그래도 한 번 도전해 보려고. '친구를 보면 그 사람을 알 수 있다'는 속담도 있듯이 그 사람도 분명히 너처럼 성격이 좋을 거야. 데이트 끝나고 어떻게 됐는지 알려줄게.

속담
18 Friends and wine improve with age.

친구와 와인은 오래될수록 좋다.

Michael, It's Jess. I had a great time with joshua thanks to you. He was so funny, pleasant and down-to-earth. I hope things are going to work out with him. Anyway I'm happy that we are still good friends. You've been my bosom friend ever since high school. Just like the saying goes "**Friends and wine improve with age.**", let's keep our friendship forever.

마이클, 나 제스야. 덕분에 죠슈아랑 정말 좋은 시간을 보냈어. 그 사람 진짜 재밌고 유쾌해. 그리고 현실적이기도 하고. 나 그 사람이랑 잘 됐으면 좋겠어. 그나저나 우리가 아직 친한 친구라는 것이 기쁘다. 넌 고등학교 때부터 나의 가장 친한 친구잖아. '친구와 와인은 오래될수록 좋다'는 속담처럼 우리 우정 평생 지키자.

원어민에게 바로 써먹는 영어표현

영어야 드루와

지은이 최창우
펴낸이 조경희
펴낸곳 경문사
펴낸날 2021년 2월 5일 1판 1쇄
등 록 1979년 11월 9일 제1979-000023호
주 소 04057, 서울특별시 마포구 와우산로 174
전 화 (02)332-2004 팩스 (02)336-5193
이메일 kyungmoon@kyungmoon.com

값 18,000원

ISBN 979-11-6073-436-2